THE EVERYDAY POLITICS OF FOOD CO-OPS

ANTHROPOLOGY OF EUROPE

Europe, a region characterized by its diversity and speed of change, is the latest area to attract current anthropological research and scholarship that challenges the prevailing views of classical anthropology. Situated at the frontier of the social sciences and humanities, the anthropology of Europe is born out of traditional ethnology, anthropology, folklore and cultural studies, but engages in innovative interdisciplinary approaches.

Anthropology of Europe publishes fieldwork monographs by young and established scholars, as well as edited volumes on particular regions or aspects of European society. The series pays special attention to studies with a strong comparative component, addressing theoretical questions of interest to both anthropologists and other scholars working in related fields.

Volume 9
The Everyday Politics of Food Co-ops
Care, Aid and Community in Austerity Britain
Celia Plender

Volume 8
Translocal Care across Kosovo's Borders
Reconfiguring Kinship along Gender and Generational Lines
Carolin Leutloff-Grandits

Volume 7
Gentrifications
Views from Europe
Marie Chabrol, Anaïs Collet, Matthieu Giroud, Lydie Launay, Max Rousseau and Hovig Ter Minassian

Volume 6
A Taste for Oppression
A Political Ethnography of Everyday Life in Belarus
Ronan Hervouet

Volume 5
Punks and Skins United
Identity, Class and the Economics of an Eastern German Subculture
Aimar Ventsel

Volume 4
In Pursuit of Belonging
Forging an Ethical Life in European-Turkish Spaces
Susan Beth Rottmann

Volume 3
All or None
Cooperation and Sustainability in Italy's Red Belt
Alison Sánchez Hall

Volume 2
European Anthropologies
Edited by Andrés Barrera-González, Monica Heintz and Anna Horolets

Volume 1
The France of the Little-Middles
A Suburban Housing Development in Greater Paris
Marie Cartier, Isabelle Coutant, Olivier Masclet and Yasmine Siblot

THE EVERYDAY POLITICS OF FOOD CO-OPS

Care, Aid and Community in Austerity Britain

Celia Plender

berghahn
NEW YORK • OXFORD
www.berghahnbooks.com

First published in 2025 by
Berghahn Books
www.berghahnbooks.com

Library of Congress Cataloging-in-Publication Data

A C.I.P. cataloging record is available from the Library of Congress

Library of Congress Cataloging in Publication Control Number: 2024059470

British Library Cataloguing in Publication Data

A catalogue record for this book is available from the British Library

ISBN 978-1-80539-981-0 hardback
ISBN 978-1-80539-982-7 epub
ISBN 978-1-80539-983-4 web pdf

https://doi.org/10.3167/9781805399810

This open access edition of *The Everyday Politics of Food Co-ops: Care, Aid and Community in Austerity Britain* has been funded by two research grants from the Economic and Social Research Council [grant numbers 1512259, ES/V011227/1].

CONTENTS

ILLUSTRATIONS

ACKNOWLEDGEMENTS

First and foremost, I would like to thank my research participants, without whom this book would not have been possible. Thank you to Fareshares and St Hilda's East and all of those involved with each for welcoming me in and allowing me to be a part of their activities as a volunteer, member, researcher and friend. Special thanks go to Jenny, Ed and Kell for their friendship, advice and support. Thank you also to all the other food co-ops, community food projects and campaigning and research groups who allowed me to visit, participate and ask questions.

Secondly, I should mention that this book has been supported by two research grants from the Economic and Social Research Council [grant numbers 1512259, ES/V011227/1]. Some content in chapters 3, 4 and 5 has previously been included in the following journal article: Plender, Celia. 2022. '"It's a Co-op in Spirit, That's What It Is": Fostering Collaboration, Collectivity, and Egalitarianism in Food Cooperatives', *Kritisk Etnografi – Swedish Journal of Anthropology* 5(1–2): 77–92. Some content in chapter 6 has previously been included in the following journal article: Celia Plender. 2024. 'The "Awkwardnesses" of Aid and Exchange: Food Cooperative Practices in Austerity Britain', *Focaal* 2024(98): 86–99.

In terms of academic support, there are many people whose input has been invaluable to the development of this research and to my academic career. In particular, I would like to thank Harry West, who has been with me since the beginning of this project, for his support, encouragement and guidance; for giving me thinking and writing space when needed, while also helping to move my thinking on when I felt stuck. Thank you for continuing to be a mentor to me on my academic journey as well as a valued colleague, and for all of the opportunities and advice you have given me over the years. At SOAS, where I started this research, I would like to thank Jakob Klein, Catherine Dolan and Lizzie Hull for their advice and encouragement. At Exeter, where I finished it, I would like to thank Charles Masquelier and Katharine Tyler for their insights, guidance and support. Thank you to Charlie, for all your warmth and positivity when I arrived at Exeter, your continued encouragement of and feedback on my research and the fantastic insights into cooperatives that you gave me. Thank you to Katharine, for the many broad-ranging conversations (academic and otherwise), detailed feedback on proposals and drafts, and mentorship during my postdoc and beyond. Thank you also to Katharine for all the different opportunities you have given me, from research projects to passing on the convenorship of the ASA Anthropology of Britain network. I would also like to thank members of the Centre for Rural Policy Research at Exeter where I am based for their insights and all the tea and cake.

In terms of other colleagues at Exeter, my thanks go to Jess Fagin, my co-convenor of the ASA Anthropology of Britain (AOB) Network who has been a great friend and colleague throughout my time here with lots of empathy, academic conversations and good laughs. I am also very grateful to Sally Atkinson and Becci Lynch at Exeter for their friendship, solidarity and many writing group sessions, which helped while I was drafting and refining various sections of this monograph. In my extended academic network, both Andrea Muehlebach and Cristina Grasseni have offered incredibly valuable feedback and opportunities. My thanks go to AOB network members for their feedback on presentations and for the stimulating conversations.

My thanks should also go to the extended network of early career food scholars I met through SOAS who continue to inspire me. These include Zosia Boni, Nese Ceren Tosun, Anna Cohen, Anna Colquhoun, Mukta Das, Lucy Dow, Nora Faltmann, Zoë Goodman, Katie Graf, Claudia Prieto Piastro, Anna Seecharan and Fran Vaghi. At Exeter, thanks also to the early career peers who gave me so much valuable feedback on my work in its early stages, and some of whom collectively proofread parts of my thesis (in true co-operative spirit). These include Charlotte Chivers, Tridibesh Dey, Beth Dooley, Jess Fagin, William Jaggard, Megan Larmer, Aimee Middlemiss, Lexie Onofrei, Lucy Osler and Elena Sharratt.

Special thanks go to Beth, Jess, Lucy, Megan and Zosia who helped me get to the finish line at different points in this research. Zosia and Megan, your unwavering support and words of encouragement and reassurance at the very final stages made all the difference.

Thank you also to all the friends and family members who cheered me on along the way especially Tom, Jess, Mum, Dad, Stephanie, Richard, Robin, Iona, Al, Maurizio, Helen, Vera, Luke, Marcin, Hanna, Sam and Gareth. Last, but by no means least, I would like to thank my sister, Lilly, who has been with me throughout this journey, offering support and encouragement at moments of doubt and advice on many of my thoughts and ideas. She heard about and met many of the people from my fieldwork and also read various drafts of this work. She also sat with me under a blanket watching RuPaul's Drag Race at points when it all felt like a bit too much. Thanks Lil.

INTRODUCTION

IN SEARCH OF THE POLITICAL

As I sat behind the old, wooden counter at Fareshares Food Co-op with Brian, he told me he was disappointed. Over the time that he had got to know Fareshares, a volunteer-run, vegan, wholefood co-op in southeast London, he had come to the conclusion that it was not all that political. He was already involved with other activist projects and had joined Fareshares out of an interest in cooperativism and activism more generally. Now he was wondering if he should have joined the Infoshop instead – the Anarchist social centre in the same building. He was sick of hearing about customers' dietary beliefs and lamented the fact that few of the conversations that took place during the Thursday evening shift on which he had been volunteering seemed to relate to activism or to politics. (Diets did not seem to fit into his understanding of the political.) He was also unhappy with the co-op's customer base. As he saw it, Fareshares was a project for elites, offering wholefoods to hippies and hipsters.

I had originally met Brian on his first shift at Fareshares just over a year earlier in 2014 while I was at the tail end of a short piece of fieldwork there. This time, it was him who was leaving and me who had just arrived (albeit for the second time). Just as I took on Brian's shift after he left a few weeks later, I also took on some of his concerns. I regularly found myself reflecting on his words as shoppers shared natural health remedies and conspiracy theories, or told me how excited they were to find a 'shop' that promoted low packaging as they were trying to go plastic free or low waste. 'Shop' was a term that Fareshares itself did not necessarily use, referring to the food co-op as an 'experiment in Community [*sic*]' on its website. A place where all users were encouraged 'to become active in running the project' (Fareshares n.d.). These co-op visitors were, perhaps, engaging with individualized, consumption-based forms of 'lifestyle politics' or ethical consumption, I thought. While these did not necessarily sit outside of Fareshares' own values as a project that supports 'patterns of consumption that promote social justice and sustainable agriculture and [that] fosters an awareness of the political and ecological effects of consumer actions' (ibid.), they did seem to involve a different relationship to collectivity, sociality and consumerism to that of cooperativism.

Like Brian, I sometimes felt disappointed in those early days – why was there so little talk about Fareshares' political goals or activism more generally? This led me to contemplate the nature of 'the political' in contemporary Britain and where its parameters are. I was also curious to know where food cooperatives fitted into this, how their activities intersected with shifts in mainstream politics and political thinking, or social and political-economic change; and whether the activities of the food co-ops I was working with reproduced or disrupted existing relations and structures of power.

Miriam Ticktin breaks the concept of politics down into two parts. She uses 'politics' to refer to 'the set of practices by which order is created and maintained', such as national or international policy as well as the daily experiences of these. She describes the realm in which the established order is disrupted as 'the political' (Ticktin 2011: 19–20; see also Mouffe 2005). Both of these components are significant to what I explore in this book.

As a basic human necessity and potentially the world's oldest commodity (Klein et al. 2012: 302), food – along with the management of its production, supply and pricing – is, and always has been, political. As Wilk (2006: 21–2) suggests, '[f]ood has long been a focus for political and social movements in many parts of the world; food is a potent symbol of what ails society, a way of making abstract issues like class or exploitation into a material, visceral reality'. Food provision and access are also deeply linked to the state and its politics. In historical terms, it has been argued that the evolution of civilizations and the adoption of agricultural practices have often developed hand in hand as increased food production created opportunities for some people to pursue work unrelated to food provisioning (Diamond 1998; see also Allen 1997). This connection also raises complex questions for any state about who should be responsible for ensuring a strong enough agricultural sector and/or trade arrangements to provide an adequate supply of food at accessible prices to its people. There are also other questions about the circumstances under which this happens: who benefits most and at what cost to producers, citizens or the economy? Food co-ops also have a role to play in politics and the political both in how they respond to the status quo in terms of political regimes, the economy, the structures of society or food systems, and in how they have become a focus of government policy and agendas at different times.

From 2015 to 2017, I spent almost two years as a volunteer-member and participant observer at two London-based, grassroots, retail food co-ops – Fareshares and St Hilda's East. Both food co-ops are located in historically deprived, multicultural and rapidly gentrifying London boroughs. I visited each on a weekly basis to become part of their routines and rhythms – selling goods, stocking shelves, placing orders, assisting shoppers and any number of other jobs as and when needed. Through these activities, and the many conversations I had with volunteers, shoppers, coordinators and others in the food co-op's networks, I learned about their practices, social organization, ideals and visions of the cooperative and of wider societal and political-economic issues. Over time, as I became embedded in the structures and practices of Fareshares and St Hilda's East food co-ops, the *politics* of each also became more visible to me. I came to see how the political-economic climate in which we were living impacted on the workings of the food co-ops and the lives of those that interacted with them. The longer I spent with the co-ops, the more I also came to see some of the everyday forms of care, aid and community building taking place within them in *political* terms. In the context of austerity Britain, small, affective acts could be deeply meaningful in many ways.

While the bold politics of mass social movements, social justice campaigning work and overt forms of direct action are more easily legible as political,[1] the comparatively mundane, or everyday, actions taking place within local, grassroots, community projects, can often be seen in more ambivalent terms, just as Brian and I had done. As Steph Lawler points out, however, 'the everyday yields insights that may slip from sight in a focus only on grand gestures and large-scale structures' (2017: 16; see also Scott 1985 on everyday resistance). As such, it makes sense to 'take the mundane seriously' (Back 2015: 822), not only as a site from which we can explore lived experiences of wider social circumstances, structures and politics, but also as a potential space of creativity, solidarity, and resistance (Lawler 2017: 14–16), as well as ambivalence, tension and contradiction.

In the wake of the financial crisis, many European and North American governments implemented austerity policies that aimed to reduce national deficits through harsh public spending cuts, the efficacy of which has since been critiqued (Blyth 2015). These processes reinforce existing forms of social stratification within countries, while eroding social cohesion and drawing a widening socio-economic group into precarious living conditions (Rakopoulos 2018). As well as social impacts, austerity has been linked to increasing physical and mental health issues, shrinking health services and growing anxieties brought on by having to manage with fewer wellbeing resources (Basu et al. 2017). The forms of moralization that accompany austerity in relation to national spending, collective responsibility for belt tightening and deficit reduction can also lead to the revaluation of everyday lives and the measurement of individual worth or deservingness in relation to welfare. This creates tensions between ideals of egalitarianism and collective burden, while also reinforcing inequalities (Powers and Rakopoulos 2019: 5; Rakopoulos 2018: 2).

As state welfare is hollowed out and outsourced to business, charity and the voluntary sector, these valuations can also produce moral discourses of deservingness in relation to limited welfare resources (Koch and James 2022). For those working within public services and the voluntary sector, there is also a considerable practical and emotional toll to keeping up the levels of care and commitment to those who use their services with squeezed funding and infrastructures. While this can lead to creativity in some cases, in others it leads to exhaustion, despondency and burnout (Clayton et al. 2015; Jupp 2022).

By the time I started my fieldwork in the autumn of 2015, the Conservative-led government's policy of austerity had been in place for more than five years, and its fall out was becoming ever more visible. Combined with the aftershocks of the 2008 global financial crisis and the food price crisis of 2007–8, austerity was impacting many people's lives, incomes and abilities to feed, clothe or house themselves and their families adequately. In London, where the extremes of wealth and poverty are often particularly severe, many people were having to face up to the inequalities that welfare reform was causing. During the period of my fieldwork, the Brexit referendum also took place (23 June 2016), causing a change of Prime Minister, a snap election and endless negotiations on the terms of departure from the EU. There was also considerable talk about the rise of populism in Britain and further afield, as well as the many legacies of the British Empire in regard to issues such as national identity, race relations and responses to migration. As a consequence of these significant political-economic shifts, mainstream politics came to feel very present, punctuating everyday lives.

The Everyday Politics of Food Co-ops explores the ways in which politics and the political intersect within contemporary, British food cooperatives, and the resonance of the everyday acts of care, aid and community building that take place within them. It examines the very nature of the cooperative, its politics, imaginary and complexities through the lens of Fareshares and St Hilda's East. Through the study and contextualization of Fareshares and St Hilda's East and their politics, the book also offers a grounded perspective on a particularly turbulent moment in British history, and how food co-op participants conceptualized and responded to experiences of austerity. In doing so, it explores some of the 'structures of feeling' within austerity Britain – the socially and historically distinct qualities and feelings attached to this period (Williams 2015: 23), which kinds of political energies this catalysed and which it suppressed. As such, the monograph assesses the power of the cooperative in this environment.

The histories of the two food co-ops I worked with speak to a longer set of political-economic processes and structures of feeling. Fareshares finds its roots in the resurgence of anarchism in the UK in the 1970s and 1980s as well as the ideals of the counterculture of the 1960s and 1970s and its cuisine. The co-op was set up in Elephant and Castle, southeast London in 1988 during the Thatcher era by a group of Anarchists, leftists and squatters. In line with the countercultural food projects of the 1960s and 1970s (see, for example, Belasco 2007), it began as a place to buy wholegrains, organic vegetables, fairly-traded foods and vegan products, while also exploring alternative practices and structures. In principle, anyone could shop and socialize there or get more involved by becoming a volunteer-member. Collective decision-making and non-hierarchical organizing were fundamental to its operation and ideology. The name also alluded to a desire for an economy (and forms of food distribution) set up on the principles of 'fair shares' for all (Cole 2018), and this ideal was accompanied by a rejection of wage labour and profit within the volunteer-run project.

St Hilda's East Food Co-op in Shoreditch, east London, comes from a very different political era and history, which speaks to the ways in which cooperatives can become folded into state agendas and development work as much as activism. This co-op was founded in 2005, at a time when the New Labour government was actively promoting community-based coping strategies as part of what has come to be known as the 'Third Way', a centrist political perspective which so often gets characterized in neoliberal terms. As state welfare services were restructured and withdrawn, this included the bolstering of the third or voluntary sector and an emphasis on citizens who not only took responsibility for themselves, but also for their communities (Rose 2000). Structurally, food co-ops started during this drive rarely conformed to the classic definition of a modern cooperative (member-owned and run), but the name still created positive associations with concepts such as 'community', 'mutuality', 'self-help', and 'empowerment'. For scholars of governmentality such as Susan Brin Hyatt, this was a moment in which the activist energies of the 1980s and 1990s that had sprung up in response to Thatcherism were increasingly tamed, losing much of their oppositional power (2012: 160).

Within the modern cooperative model itself, there is a desire to 'transform the organization of production and consumption through new, democratic organizational forms'; and if cooperatives are 'people-centred enterprises owned, controlled and run by and for their members to realise their common economic, social, and cultural needs and aspirations' (International Cooperative Alliance n.d.), then this variation in models raises questions about ownership, autonomy and practices of collective care – all of which can have deep political resonance within the social imaginaries of cooperatives. Working with two food co-ops born of different traditions, and across the boundaries of community action and seemingly more explicitly politicized provisioning, also helps to look at the complex relationship between neoliberal 'incorporation' and 'resistance' within these spaces (Cloke et al. 2017: 721; Jupp 2022: 4). This offers insights into the possibilities, tensions and contradictions that lie within them as well as the role of their differing histories, structures and entangled imaginaries in this.

As Charles Taylor (2003: 27) argues, social imaginaries, or in the case of this book cooperative social imaginaries, are more than a set of ideas. Through the ways in which they attempt to make sense of society, they also enable its practices, structures and norms. They help us to understand the moral and social order, and where we stand within this and within space and time, that is, how these orders and imaginaries are formed and how they relate to other social orders. Social imaginaries are also interwoven with possibility – with ideas about how things *could* be as well as how they are or have been. Within this space of possibility, there are opportunities to foster more radical imaginations, practices and sites of alternative social reproduction (Asara 2020: 5; see also Haiven and Khasnabish 2014). In the context of the food cooperative, much of this imaginative work happens through seemingly small, everyday acts of care, aid and community building within these food retail spaces.

EVERYDAY POLITICS

Working from a feminist perspective, Jupp suggests that local forms of activism are often overlooked, not only due to their small scale, but also their ordinary, everyday nature. While much more low-key and ambiguous than actions more easily narrativized as resistance, Jupp argues that everyday, community practices still offer 'new understandings of local collective action' (Jupp 2012: 3032) and the power of the work it does to cultivate local capacities for change. From Gibson-Graham's perspective, this is also about cultivating capacities to 'imagine, desire, and practice' different, more collective and interdependent, ways of being (2003: 54).

Silvia Federici argues that we can 'begin to do things in our everyday lives to start to reclaim control' (Federici in Carenotes Collective 2020: xi). For Federici (2012), practices of collective, or community, capacity building, resonate with notions of the commons and its emphasis on the reproduction of everyday activities and social relations grounded in social cooperation, mutuality and collective responsibility. Federici defines the commons as 'the creation of social relations and spaces built on solidarity, the communal sharing of wealth, and cooperative work and decision-making' (Federici 2018: 183). She frames these acts in the language of prefiguration, arguing that the collective capacities fostered by commoning must be at the heart of change as 'our struggles cannot only be oppositional, they must also be constructive and create the seeds of the society in which we want to live' (Federici in Carenotes Collective 2020: xii). Such activities, Federici argues, not only 'require', but also 'produce, community' (Federici 2018: 166).

Within the context of austerity, Jupp suggests that the everyday nature of community action responds to the ways in which austerity '"hits" at the level of the body, the family and domestic sphere, the household and the home' (2017: 352). She describes these practices as 'low-key, seemingly non-confrontational' and 'consisting of embodied practices based on care, intergenerational exchange, everyday coping and support' (2017: 353). She argues that care is central to the politics of the everyday. And that 'matters of care always involve embodied practices and emotions, but also politics and ethics' (2022: 15).

A focus on affective politics also connects with anthropological work on grassroots responses to austerity. In Matt Wilde's research with urban housing activists in the UK he suggests that caring practices within such community spaces can create 'moral spheres that engender alternative forms of personal and social worth' (Wilde 2022: 24). Such approaches can become all the more significant in the face of deepening inequalities and entrenched political and economic power. Here, there is an attempt to reclaim the political power of care (Ticktin 2021), offering 'a set of vital but underappreciated strategies for enduring precarious worlds' (Hobart and Kneese 2020: 2).

Letizia Bonanno's work engages with the volunteer-run social pharmacies in austerity Greece which developed in response to the considerable financial challenges people faced in accessing the medicines they needed. She frames the pharmaceuticals and the work of sorting and distributing them as a form of care, which communicates emotions, reinforces social relations and extends these beyond the domestic to something more collective (Bonanno 2023). Arguably food can have a similar role.

Collective care itself has long been understood as a radical concept which acknowledges interdependence, while reimagining society along more equal lines (see, for example, Tronto 1993). Working from the perspective of a feminist 'ethic of care', '"caring" is a central and defining human activity' that can also have 'radical political potential' (Kneafsey et al. 2008: 41–3). It is within this relationality, and the desire to make the needs of others as well as selves the basis for action, that its political potential lies. The Care Collective suggest that care is 'our individual and common ability to provide the political, social, material, and emotional conditions that allow the vast majority of people and living creatures on this planet to thrive' (The Care Collective 2020: 6). Caring speaks to a sense of connection to and responsibility for others – both human and non-human (Alber and Drotbohm 2015; Kneafsey et al. 2008; Puig de la Bellacasa 2017; The Care Collective 2020; see also Tronto 1993). By acknowledging that we 'are all recipients of "care"' we recognize that it is a 'social responsibility' (Kneafsey et al. 2008: 43; see also Lawson 2007).

This also chimes with the Cooperativist and Anarchist ideal of mutual aid in attempting to create equality through co-dependency (Kropotkin 2014) and radical collective care (Ticktin 2021). As Jamie Heckert points out, with the ethos of Anarchist mutual aid, which also entails non-hierarchical organizing, should come a 'radical commitment to care' (2011: 188). This Anarchist form of care eschews the hierarchical relationships of giver and receiver inherent in models of charity, instead emphasizing 'equality, mutuality, embodiment and interdependence' (ibid. 2011: 194).

For Ticktin (in Woodly et al. 2021), the materially grounded forms of care that have emerged in recent years are 'co-constitutive of a new set of political formations', which she frames as a feminist commons. As she puts it, 'there is a version of care at the heart of the commons, insofar as the commons are about radical resource distribution and undoing forms of domination and enclosure to produce horizontal relationships of equality, mutuality and responsibility' (ibid.). A feminist commons is, therefore, a means of prefiguring alternative ways of being, acting and imagining together. I build on these feminist and Anarchist approaches to the political in my understanding of the everyday politics of food co-ops and its connection to care, aid and community. These things are both social and economic in their material practices and visions of alternative forms of reproduction. These allude to the caring practices of the state and civil society, the relationship between these and the kinds of visions of society and citizenship they represent. They also ask 'how care can and should be organised in society, including the reach and role of the state and other institutions and infrastructures (Jupp 2022: 4).

As such, care is an 'important aspect of moral reasoning' (Kneafsey et al. 2008: 41–3), offering clues about cultural values, forms of relationality and visions of society. Indeed, care practices 'feed into the (re)making of social order as well as the shaping of social change' (Thelen 2015: 498). Thelen, therefore, argues that these practices are fundamental to social organization. Through their connection to our 'self-understandings and moral sensibilities', they can tell us much about how a 'good life' or a 'good society' is envisioned and practised (ibid.). This understanding is key to how I view care within this monograph and its connection to the politics of each co-op – themselves micropolitical social organizations.

While Fareshares' Anarchist, Cooperativist roots make mutual aid, or collective care, a fundamental aspect of its organizing logics, at St Hilda's East Food Co-op and Community Centre, its caring practices come from a different tradition. This speaks to St Hilda's East's own history as a Victorian settlement community, founded to support people living in deprivation, while also fostering relationships across the divides of class, ethnicity and gender. During my fieldwork, much of the assistance provided by the centre came in the form of 'care as work' (Alber and Drotbohm 2015), through the actions of the food co-op coordinator, Jenny. It was her job to support and facilitate the scheme's volunteers and customers, and the affective, intersubjective forms of care and respect created within the space by her and those who participated in the food co-op's activities.

Within the context of food co-ops, food itself is also an important site of care. Food is integral to the 'construction and maintenance of our bodies, selves and environments and is deeply implicated in ethics of care at individual and societal levels' (Kneafsey et al. 2008: 45). Indeed, as Kneafsey et al. (ibid.) argue, it is 'a marker of who we are, what and who we care about'. This can be extended across any number of human and non-human actors from people to animals, objects and the environment (an increasing site of care and concern for many within a period of heightened anxiety about climate change).

One of the most typical forms of caring through food is provisioning – how we buy, and who for, how we cook and share food. The act of food provisioning can be a form of emotional labour, involving caring and providing nourishment for others (as well as selves) (Som Castellano 2015). Miller goes so far as to argue that food shopping is an expression of love towards those it is bought for (Miller 2001). As others have noted, however, as with other forms of social reproduction, the dynamics of food provisioning can also be laden with power, reinforcing hierarchies and differences as much as showing care or reinforcing shared identities (Appadurai 1981). As a consequence, food provisioning can tell us much about the 'production of particular meanings and identities and the reproduction of the social and economic system as a whole' (Narotzky 2013: 78).[2]

Within the context of Fareshares and St Hilda's East, the co-ops often found themselves in negotiation with competing values derived from Capitalist and neoliberal logics and structures of feeling, societal norms or humanitarian desires. These could produce more 'liberal' (Ticktin in Woodly et al. 2021) rather than radical forms of care, highlighting the ways in which these things are inevitably messy and entangled (Jupp 2022: 4).

As Greenhouse notes, neoliberal[3] reform 'has restructured the most prominent public relationships that constitute *belonging*: politics, markets, work, and self-identity' (2012: 2 emphasis original). For the Care Collective, such restructuring represents a form of carelessness built into neoliberal Capitalist logics, which prioritize 'growing the economy ... over ensuring the well-being of citizens' (2020: 8). Community-based responses to crisis and welfare withdrawal highlight the intimate link between community action and shifting state economic and welfare visions, practices and policies (Jupp 2022: 2) – '[w]hat kinds of care are being offered or withdrawn by the welfare state, and what ... this mean[s] for the caring practices and interventions of community activists' (Jupp 2022: 2). In the context of Greek austerity, for example, Cabot (2016) foregrounds the interconnections between solidarity and neoliberal reform, arguing that counter-movements are an integral part of how neoliberalism unfolds, with solidarity and crisis acting as two sides of the same coin (see also Carney 2021 on Sicily). While Andrea Muehlebach (2012), in her work on volunteerism in post-Fordist Italy, argues that many of the caring acts that volunteers perform in attempts to ameliorate some of the consequences of neoliberalism are themselves aspects of a neoliberal subjectivity – a 'moral neoliberal'.

Focusing on these more liberal forms of care, Ticktin argues in her work on humanitarian aid in France (2011: 3) that compassion and care have become deeply entwined with politics in the contemporary period in unexpected ways. People who fall outside of the remit of state aid, whose numbers are growing as welfare retracts, are often the primary targets of alternative regimes of aid and compassion (11). While Ticktin focuses on immigrants in France, I argue here that those suffering from 'food poverty'[4] in Britain are no exception, as highlighted by the rise and roll out of emergency food aid schemes such as food banks in the UK.[5] Within the public consciousness, food became a particularly potent symbol of the extreme inequalities evident in Britain after the economic crisis of 2008 and the implementation of austerity policies in Britain that followed. In this book, I argue that this growth in humanitarian approaches to relieving hunger or other inequalities, which became much harder to ignore in times of austerity, also seeped into other value systems, ideologies and models of aid within society as well as the food cooperative imaginary.

Within the changing political-economic climate of neoliberal capitalism, austerity and rising humanitarian sensibilities, Fareshares, St Hilda's East and their participants were obliged to constantly negotiate diverse forms of politics while practising different kinds of aid and care, which called on a mixture of ideological and moral values drawn from many different aspects of their lives. Working with two food co-ops, born of different political-economic moments and the logics and discourses that came with them, helped me to identify this connection between politics, aid, care and community-making, and the complex ways in which different value systems interacted within them. Such an exploration raises questions about how more radical forms of collective care can be enacted, which do not rely on more liberal 'sentiments such as compassion, sympathy or pity, or the more moralized judgements, such as deserving or undeserving' (Ticktin 2021), which have become heightened in recent years. As such, a key question within this book is how the moral neoliberal interacts with the more radical components of cooperativism in austerity Britain.

Within the activities and structures of Fareshares and St Hilda's, there are also important questions about who is responsible for the welfare of others, how it should be delivered and who is and is not included in each vision. This becomes all the more pressing at a time when state welfare (the most significant system of aid and care in the country for over 70 years) is being eroded. While each co-op approached these questions from a different starting point, both had to navigate competing narratives and values reflecting aspects of the micro- and macro-political, the changing nature of welfare, and of capitalism, and the relationship of each to morality. Within this there are also questions about rights, responsibilities, models of democracy and the social contracts by which these are derived. This book, then, also speaks to different forms of power and authority, and how these are enacted, accepted and resisted through care, aid and community building within the co-ops.

THE COOPERATIVE IMAGINARY

A month or so after Brian had stopped volunteering at Fareshares, I bumped into him again at a talk on transformative politics and solidarity economies, in which cooperatives – including food cooperatives – were a part of the speakers' visions of a post-Capitalist world (Williams and Satgar 2016; see also Satgar 2014). In Vishwas Satgar's work, the solidarity economy, which he and Michelle Williams discussed in the talk, is framed as a 'counter hegemonic alternative [to global capitalism] driven from below, synthesising emancipatory utopian possibilities while gaining definition through dynamic grassroots practices' (Satgar 2014: 12; see also Rakopoulos 2014). After the talk we chatted enthusiastically about other inspirational moments in the history of cooperatives and of anarchism, reminded of the cooperative's political potential and aspirational nature.

Williams and Satgar are not the only ones who see cooperation as part of an alternative economic vision. In their often-cited model of a 'diverse economy', for example, feminist geographers J. K. Gibson-Graham (2006: 77) focus on activities which can be said to sit outside the dominant 'Capitalist economy' in some ways, including cooperatives. This, too, is seen as prefigurative work. It is a way 'to dis-order the capitalist economic landscape, to queer it and thereby dislocate capitalocentrism's hegemony'. In the spaces this leaves, Gibson-Graham envisage new 'sites where ethical decisions can be made, power can be negotiated, and transformations forged'.

Inherent in the alternative structures that Williams and Satgar or Gibson-Graham propose is a more 'just' or 'moral' form of economy, reminiscent of E. P. Thompson's classic work *The Moral Economy of the English Crowd in the Eighteenth Century* (1971), in which he explores the ways in which food riots have been used to recalibrate the market following price rises, reflecting a common consensus among revolting citizens about what were and were not legitimate practices within the market. As Edelman (2015: 55) argues, Thompson's use of the term 'moral' not only refers to the mores or customs that people were used to, but also 'a principled stance vis-à-vis society, the world, and especially the common good, with the latter defined both in terms of customary rights and utopian aspirations'. It is this future-orientated, utopian stance that is particularly relevant to these visions of an alternative economy and society and to the cooperative imaginary. In this vein, sociologist Erik Olin Wright (2010: 6) has claimed that cooperatives are an example of 'real utopias'. While he acknowledges the tension between 'dreams and practice' inherent in this phrase, he suggests that, 'a vital belief in a utopian ideal may be necessary to motivate people to set off on the journey from the status quo in the first place, even though the likely actual destination may fall short of the utopian ideal'.

In a similar vein, Bauman (1976: 13) argues that utopias 'relativise the present', and by 'exposing the partiality of current reality', pave 'the way for a critical attitude and a critical activity which alone can transform the present predicament of man'. If classical utopias are 'little concerned with pragmatically conceived realism', however, the cooperative imaginary balances the practical with the imagined. In doing so, the future is collapsed into the present through practice in order to start to make these desired outcomes into realities (Bryant and Knight 2019: 14).

In historical terms, the cooperative movement has also been political and prefigurative. The cooperative imaginary in Britain has been tied to left-wing ideals of social transformation ever since the early nineteenth century Welsh factory owner and social reformer Robert Owen converted his cotton mill in New Lanark, Scotland, into a communitarian 'model factory' where workers and their families had better working conditions and access to education, leisure facilities and a cooperative shop. Owen's ultimate project, often called utopian socialism, was to create a mutual form of society made up of cooperative communities, or 'villages of cooperation', where working-class people could free themselves from Capitalist society and the poverty it created, living instead in a 'New Moral World' where they grew their own food, made their own clothes, and, in the long run, became self-governing (Birchall 1994: 20; Restakis 2010: 29). For Owen, therefore, cooperativism was 'the key to both wealth creation and a just society' (Restakis 2010: 29).[6]

More broadly, cooperativism has had a role in various left-wing political philosophies, ranging from Socialist to Anarchist. Marcel Mauss – a long-time consumer cooperative member – believed that cooperatives created a kind of 'practical socialism' through which economic experiments were not just planned or imagined, but actually experienced (Rakopoulos 2014). As he saw it, 'they are the strength and the resistance of socialism; they are the means by which socialism creates' (Mauss in Nash and Hopkins 1976: 3). By bringing visions of a different political economy into being through practice, this lent the cooperative a prefigurative quality (Graeber 2009, 2014; Maeckelbergh 2011). Rather than an attempt to completely overhaul the existing system, however, Mauss saw cooperation as a means of change from within, in which reform 'is and will be made by a process of building new groups and institutions along and on top of the old ones' (Mauss in Hart et al. 2010: 8).

Karl Marx was more ambivalent, however (Wright 2010: 235). He was dismissive of utopian socialism, and while he was positive about the cooperative movement on some occasions, suggesting that '[t]he value of these great social experiments cannot be overrated' (Marx 1864 in Wright 2010: 235), on others, he pointed out the ways in which cooperatives were still embroiled within a repressive global market (Sharzer 2017: 456).[7] Focusing on worker cooperatives, in particular, he suggested that they might deal with the issue of alienated labour, but not with capital. The workers, therefore, became their own Capitalists rather than overthrowing capitalism (Marx 1992: 571). As such, from Marx's perspective cooperatives could be a (perhaps more 'caring') aspect of capitalism rather than always an alternative. This highlights a significant tension that has long existed within the cooperative movement around whether cooperatives are simply more caring or alternative enclaves within a Capitalist system or a means of wider social transformation.

The differences between Marx and Mauss or Owen's position also speak to a broader tension within the left between gradualist and revolutionary approaches to social transformation, and between more authoritarian and libertarian visions of a Socialist society (Restakis 2010: 43–9); the former of which clearly became dominant in the forms of state socialism enacted in the twentieth century. Despite the cooperative's association with grassroots activities and less top-down structures, they have been a common component of state and overseas development efforts in many parts of the world since the twentieth century. These range from the 'New Deal' United States of the 1930s to the Soviet Union and other Soviet influenced contexts, where the collectivization of peasant farmers has been a common strategy (however challenging it may have been to integrate into local cultural and agricultural practices). Cooperatives have also become entangled with other ideologies and political agendas, becoming technologies of government rather than the more egalitarian enterprises that many grassroots groups or social movements would wish for them to be (Rakopoulos 2023), as New Labour's interest in food co-ops highlights.

From the late 1940s onwards cooperatives started to emerge in newly formed Israel, postcolonial India, and much of Africa, Asia and Latin America (Attwood 1991 on India; Bowen 2000 on Mozambique; Evans 1990 on Lao; Goldschmit 1978 on the US; Hyden 1992 on Tanzania; Russell 1995 on Israel; Stahl 2007 on Ethiopia; Stanford 2018 on China; Vargas-Cetina 2005: 231 on Mexico). When encouraged by central government, this has often been a means of increasing control and bureaucratic regulation of the countryside and its resources. In Capitalist-orientated countries this has also been a means of bolstering national trade with other countries (Nash and Hopkins 1976: 14).

In some contexts, cooperatives have also been a way for local communities to 'fend off the desires of the national government to interfere' (Nash and Hopkins 1976: 15), in order to protect Indigenous rights, or to address issues of poverty and marginalization (Vargas-Cetina 2005: 234). They also still play a part in contemporary, radical experiments in autonomy, equality and Indigenous or minority rights, such as the Mexican Zapatista movement (Juris and Khasnabish 2013) or the de facto autonomous region of north-eastern Syria known as Rojava (Leezenberg 2016). This highlights the ways in which cooperative practices and values still capture imaginations in the contemporary period of globalized forms of neoliberal capitalism just as they did in Robert Owen's era of industrial capitalism.

FOOD COOPERATIVE HISTORY AND IMAGINARY

The history of the food cooperative also speaks to grassroots responses to particular political-economic moments. Focusing in on Britain, during the late eighteenth and early nineteenth century small waves of cooperative activity rippled across the country, and much of it revolved around food provisioning. Pushing back on more charitable visions of aid also factored into conceptualizations of the cooperative for those involved. While Robert Owen was key in the creation of a holistic vision of a cooperative society, English doctor William King did much to foster cooperative enterprise in Britain. Both men saw cooperation as an emancipatory force which could fund the creation of communities in which poor people could be educated, empowered and improved through a positive environment (Owen) or self-help (King) (for more see Birchall 1994; Restakis 2010; Wilson et al. 2013).

If Owen's top-down model was more idealistically utopian in approach,[8] King was, perhaps, more pragmatic. King felt that working-class people should be facilitated to help themselves. He started by organizing a friendly society in order to support poorer people to meet their own needs through mutual aid rather than reliance on charity. Then, in the late 1820s, King turned his attention to consumer cooperatives. The idea was that as grocery shopping was a daily necessity, collectively owned shops were a good starting point for social transformation in which the surplus generated could be used to build a cooperative community – 'a new society-within-society' that would be 'independent of both capitalists and of welfare' (Restakis 2010: 36). He set out a practical template for how to run a cooperative shop in the service of a wider cooperative vision, promoting this locally by setting up a consumer cooperative, and nationally through his newspaper – *The Co-operator*.[9]

The culmination of these initiatives and ideologies paved the way for the official beginning of the modern cooperative movement (and first wave of food co-ops (Sustain 2012)) in 1844 with the foundation of the Rochdale Equitable Pioneers Society in the northwest of England. During the 1930s there had been a cooperative society in Rochdale in which two of the Rochdale Pioneers had participated and half of the Pioneers were also Owenites (Birchall, 1994: 40–1). The 28 original members of the consumer cooperative were a group of working-class men whose incomes had been adversely affected by the mechanization and industrialization of traditional crafts such as weaving – the main trade in Rochdale at the time. Food prices were also rising, and supply was monopolized by profiteering local shopkeepers who often adulterated their products with potentially lethal ingredients (Birchall 1994: 13).

What the Pioneers did was clearly practical, a means of accessing safe and affordable food through direct relationships with wholesalers, the greater bargaining power this afforded them, and the cost benefits of bulk buying. It was also highly ideological. The consumer cooperative ran on the principles of participatory democracy; open membership; profit sharing among members; and the promotion of education. Through these principles, the Pioneers attempted to democratize their everyday practices, seeking the 'benefit and the improvement of the social and domestic conditions of its members' (Robertson 2010: 1). Restakis suggests that at the heart of the Pioneers' action there was a desire for dignity in the face of declining living and working conditions (2010: 40). Rakopoulos (2017: 44) reinforces this idea, suggesting that the Pioneers' actions were a direct response to the Poor Law of 1834 and the ways in which this institutionalized poverty. As such, they were a means of pushing back against notions of the 'undeserving poor' through practices of mutual aid and self-help. In doing so, they responded to the entangled caring practices of the state and economic system (or lack thereof) and liberal forms of charitable aid that were typical in the country.

For Caffentzis and Federici (2014: i95), nineteenth-century mutual aid societies such as these were a form of 'commons "outside" of capitalism', which they suggest 'can play a key role in the class struggle, feeding the radical imagination' and in many cases also the bodies of commoners – as was the case with nineteenth-century food co-ops. The actions of the Pioneers and the subsequent waves of cooperative societies that followed marked a significant moment in social movement history and cooperative imaginaries. In Restakis' words, their model 'became the blueprint for the largest, most durable and most successful movement for economic reform in history' (2010: 36–7). It was also with the Pioneers that 'the modern conception of the cooperative as a democratically controlled enterprise took form' thanks to the influence of King (ibid.). By the turn of the twentieth century countless other working-class people had taken up the Pioneers' principles and practices in the 1,439 cooperative societies in operation within Britain (Wilson et al. 2013: 138). Although the motivations and vision behind each may have varied slightly (Birchall, 1994: 63), they were still based on the Pioneers' principles. The 'Rochdale Principles' are also still used widely by cooperatives around the world today.

If first wave food cooperatives were instrumental in creating governance structures that promoted equality, democratic decision-making and open membership, then arguably the second wave did much to inform the contemporary movement's conception of 'good food'. These co-ops developed as part of the counterculture of the 1960s and 1970s, first in the US, before spreading to other countries such as the UK. Countercultural co-ops attempted to promote a left-wing vision of a less consumer Capitalist and more sustainable society through collective lifestyle choices and everyday actions. The means of food production, acquisition and cooking became increasingly important signifiers of countercultural ideals, in opposition to the increasingly industrialized food system, rapidly expanding supermarket sector, mass production, and other aspects of Fordism. As well as providing the minimally processed, local, organic wholefoods favoured by many members of the counterculture, food co-ops were spaces from which to disseminate information about countercultural cuisine and left-wing ideology in a non-hierarchical setting (Belasco 2007). They did this with a view to sharing their message beyond the immediate movement, again, through the 'quiet example' of participatory democracy (Belasco 2007: 89).

As Cox notes, however, second wave food co-ops often 'lacked political cohesiveness and ideological discipline' and the aims and interests of cooperators could vary widely from what he describes as 'good' cheap food to challenging the supermarket industry or the empowerment of local neighbourhoods (1994: 5). Nonetheless, Cox suggests that one interest that strongly connected co-ops was a commitment to, and belief in, 'the value of personal and community empowerment', and of mutual aid, which he defined as 'the notion that people working together would strengthen the community as well as the individual' (1994: ibid). Despite this heterogeneity, countercultural food co-ops spread from the US to many other parts of the Western world and the food-based ideals and practices of the counterculture are also seen as important precursors to the forms of alternative food networks present in much of the West and beyond today (Goodman et al. 2014).

More broadly, the 1960s and 1970s are seen as a turning point in sites and forms of political action due to the nature and quantity of mobilization that took place, ranging from civil rights activism to environmentalism, feminism and anti-war protests. Where the Labour Movements, which find their origins in responses to the impacts of industrial capitalism on its workers, are often associated with collective action and class conflict, these 'new social movements', as they are often characterized, are linked with culture, identity politics and more individualized acts (Edelman 2001; Nash 2004; Sörbom and Wennerhag 2013: 454). Following the creation of the 'post-war liberal-democratic welfare society', in part as a consequence of the Labour Movements' work, Sörbom and Wennerhag (2013: 456–7) argue that these forms of activism 'aimed much of their criticism at the hierarchies, privileges, and exclusions of that order'. They also questioned the nature of the political, attempting to seek out and create new forms and spaces for political action '*outside of* parliamentary democracy and party politics' (456–7 emphasis original). In relation to second wave food co-ops, Cox suggests that it was about a 'politics of personal choice and freedom, spiritual awakening and liberation. Everything else – electoral politics, distribution of wealth, class warfare – was secondary' (Cox 1994: 10–1). In essence, it was about an individual process of politicization and emancipation.

While some celebrate the ways in which political possibility has expanded, others suggest that it has led to too great an individualization of practices, both in everyday life and in activism (Sörbom and Wennerhag 2013: 457). Ghosh (2017: 128–33) argues that due to this shift, politics is coming to be conceived of as an 'individual moral adventure', guided by one's conscience and belief in self-actualization. He asserts that many of the moral acts performed today, ranging from ethical consumption to clicktivism (signing online petitions), can simply end up as forms of personal expression rather than intervention. Attempts at ethical citizenship such as this, emphasize the role of sovereign subjects and their sense of spontaneous will in social or political change (Muehlebach 2012: 49–50). Federici might argue that they are 'manifestations of the rise of a new individualism pursuing the "good life", but not through a social struggle for the "common good"' (Federici 2018: 180).

The forms of consumption-based political action that food co-ops adopt can also fall into these debates as Fareshares member Brian's concerns highlighted. Some question whether 'ethical' consumption represents any real resistance to the mainstream economic, political and environmental processes it wishes to oppose (Littler 2011: 33). They suggest that it is simply a form of conspicuous consumption or a way to mark out distinction due to the, often, higher prices of organic, fairly-traded and other goods perceived to be ethical (see also Bourdieu 2010 on distinction; Carrier and Luetchford 2012; Littler 2011). Others make arguments about new sites of political action, more accessible to everyday citizens than other forms might be (Barnett et al. 2010), or suggest that within the context of cooperative activity, such practices have the potential to become genuinely 'radical' (Littler 2011: 32). These dynamics and dilemmas undoubtedly played out in the personal and collective practices and values of Fareshares and St Hilda's East food co-ops during my fieldwork.

What of the food cooperative today? Within the British context, the term has come to be used for a wide range of community food initiatives, including fruit and vegetable box/bag schemes, worker- and consumer-run grocery shops, collective purchasing groups, and charitable or social enterprise-oriented community food projects. Each has its own agenda, socio-economic make-up and organizational structure. Each tells a different, yet complementary, story about contemporary British society, the global food system and the political-economic situation in Britain. As Fareshares and St Hilda's highlight, they can also come from very different political backgrounds.

Rather than attempt to create a typology for these food co-ops, or identify them as or within a specific social movement, I prefer to look at each in situ and on its own terms (Negri et al. 2017: 519). Equally, while a representative of Co-ops UK that I spoke to during my fieldwork was happy to include all of these different enterprises named 'food co-ops' in the cooperative movement (whether they are structured along lines of member-ownership and management or not), participants rarely spoke in movement terms, instead engaging with the individual practices of the project and its logics, the forms of social change it and its members desired or with specific political ideologies or issues that they were facing and trying to respond to.

OBSTACLES, POSSIBILITIES AND DILEMMAS

In a similar vein to Mauss, Satgar and Gibson-Graham, I see the cooperative's potential as a form of 'alter-politics', which works not simply to oppose the structures that it disagrees with (anti-capitalism, anti-racism, etc.), but also to envision new possibilities and lay 'the grounds for new modes of existence' (Hage 2015: 4).[10] Bauman (1976: 36) argues that modern socialism has been 'the counter-culture of capitalist society, if by counter-culture one means the fulcrum on which the emancipatory criticism-through-relativization of the current reality rests'. The two have evolved together, with one pushing against the other. In many ways, the modern cooperative has also been enacted as a countercultural form in relation to capitalism, whether as part of socialism, or as its own alternative vision of economy and society. Clearly, this is not without its complications and ambivalences, however.

Wright (2010: 6) suggests that we need '"real utopias": utopian ideals that are grounded in the real potentials of humanity, utopian destinations that have accessible waystations, utopian designs of institutions that can inform our practical tasks of navigating a world of imperfect conditions for social change'. Since the era of industrial capitalism, the cooperative has been one of these 'accessible waystations' (ibid.). In line with the thinking of Gibson-Graham and Wright, I see this as a means of opening up the capacity to imagine and hope for something better. As Haiven and Khasnabish put it (2014: 4), '[w]e create, with those around us, multiple, overlapping, contradictory, and coexistent imaginary landscapes, horizons of common possibility and shared understanding'. Such shared landscapes shape and are shaped by the imaginations and actions of those involved in complex ways, which speak to how individual imaginations are informed by experiences as 'embodied subjects who are intersected by race, class, gender, sexuality, nationality, ethnicity and other differences' (ibid.: 7).

Bauman suggests that the 'driving force behind the search for utopia is neither the theoretical nor the practical reason, neither the cognitive nor the moral interest, but the principle of hope ... Hope supplies the missing link between practical and theoretical interests because it is intrinsically critical of the reality in which it is rooted' (Bauman 1976: 13–14). In times of political-economic unrest, the cooperative idea has often offered such hope, compelling people to start to imagine and prefigure something better for themselves.[11]

While an initiative such as a food co-op may seem small in the face of current political-economic challenges, Federici argues that within the 'context of a growing impoverishment and the militarization of everyday life, leading to paralysis, withdrawal, and distrust of neighbours, these signs of a will to cooperate are an encouraging' symbol of 'our capacity to transform everyday practices into a terrain of collective struggle' (Federici 2018: 184). At the heart of this struggle is anti-capitalism, but also radical forms of care, aid and interconnection. The purpose of this struggle 'is to begin to construct new forms of being, new structures – even if they are small' (Federici in Moraes and Brant 2016: 212). Ticktin suggests that 'if expanded, a feminist commons could replace the exclusionary format of nation-states and borders with capacious structures and infrastructures of political care' (Ticktin 2021; see also The Care Collective 2020).

'Each of us has to decide where we can give our best contribution, which movement, which struggle' according to Federici (in Moraes and Brant 2016: 212). '[T]he challenge is to bring the struggles together. Not only protest'. Within these forms of social reproduction, which Federici describes as 'the micro politics of production', she argues that people begin to ask what kind of society they want to live in, how the activities they are involved with might make things better for them and others and how they might give people more power today and tomorrow. Through these acts, therefore, there is the potential to foster new practices, skills, imaginations and relationships. As Ticktin puts it (in Woodly et al. 2021), within the context of a feminist commons, care helps to bring 'new political formations' and 'new collective subject[s] into being'.

'Anti-capitalist commons' Caffentzis and Federici suggest (2014: i103), should not be seen as the end point for a 'non-Capitalist world', however, but the 'means' of getting there. As they explain, 'no struggle will succeed in changing the world if we do not organize our reproduction in a communal way and not only share the space and time of meetings and demonstrations but put our lives in common, organizing on the basis of our different needs and possibilities, and the rejection of all principles of exclusion or hierarchization'.

An important question here is what this new society might actually look like. While Utopian Socialists such as Owen supplied detailed blueprints (Levitas 2010: 52), I align with more process-orientated, bottom-up and prefigurative approaches to transformation. Instead, of blueprints, key organizing principles can be worked out and tested through trial and error and adaptation to changing circumstances. This attention to process and adaptability provides opportunities to explore political and practical 'virtues' (Wright 2010: 7–8) as well as the resilience of particular models such as the cooperative. It can also lead to unintended consequences, however, as the discussion above on the adoption (or co-option) of the cooperative and the food co-op for less radical or egalitarian purposes highlights.

Wright (2010: 10) argues that 'any emancipatory social science faces three basic tasks – elaborating a systematic diagnosis and critique of the world as it exists; envisioning viable alternatives; and understanding the obstacles, possibilities, and dilemmas of transformation'. Building on Wright, in many ways this book is guided by questions of what hope the food cooperative might offer in the context of austerity Britain, and what 'obstacles, possibilities, and dilemmas' it encounters along the way.

In addition to the possibilities engendered by particular models and practices (such as the cooperative), context also matters. As Wright (2010: 22) puts it, considerations of viability need to include 'discussions of the contextual conditions-of-possibility for particular designs to work well'. In this book, I consider how the food co-op fares in austerity Britain. Ethnographically exploring the structures of feeling within a specific time and place highlights how dominant structures are experienced as well as what everyday people do to resist them and how.

As Wright suggests, 'what is pragmatically possible is not fixed independently of our imaginations, but is itself shaped by our visions' (Wright 2010: 6). Better understanding the affective qualities of such an era is, therefore, important in analysing the kinds of imaginations and radical actions that this facilitates and obstructs; the kinds of structures of feeling that are emergent and residual (Vanke 2024: 26); and how these shape relationships, actions and visions. I focus on the entanglement of care, aid and community in my conceptualization of everyday politics as these are not only key practical and ideological components of the food cooperative, but also areas in which the obstacles, possibilities and dilemmas of alter-political practice became most apparent during my fieldwork.

Clearly Fareshares and St Hilda's East are very different projects, born of different values, aims and structures of feeling. Rather than a like-for-like comparative, therefore, this book explores the forms of everyday politics that took place within each, what these different models (re)produced in terms of actions and imaginations and what this helps us to understand about everyday forms of political action and the meaning of the food cooperative.

PERSONAL ANTHROPOLOGY

My interest in food co-ops has been shaped in many ways by my life experiences, personal politics and concerns for the contemporary political-economic and food systems. Spurred on by a dissatisfaction with housing conditions in the UK, I made the decision to move into a housing co-op in London in 2012. I saw this as both a socially and politically driven act. Idealistically, I wanted to be a part of some form of 'community', in a city and time where such things felt fragmented. I was interested in queering notions of the family in terms of where care, support and a sense of belonging or shared values are sought.[12] I also hoped that the successful foundation of a new housing co-op in a prohibitively expensive city would demonstrate that alternatives to the deeply problematic housing system were possible and doable without having to be wealthy (none of the members put capital into the purchase of the property – instead it was supported by loan stock from other cooperatives and like-minded people). Within the co-op our practices worked to enact a more direct form of democracy through the use of consensus decision-making and principles built around equality, tolerance and inclusiveness. This also appealed to me, as I have long had an uncomfortable relationship with hierarchical authority. As is often the case with such projects, however, the reality was different to the ideal. There were many arguments within the co-op, protracted meetings and multiple instances of 'bad-consensus' (where members were not willing to shift their position for the good of the group). While caring about the upkeep of the building, the finances, the shopping and cooking rotas or other practicalities, the need to invest time in fostering forms of sociality built around mutuality, care and fun were often left to one side. Instead, the 'business' of the co-op often spilled over into evening meals and other everyday interactions. In many ways, we were caring for the co-op, but not sufficiently for each other or ourselves as its residents and members. Such an experience will, no doubt, be familiar to many who have engaged in non-hierarchical organizing, whether in housing co-ops, activist networks (see, for example, Freeman 1972; Graeber 2009) or food co-ops. All in all, this did not make for a particularly relaxing living situation. Although I chose to leave the housing co-op, I did not feel that I had fully satisfied my interest in cooperatives either personally or academically.

As a consequence of this personal interest in cooperatives and my concerns about aspects of the mainstream political-economic and food systems, I characterize this research project as an engaged form of anthropology. This is reflective of my shared interest in and commitment to aspects of food cooperatives' visions of social justice and social change (Low and Merry 2010: S208), although these can, admittedly, vary considerably. Engaged anthropology can work in various registers, ranging from sharing and support to collaboration, advocacy or activism, and some of these may be more subtle than others (Low and Merry 2010). I choose the term 'engaged' over others such as 'activist' (Lyon-Callo and Hyatt 2003) or 'militant' (Scheper-Hughes 1995) anthropology as I feel it leaves more space for the subtleties and complexities of ethnographic engagement, and the ways in which my own ethics and positionality may not have always perfectly aligned with those of my research participants (just as each of theirs may not align with each other's) despite my desire to take a supportive approach, which attempted solidarity. Due to my stance on engagement, I also attempt to make my writing as accessible as I can within the confines of academic standards. As such, at times, I choose less formal wording.

Through my ethnographic work, I engage with some forms of cultural critique by 'studying up' in order to highlight the ways in which macroeconomic and political factors impacted the microsocial spaces in which I worked during a politically turbulent period (Low and Merry 2010), which saw many harsh consequences of austerity and welfare reform. As Lyon-Callo and Hyatt (2003: 177–9) suggest, studying localities 'from below' can be a way of '"ethnographizing" and therefore demystifying' wider structures, such as neoliberal state practices, and the ways in which processes of neoliberalization and globalization can impact grassroots attempts at social change. This also feeds into Wright's conceptualization of 'emancipatory social science' in which 'diagnosis and critique of the world as it exists' is necessary as part of a process of challenging oppression, envisioning 'viable alternatives' to the current situation and 'understanding the obstacles, possibilities, and dilemmas of transformation' as discussed above (2010: 10).

Identifying with a spirit of mutual aid or a feminist ethic of care, I have attempted to acknowledge in this work and in the way I conducted my fieldwork that we *all* need care and also give it. In other words, we all have our vulnerabilities (O'Neill 2018) and interdependencies (Puig de la Bellacasa 2017: 4). In this vein, I attempted to be open about my own vulnerabilities in my fieldwork while also trying to acknowledge those of others through the care I offered and received as a volunteer, colleague, friend and ethnographer; and now through the ways in which I represent the people and the projects I worked with.

As a consequence of my stance on engagement, and the nature of the organizations I worked with, at times I was very much an 'observing participant' (Kadir 2016: 40) who actively fed into the decision-making practices of each food co-op and therefore shaped the spaces in which I worked. In line with 'an ethic of openness and flexibility' (Juris and Khasnabish 2013: 9), the ethnographic process, which itself can be a transformative experience, also shaped me in many ways (Malkki 2015: 12). This more active form of 'observing participation' was an important tool in fully understanding what it meant and felt like – practically, physically and affectively – to be a volunteer-member of Fareshares and St Hilda's East. I felt that this approach was necessary to fully understand the practices, ideology and social imaginary of each food co-op, as well as how it felt to care and be cared for in these spaces. At times, when a situation appeared to be ethnographically rich, I also tried to allow others to take the lead, however, provided that this did not put additional pressure on them or create an uncomfortable situation. This allowed me to better understand the logics and decision-making processes within each space. At Fareshares, in particular, a project attempting non-hierarchical organizing and consensus decision-making, being a fully participating observer proved instrumental in my understanding of the structures and hierarchies within the food co-op – even as I became embroiled in them.

While I name many of the sites I worked with, in particular St Hilda's and Fareshares, and the managerial figures within the former, such as the director and coordinators, I use pseudonyms and, at times, anonymization for the other people involved with each co-op, unless they expressly gave consent for their names to be used in this research. When discussing contentious issues, I sometimes still use pseudonyms and anonymization for those who gave consent in order to protect my research participants' privacy, dignity or social relations within each co-op.

CRISIS ON CRISIS

While the research for this book was primarily conducted between 2015 and 2017, a time in which austerity was having serious impacts on people's lives in the UK, less than three years later, the coronavirus pandemic started in March 2020. This marked the beginning of another period of extended global, social, political and economic crisis. Since 2021, food prices have increased continuously, energy prices have sky-rocketed and inflation has also risen. The economic turmoil that the pandemic created has also been further compounded by the Russian invasion of Ukraine in February 2022 and climate-related poor harvests, all of which led to shortages of goods and workers.[13] This threw many countries, including the UK, into a severe cost of living crisis (The Institute for Government 2022), the impacts and extent of which are yet to be fully understood.

In September 2020, one of the key architects of British austerity, former Prime Minister David Cameron, released the paperback version of his memoir, updated with a foreword commenting on the coronavirus pandemic. In it, he claimed that cuts introduced when he came to power in 2010 fixed 'the roof when the sun was shining in preparation for the next crisis that should hit'. Ten years on, he stated 'COVID-19 was the rainy day we had been saving for' (Cameron 2020: xv). Yet these cuts to welfare and the public sector also hollowed out the National Health Service (NHS) so vital to the response to Covid-19, reformed welfare in ways that left ever growing numbers of people unable to afford food, housing or the energy needed to heat and power their homes. As I write, these issues are now being further compounded by the latest set of crises.

While Cameron and others from his cabinet have fiercely defended austerity politics, its success in relation to the alleviation of sovereign debt has been called into question (see, for example, Blyth 2015; Koch and James 2022). The UN also raised concerns about the social impacts of the severe austerity cuts implemented in the UK (Booth and Butler 2018). While austerity as a fiscal policy officially ended in the UK in 2019, the latest set of crises has exacerbated many of the forms of insecurity and inequality that British austerity catalysed in the preceding decade. This period has also galvanized action around needs, inequalities and various forms of insecurity, whether through pre-established community projects, the swathe of new mutual aid groups that were set up around the globe during the pandemic

(Solnit 2020) or the resurgence of the Black Lives Matter Movement following the murder of George Floyd. The kinds of mass mobilization seen during the pandemic highlight the imperative to study welfare, aid and political action in the current era.

Although this book deals with a period before 2020, it highlights some of the ways in which welfare provisions were hollowed out, the nature of citizenship shifted, and everyday political action was informed by a prolonged period of economic turbulence, austerity and decades of neoliberal policy. In doing so, it offers vital context to the impacts that these more recent crises are having, and to the forms of community organizing and political action they engender.

OVERVIEW OF CHAPTERS

In chapter 1, I tell the story of the foundation of Fareshares and St Hilda's East Food Co-ops. I show how each is connected to specific political regimes and ideologies, arguing that these and the structures of feeling within the given era of their formation are fundamental to the food co-op's modes of organizing and imaginaries. In chapter 2, I explore the material and social worlds of each food co-op today – their looks, foods, daily rhythms and aims as well as how these are experienced by their participants. I engage, in particular, with themes of community, inclusion and alternative economic practice and how these articulate elements of the food co-ops' contemporary imaginaries and politics. In chapter 3, I move onto the social organization of each co-op, its relationship to notions of hierarchy, horizontality and work, as well as the tensions that attempts at collective organizing can create. I focus in on the practices and ideals around care and political action that these represent, the different ideologies that these are drawn from and the ways in which other value systems and experiences can conflict with ideal typical models of ownership, autonomy and unalienated labour. In chapter 4, I contextualize the political-economic climate and structures of feeling in austerity Britain, exploring how this interacted with the practices and experiences of the food co-ops and their members. I focus, in particular, on each co-op's relationship to changing needs and interests, showing some of the tensions that were felt in relation to issues such as resilience (at St Hilda's); and diverse values and motivations among members (at Fareshares), as well as the ways in which austerity Britain could be experienced as closing down imaginations. I also look at some members' direct experiences of and feelings about austerity and the punitive climate it has created, highlighting some of its affective as well as material impacts. In chapter 5 I explore the food co-ops' practices of community building and boundary-making along with the forms of inclusion or exclusion that each of these can entail. I also look outwards from the food co-ops to contextualize them more thoroughly within two areas deeply impacted by housing reform and regeneration. I show the ways in which this has inspired both nostalgia for past communities, and heightened desires to create inclusive spaces in terms of class, race, ethnicity and alternative lifestyles – however tension ridden this may be. In chapter 6, I engage with the social and financial value of the goods Fareshares and St Hilda's East stock, the ideologies that the food co-ops attempt to work by and the ways in which these ideologies interact and push back against forms of Capitalist exchange and charity, as well as the 'awkwardnesses' that can occur between ideals and the reality of austerity Britain in which charitable feeding and humanitarian imaginaries were both on the rise. In the conclusion, I return to the subject of everyday politics, engaging with how the political is experienced and understood at each food co-op. I argue again for the importance of taking seriously such small everyday acts as food provisioning in our understanding of the political as these can be deeply resonant within the lives of those involved in terms of personhood and political imaginations.

NOTES

1. At times even more so with the benefit of hindsight.
2. With food cooperatives, this provisioning comes in two forms – the act of choosing what to provide for sale at the co-op, who these goods are aimed at, and at what price goods are sold; and the purchase of goods for friends, family and selves. In the context of alternative food schemes, such as grassroots, retail food co-ops, household food provisioning is, like elsewhere, still often performed by women despite the common desire of such schemes to challenge some of societies structures (Som Castellano 2015; see also Miller 2001 on food shopping and gender). This gendered dynamic no doubt also impacts on who chooses, or is encouraged, to get involved with schemes such as food co-ops. Many of the volunteers in both of the food co-ops I worked with identified as women. While Fareshares stretched some of the normative assumptions about who we care for through food provisioning a little further as a more queer space, at St Hilda's many of the women who volunteered were also mothers or wives. To date, the majority of the food co-op coordinators at St Hilda's have also been women. The act of food provisioning and the prevalence of women in these sites speaks to some of the ways in which caring responsibilities can and often are gendered, with women doing much of the practical and emotional (although not necessarily paid) labour (Alber and Drotbohm 2015; Kneafsey et al. 2008; Thelen 2015).
3. As many have pointed out, neoliberalism is contradictory and heterogeneous, neither complete nor timeless (Brenner and Theodore 2002; Hilgers 2010; Masquelier 2017; Peck and Tickell 2002). Here I understand it as 'process' and as 'experience' (Greenhouse 2012: 2), attending to some of the impacts it has had on food cooperative participants and wider British society.

4. I use inverted commas in recognition of the fact that despite its wide usage, the term food poverty is also criticized by some of the practitioners I met during fieldwork for running the risk of obfuscating the wider issue of poverty by focusing only on one aspect of it.
5. Within a British context, food banks are charitable organizations that offer food parcels to 'the hungry'.
6. It is worth noting that there were also other Utopian Socialists such as Saint-Simon and Fourier with their own visions of a new Socialist society, but Owen is the most influential to the British cooperative movement. I therefore focus, in particular, on his work here. For more on the others, their influence on Socialist thought and tensions between such thinkers and Marxist thought, see Levitas 2010.
7. Restakis (2010: 44) suggests that Marx and Engels were more positive towards cooperatives in earlier writings as 'the conditions for a class-based strategy for revolution were not fully developed'. Once these conditions were developed, he suggests that they became more critical of cooperativism.
8. Wilson et al. (2013: 30) suggest that he was critical of any who viewed cooperation and co-ops in practical rather than ideological terms.
9. Despite its initial successes, by 1834 King's wave of cooperation had all but subsided due to: the turbulence of the economy; the precariousness of the legal status of co-ops – which could only be registered in one member's name, making them vulnerable to maladministration and fraud; and the fact that not all cooperators were committed to the dream of cooperative communities, giving them less incentive to continue with their membership (Wilson et al. 2013: 33).
10. Although the 'alter-political' and the more oppositional approaches that Hage calls 'anti-political' need not be mutually exclusive (Hage 2015: 4).
11. Significant contemporary examples include the workers' cooperative movement in Argentina, in which workers collectively 'recovered' or reopened companies that closed during the economic and social crisis of 2001 (Bryer 2012; Sitrin 2012) in order to take control of their own livelihoods, while also addressing some of the perceived issues with the economy and structures of work. Another notable example is the food cooperatives involved with the anti-middleman movement in Greece, which attempted to create more direct connections between producers and consumers, while creating better access to affordable food in a period of austerity (Rakopoulos 2014). Rakopoulos argues that the financial crisis of 2008 'rejuvenated interest in the long-standing debate on the multiple range of human economic practices' (Rakopoulos 2014: 198), giving rise to various cooperative initiatives, including food cooperatives.
12. Although I would not necessarily have articulated that in these exact terms at the time.
13. In the British context, Brexit has also contributed to these issues.

REFERENCES

Alber, Erdmute, and Heike Drotbohm (eds). 2015. *Anthropological Perspectives on Care: Work, Kinship, and the Life-Course*. New York: Palgrave Macmillan.

Allen, Robert C. 1997. 'Agriculture and the Origins of the State in Ancient Egypt', *Explorations in Economic History* 34(2): 135–54.

Appadurai, Arjun. 1981. 'Gastro-Politics in Hindu South Asia', *American Ethnologist* 8(3): 494–511.

Asara, Viviana. 2020. 'Untangling the Radical Imaginaries of the Indignados' Movement: Commons, Autonomy and Ecologism', *Environmental Politics:* 1–25.

Attwood, Donald W. 1991. *Raising Cane: The Political Economy of Sugar in Western India.* Boulder: Routledge.

Back, Les. 2015. 'Why Everyday Life Matters: Class, Community and Making Life Livable', *Sociology* 49(5): 820–36.

Barnett, Clive et al. 2010. *Globalizing Responsibility: The Political Rationalities of Ethical Consumption.* Chichester, West Sussex: Wiley-Blackwell.

Basu, Sanjay et al. 2017. 'Ten Years after the Financial Crisis: The Long Reach of Austerity and Its Global Impacts on Health', *Social Science & Medicine* 187: 203–7.

Bauman, Zygmunt. 1976. *Socialism: The Active Utopia.* Plymouth: Allen & Unwin.

Belasco, Warren. 2007. *Appetite for Change: How the Counterculture Took on the Food Industry.* Ithaca, NY: Cornell University Press.

Birchall, Johnston. 1994. *Co-op: The People's Business.* Manchester: Manchester University Press.

Blyth, Mark. 2015. *Austerity: The History of a Dangerous Idea* (Illustrated edition). Oxford; New York: Oxford University Press.

Bonanno, Letizia. 2023. 'The Work of Pharmaceuticals in Austerity-Burdened Athens: Modes and Practices of Care in Times of Crisis', *Ethnos* 88(5): 1054–72.

Booth, Robert, and Patrick Butler. 2018, 16 November. 'UK Austerity Has Inflicted "Great Misery" on Citizens, UN Says', *The Guardian.*

Bourdieu, Pierre. 2010. *Distinction: A Social Critique of the Judgement of Taste.* London: Routledge.

Bowen, Merle L. 2000. *The State against the Peasantry: Rural Struggles in Colonial and Postcolonial Mozambique.* Virginia: University of Virginia Press.

Brenner, Neil, and Nik Theodore. 2002. 'Cities and the Geographies of "Actually Existing Neoliberalism"', *Antipode* 34(3): 349–79.

Bryant, Rebecca, and Daniel M. Knight. 2019. *The Anthropology of the Future.* Cambridge; New York: Cambridge University Press.

Bryer, Alice Rose. 2012. 'The Politics of the Social Economy: A Case Study of the Argentinean Empresas Recuperadas', *Dialectical Anthropology* 36(1): 21–49.

Cabot, Heath. 2016. '"Contagious" Solidarity: Reconfiguring Care and Citizenship in Greece's Social Clinics', *Social Anthropology* 24(2): 152–66.

Caffentzis, George, and Silvia Federici. 2014. 'Commons Against and Beyond Capitalism', *Community Development Journal* 49: i92–105.

Cameron, David. 2020. *For the Record.* Glasgow: William Collins.

The Care Collective. 2020. *The Care Manifesto: The Politics of Interdependence.* London; New York: Verso.

Carenotes Collective (ed.). 2020. *For Health Autonomy: Horizons of Care Beyond Austerity – Reflections from Greece.* Brooklyn: Common Notions.

Carney, Megan A. 2021. *Island of Hope: Migration and Solidarity in the Mediterranean.* Berkeley: University of California Press.

Carrier, James, and Peter Luetchford. 2012. *Ethical Consumption: Social Value and Economic Practice.* Oxford: Berghahn Books.

Clayton, John et al. 2015. 'Emotions of Austerity: Care and Commitment in Public Service Delivery in the North East of England', *Emotion, Space and Society* 14: 24–32.

Cloke, Paul et al. 2017. 'The Geographies of Food Banks in the Meantime', *Progress in Human Geography* 41(6): 703–26.

Cole, G. D. H. 2018. *The British Co-operative Movement in a Socialist Society*. London: Routledge.

Cox, Craig. 1994. *Storefront Revolution: Food Co-ops and the Counterculture*. New Brunswick: Rutgers University Press.

Diamond, Jared. 1998. *Guns, Germs and Steel: A Short History of Everybody for the Last 13,000 Years* (New edition). London: Vintage.

Edelman, Marc. 2001. 'Social Movements: Changing Paradigms and Forms of Politics', *Annual Review of Anthropology* 30: 285–317.

———. 2015. 'E. P. Thompson and Moral Economies', in Didier Fassin (ed.), *A Companion to Moral Anthropology*. Malden, MA: John Wiley & Sons, pp. 49–65.

Evans, Grant. 1990. *Lao Peasants under Socialism*. New Haven: Yale University Press.

Fareshares. (n.d.). 'Welcome to Fareshares'. Retrieved 13 September 2022 from https://fareshares.org.uk/front-page.

Federici, Silvia. 2012. 'Feminism and the Politics of the Common in an Era of Primitive Accumulation', in Silvia Federici, *Revolution at Point Zero: Housework, Reproduction, and Feminist Struggle*. Oakland, CA; Brooklyn; London: PM Press, pp. 138–48.

———. 2018. *Re-enchanting the World: Feminism and the Politics of the Commons*. Oakland, CA: PM Press.

Freeman, Jo. 1972. 'The Tyranny of Structurelessness'. Retrieved 10 December 2023 from http://www.jofreeman.com/joreen/tyranny.htm.

Ghosh, Amitav. 2017. *The Great Derangement: Climate Change and the Unthinkable*. Chicago; London: University of Chicago Press.

Gibson-Graham, J. K. 2003. 'An Ethics of the Local', *Rethinking Marxism* 15(1): 49–74.

———. 2006. *A Postcapitalist Politics*. Minneapolis; London: University of Minnesota Press.

Goldschmit, Walter Rochs. 1978. *As You Sow: Three Studies in the Social Consequences of Agribusiness*. Montclair: Rowman & Littlefield.

Goodman, David et al. 2014. *Alternative Food Networks: Knowledge, Practice, and Politics*. Abingdon: Routledge.

Graeber, David. 2009. *Direct Action: An Ethnography*. Edinburgh: AK Press.

———. 2014. *The Democracy Project: A History, a Crisis, a Movement*. London: Penguin.

Greenhouse, Carol J. (ed.). 2012. *Ethnographies of Neoliberalism*. Philadelphia; Oxford: University of Pennsylvania Press.

Hage, Ghassan. 2015. *Alter-Politics: Critical Anthropology and the Radical Imagination*. Carlton, Victoria: Melbourne University Publishing.

Haiven, Max, and Alex Khasnabish. 2014. *The Radical Imagination: Social Movement Research in the Age of Austerity*. Halifax; Winnipeg; London: Zed Books Ltd.

Hart, Keith et al. 2010. *Human Economy: A Citizen's Guide*. Cambridge: Polity Press.

Heckert, Jamie. 2011. 'Listening, Caring, Becoming: Anarchism as an Ethics of Direct Relationships', in Benjamin Franks and Matthew Wilson (eds), *Anarchism and Moral Philosophy*. Basingstoke: Palgrave, pp. 186–207.

Hilgers, Mathieu. 2010. 'The Three Anthropological Approaches to Neoliberalism*', *International Social Science Journal* 61(202): 351–64.

Hobart, Hi'ilei Julia Kawehipuaakahaopulani, and Tamara Kneese. 2020. 'Radical Care: Survival Strategies for Uncertain Times', *Social Text* 38(1 (142)): 1–16.

Hyatt, Susan Brin. 2012. 'The Work of Being Governed: From the Welfare State to the "Big Society" in Britain', in Kendra Coulter and William R. Schumann (eds), *Governing Cultures: Anthropological Perspectives on Political Labor, Power, and Government*. New York: Palgrave Macmillan, pp. 159–81.

Hyden. 1992. *Beyond the Ujamaa in Tanzania: Underdevelopment and an Uncaptured Peasantry* (New edition). Berkeley: University of California Press.

The Institute for Government. 2022, 7 February. 'Cost of Living Crisis', *The Institute for Government*. Retrieved 3 June 2022 from https://www.instituteforgovernment.org.uk/explainers/cost-living-crisis.

International Co-operative Alliance. (n.d.). 'What is a Cooperative?' Retrieved 13 September 2022 from https://www.ica.coop/en/cooperatives/what-is-a-cooperative.

Jupp, Eleanor. 2012. 'Rethinking Local Activism: "Cultivating the Capacities" of Neighbourhood Organising', *Urban Studies* 49(14): 3027–44.

———. 2017. 'Home Space, Gender and Activism: The Visible and the Invisible in Austere Times', *Critical Social Policy* 37(3): 348–66.

———. 2022. *Care, Crisis and Activism: The Politics of Everyday Life*. Bristol: Policy Press.

Juris, Jeffrey S., and Alex Khasnabish (eds). 2013. *Insurgent Encounters: Transnational Activism, Ethnography, and the Political*. Durham, NC; London: Duke University Press.

Kadir, Nazima. 2016. *The Autonomous Life? Paradoxes of Hierarchy and Authority in the Squatters Movement in Amsterdam*. Manchester: Manchester University Press.

Klein, Jakob A. et al. 2012. 'New Directions in the Anthropology of Food', in Richard Fardon et al. (eds), *The SAGE Handbook of Social Anthropology*. London: SAGE Publications Ltd, pp. 293–302.

Kneafsey, Moya et al. 2008. *Reconnecting Consumers, Producers and Food: Exploring Alternatives*. Oxford; New York: Berg Publishers.

Koch, Insa, and Deborah James. 2022. 'The State of the Welfare State: Advice, Governance and Care in Settings of Austerity', *Ethnos* 87(1): 1–21.

Kropotkin, Peter. 2014. *Mutual Aid: A Factor in Evolution* (W. Jonson, ed.). Charlestown, SC: CreateSpace Independent Publishing Platform.

Lawler, Steph. 2017. 'Studying Britain: A British Sociologist's View' (C. Degnen and K. Tyler, eds), *The Sociological Review* 65(1_suppl): 13–19.

Lawson, Victoria. 2007. 'Geographies of Care and Responsibility', *Annals of the Association of American Geographers* 97(1): 1–11.

Leezenberg, Michiel. 2016. 'The Ambiguities of Democratic Autonomy: The Kurdish Movement in Turkey and Rojava', *Southeast European and Black Sea Studies* 16(4): 671–90.

Levitas, Ruth. 2010. *The Concept of Utopia: 3* (New edition). Oxford; New York: Verlag Peter Lang.

Littler, J. 2011. 'What's Wrong with Ethical Consumption?', in T. Lewis and E. Potter (eds), *Ethical Consumption: A Critical Introduction*. London: Routledge, pp. 27–39.

Low, Setha M., and Sally Engle Merry. 2010. 'Engaged Anthropology: Diversity and Dilemmas: An Introduction to Supplement 2', *Current Anthropology* 51(S2): S203–26.

Lyon-Callo, Vincent, and Susan Brin Hyatt. 2003. 'The Neoliberal State and the Depoliticization of Poverty: Activist Anthropology and "Ethnography From Below"', *Urban Anthropology and Studies of Cultural Systems and World Economic Development* 32(2): 175–204.

Maeckelbergh, Marianne. 2011. 'Doing is Believing: Prefiguration as Strategic Practice in the Alterglobalization Movement', *Social Movement Studies* 10(1): 1–20.

Malkki, Liisa. 2015. *The Need to Help: The Domestic Arts of International Humanitarianism*. Durham, NC: Duke University Press.

Marx, Karl. 1992. *Capital: Critique of Political Economy v. 3*, (D. Fernbach, trans.) (3rd edition). New York: Penguin Classics.

Masquelier, Charles. 2017. *Critique and Resistance in a Neoliberal Age: Towards a Narrative of Emancipation*. London: Palgrave Macmillan.

Miller, Daniel. 2001. *The Dialectics of Shopping*. Chicago: University of Chicago Press.

Moraes, Alana, and Maria A. C. Brant. 2016. 'SILVIA FEDERICI: "Our Struggle Will Not Succeed Unless We Rebuild Society": An Interview with Silvia Federici', *Sur – International Journal on Human Rights* 13(23): 203–13.

Mouffe, Chantal. 2005. *On the Political*. London; New York: Routledge.

Muehlebach, Andrea. 2012. *The Moral Neoliberal: Welfare and Citizenship in Italy*. Chicago: University of Chicago Press.

Narotzky, Susana (ed.). 2013. 'Provisioning', in James G. Carrier, *A Handbook of Economic Anthropology* (2nd edition). Cheltenham: Edward Elgar Publishing Ltd, pp. 78–3.

Nash, June. 2004. *Social Movements: An Anthropological Reader*. Malden, MA: John Wiley & Sons.

Nash, June, and Nicholas S. Hopkins. 1976. 'Anthropological Approaches to the Study of Cooperatives, Collectives, and Self-Management', in June Nash et al. (eds), *Popular Participation in Social Change: Cooperatives, Collectives, and Nationalized Industry*. The Hague; Paris: Mouton Publishers, pp. 3–32.

Negri, Antonio et al. 2017. 'Living Labour and Social Movements: A Dialogue with Antonio Negri', *Anthropological Theory* 17(4): 518–25.

O'Neill, John. 2018. 'Food, Needs and Commons', in Jose Luis Vivero-Pol et al. (eds), *Routledge Handbook of Food as a Commons*. Abingdon, Oxon; New York: Routledge, pp. 103–20.

Peck, Jamie, and Adam Tickell. 2002. 'Neoliberalizing Space', *Antipode* 34(3): 380–404.

Powers, Theodore, and Theodoros Rakopoulos. 2019. 'The Anthropology of Austerity', *Focaal* (83): 1–12.

Puig de la Bellacasa, María. 2017. *Matters of Care: Speculative Ethics in More than Human Worlds*, Posthumanities. Minneapolis: University of Minnesota Press.

Rakopoulos, Theodoros. 2014. 'The Crisis Seen From Below, Within, and Against: From Solidarity Economy to Food Distribution Cooperatives in Greece', *Dialectical Anthropology* 38(2): 189–207.

———. 2017. *From Clans to Co-ops: Confiscated Mafia Land in Sicily*, The Human Economy (Vol. 4). Oxford: Berghahn Books.

———. 2018. 'Introduction: Austerity, Measured', in Theodoros Rakopoulos (ed.), *Global Life of Austerity: Comparing Beyond Europe: 17*. New York: Berghahn Books, pp. 1–16.

———. (2020) 2023. 'Cooperatives', in Felix Stein (ed.), *The Open Encyclopedia of Anthropology*. Facsimile of the first edition in *The Cambridge Encyclopedia of Anthropology*. Retrieved 5 November 2024 from http://doi.org/10.29164/20coops.

Restakis, John. 2010. *Humanizing the Economy: Co-operatives in the Age of Capital*. Gabriola, BC: New Society Publishers.

Robertson, Nicole. 2010. *The Co-operative Movement and Communities in Britain, 1914-1960: Minding Their Own Business*. Farnham; Burlington, VT: Ashgate.

Rose, Nikolas. 2000. 'Community, Citizenship, and the Third Way', *American Behavioral Scientist* 43(9): 1395–411.

Russell, Raymond. 1995. *Utopia in Zion: The Israeli Experience with Worker Cooperatives.* Albany: State University of New York Press.

Satgar, Vishwas (ed.). 2014. *The Solidarity Economy Alternative: Emerging Theory and Practice.* KwaZulu-Natal: University of KwaZulu-Natal Press.

Scheper-Hughes, Nancy. 1995. 'The Primacy of the Ethical: Propositions for a Militant Anthropology', *Current Anthropology* 36(3): 409–20.

Scott, James C. 1985. *Weapons of the Weak: Everyday Forms of Peasant Resistance* (New edition). New Haven: Yale University Press.

Sharzer, Greg. 2017. 'Cooperatives as Transitional Economics'. *Review of Radical Political Economics* 49(3): 456–76.

Sitrin, Marina A. 2012. *Everyday Revolutions: Horizontalism and Autonomy in Argentina.* London; New York: Zed Books Ltd.

Solnit, Rebecca. 2020, 14 May. '"The Way We Get Through This is Together": Mutual Aid Under Coronavirus', *The Guardian.* Retrieved 2 December 2020 from http://www.theguardian.com/world/2020/may/14/mutual-aid-coronavirus-pandemic-rebecca-solnit.

Som Castellano, Rebecca L. 2015. 'Alternative Food Networks and Food Provisioning as a Gendered Act', *Agriculture and Human Values* 32(3): 461–74.

Sörbom, Adrienne, and Magnus Wennerhag. 2013. 'Individualization, Life Politics, and the Reformulation of Social Critique: An Analysis of the Global Justice Movement', *Critical Sociology* 39(3): 453–78.

Stahl, Michael. 2007. 'Capturing the Peasants through Cooperatives – the Case of Ethiopia', *Review of African Political Economy* 16(44): 27–46.

Stanford, Mark. 2018. 'Problems in the New Cooperative Movement: A Window onto Changing Cooperation Mechanisms', in Mark Stanford, *Cooperation in Chinese Communities: Morality and Practice.* London: Bloomsbury Academic, pp. 211–29.

Sustain. 2012. *Food Co-ops Final Report – Draft.* London: Sustain, unpublished.

Taylor, Charles. 2003. *Modern Social Imaginaries.* Durham, NC: Duke University Press.

Thelen, Tatjana. 2015. 'Care as Social Organization: Creating, Maintaining and Dissolving Significant Relations', *Anthropological Theory* 15(4): 497–515.

Thompson, E. P. 1971. 'The Moral Economy of the English Crowd in the Eighteenth Century', *Past & Present* (50): 76–136.

Ticktin, Miriam. 2011. *Casualties of Care: Immigration and the Politics of Humanitarianism in France.* Berkeley: University of California Press.

———. 2021. 'Building a Feminist Commons in the Time of COVID-19', *Signs: Journal of Women in Culture and Society.* Retrieved 1 June 2022 from http://signsjournal.org/covid/ticktin/.

Tronto, Joan C. 1993. *Moral Boundaries: A Political Argument for an Ethic of Care.* London: Routledge.

Vanke, Alexandrina. 2024. *The Urban Life of Workers in Post-Soviet Russia: Engaging in Everyday Struggle.* Manchester: Manchester University Press.

Vargas-Cetina, Gabriela. 2005. 'Anthropology and Cooperatives: From the Community Paradigm to the Ephemeral Association in Chiapas, Mexico', *Critique of Anthropology* 25(3): 229–51.

Wilde, Matt. 2022. 'Eviction, Gatekeeping and Militant Care: Moral Economies of Housing in Austerity London', *Ethnos* 87(1): 22–41.

Wilk, Richard. 2006. 'From Wild Weeds to Artisanal Cheese: An Introduction to Slow and Fast Food', *Fast Food/Slow Food: The Cultural Economy of the Global Food Sys-*

tem, Society for Economic Anthropology Monograph Series. Lanham: Altamira Press.

Williams, Michelle, and Vishwas Satgar. 2016, 2 February. *Transformative Politics and the Solidarity Economy*. Seminar presented at the Department of Development Studies Seminar.

Williams, Raymond. 2015. 'Structures of Feeling', in Devika Sharma and Frederik Tygstrup (eds), *Structures of Feeling: Affectivity and the Study of Culture*. Berlin: De Gruyter, pp. 20–5.

Wilson, John. F. et al. 2013. *Building Co-operation: A Business History of the Co-operative Group, 1863–2013*. Oxford: Oxford University Press.

Woodly, Deva et al. 2021. 'The Politics of Care', *Contemporary Political Theory* 20(4): 890–925.

Wright, Erik Olin. 2010. *Envisioning Real Utopias*. London; New York: Verso.

CHAPTER

1

ORIGINS

SLEDGEHAMMERS AT DAWN

As the police and bailiffs attempted to enter the Pullens Estate, a noxious slurry of rotten apples, vegetable peelings and manure from the local city farm rained down on them. The squatters inside had been filling buckets and tin baths for several weeks, all stored on the roofs of the housing estate in preparation for the planned, mass eviction. From 6.30am onwards, the day pulsated with the rhythm of bailiffs' sledgehammers and New Orleans Jazz, which came from the crowd that had assembled on the street in solidarity with the squatters. As Adina, one of the founder members of Fareshares and a squatter on the estate at the time, recounted to me, people inside and out also sang in peaceful protest. Vanloads of police with riot shields arrived for the eviction, 'but a little bit of manure on their head and they all went', Adina chuckled.

The bailiffs stayed and once they had made it through the shower of rotten vegetables and shit, they started the arduous job of dismantling barricades. Both the stairwells and the doors to many flats had been blocked – nailed shut and stopped up with anything from boards to steel, barbed wire or concrete blocks (SNOW 1986). Door numbers were painted over, too, making it all the more difficult for the bailiffs to work out which flats to evict (mudlark121 2018). All this made their pace of progress through the estate slow. By noon, just sixteen of the thirty planned squat evictions had been completed (mudlark121 2018). The bailiffs, riot police and council representatives started to dissipate, and the squatters began to organize again. Within hours, many of them had returned to the Pullens Estate, moving furniture back in and fixing smashed-up doors.

The year was 1986, and as novelist Hanif Kureishi (2008: 190) put it, 'revolution had come at last: Margaret Thatcher was its figurehead'. Others also characterize Thatcher in revolutionary terms as one of the key actors in the promotion of neoliberalism, as the guiding principle of political-economic practices, along with President Ronald Reagan in the US and the paramount leader Deng Xiaoping of the People's Republic of China (Harvey 2007: 1–2). As well as creating changes in terms of economic policies and modes of governing, neoliberal processes have also had profound impacts on culture, citizenship, welfare and political action in the UK, some of which are apparent in the origin stories of Fareshares and St Hilda's East. In this chapter, I explore the intersection between these mainstream political shifts in the UK (what Ticktin might describe as *politics*), the changing nature of political action (the *political*) and the different imaginaries apparent within each food co-op.

The social histories I present here help to contextualize how Fareshares and St Hilda's East have been structured and informed by the social worlds around them, and how their foundations (organizational logics, politics, imaginaries) were moulded by a particular moment in time and its structures of feeling. Raymond Williams describes structures of feeling as the 'particular quality of social experience and relationship, historically distinct

Figure 1.1. The Pullens eviction, United Kingdom, 1986. © Crispin Hughes

Figure 1.2. 'Welcome to Southwark a Homeless Zone' – The Pullens eviction, United Kingdom, 1986. © Crispin Hughes

from other particular qualities, which gives the sense of a generation or a period' as well as how 'meanings and values . . . are lived and felt' within that period (Williams 2015: 23). As Vanke frames it, structures of feeling are 'an affective principle regulating senses, imaginaries and practical activities of local communities' (Vanke 2024: 8). Inevitably, these structures of feeling feed into political moods and atmospheres (Highmore 2016: 145–6) as well as actions and imaginations. Working through the lens of everyday politics, they help us to understand the political resonances of everyday actions such as food provisioning and of a model such as the food co-op within a specific place and time. In this case, the eras of Thatcherism and New Labour, in which state infrastructures of care were being reduced and withdrawn. Key focuses of this chapter are what catalysed the food cooperative activities of Fareshares and St Hilda's East; how politics and the political interact within each project; and what this interaction does to the political within food cooperatives.

THATCHERISM AND ANARCHISM

Margaret Thatcher became the first female Prime Minister of the UK in 1979 as the leader of the Conservative Party, and by the time of the attempted eviction of the Pullens Estate in the mid-1980s, the country had seen the deregulation of financial services (the 'Big Bang'), the privatization of national institutions such as British Telecom, British Gas and British Airways and an accelerated programme to sell off council housing (i.e. social housing) known as 'right to buy'[1] (Jackson and Saunders 2012: 7). Union power and local government, both seen as bastions of the left, were curbed through caps on local taxation, the abolition of the Greater London Authority, a ban on union membership at the Government Intelligence Communication Centre – and the 1984 Trade Unions Act, which removed legal immunity for unions that held strikes without balloting their members first (Jackson and Saunders 2012: 7–8). Thatcher described the unions as the 'enemy within', and 'dangerous to liberty' (Travis 2013). One of the most famous symbols of her campaign to break their power was the lengthy Miners' Strike of 1984–5, the failure of which many saw as a nail in the coffin for trade unionism in Britain.

Beswick (2022) suggests that the rise of the New Right, which figures such as Reagan and Thatcher and their implementation of neoliberal policy represented, was a form of 'counterrevolution' to the volume of activism and social movements in the 1960s and 1970s. In both the US and the UK, the New Right's approach squashed the organized left, as Thatcher's destruction of the unions in Britain highlights. Beswick frames neoliberalism itself as both 'an attempted restoration of an imagined age of *laissez-faire* capitalism *and* the creation of a new society marked by a co-articulation of free market fundamentalism and massive state violence in the name of law and order' (2022: 34 emphasis original).

Thatcher and her party's policies were in stark contrast to those of the post-Second World War Labour government, famous for implementing the welfare state, nationalizing industries such as manufacturing, and resources such as the Bank of England and the national rail system. In the name of Socialist values, the post-war period had also seen the introduction of the NHS, social security provisions,[2] and the construction of hundreds of thousands of council houses. Thatcher characterized this welfare system as a 'nanny state', which had supressed '"indigenous" forms of self-help' (Hyatt 2012: 164–5). In its place she promoted the idea of an 'enterprise culture', which put a greater emphasis on self-reliance and entrepreneurialism. These discourses and Thatcher's self-proclaimed interest in Victorian values (Evans 2004), invoked 'a fantasy of a return to a past state of spontaneous welfarism willed from "below" rather than pushed from "above"' (Muehlebach 2012: 62). Through the withdrawal of public services, there was an expectation that, rather than relying on the state, poor communities would improve their own situations through a 'duty' as individuals to look after themselves, their families and their neighbours (Thatcher in 'Margaret Thatcher' 2013). This stance was immortalized in Thatcher's pronouncement that 'there's no such thing as society', which was made in an interview with *Woman's Own* magazine in the autumn of 1987. As public services became privatized, individuals were also expected to be discerning and rational about which of the new, non-state services they chose to consume (Hyatt 2012: 164). The aspiration, therefore, was for a more consumer-focused, active, entrepreneurial and 'responsibilized' citizen (Barry et al. 1996: 12).

Following on from an era in which the Labour Party had celebrated their 1975 election victory by singing the Socialist anthem *The Red Flag* (Brown 2001), by the mid-1980s, the term 'socialism' had more or less dropped out of the vocabulary of mainstream party politics (Jackson and Saunders 2012: 16). This was thanks to the Cold War between the communist East and Capitalist West, and Thatcher's move towards a more neoliberal mode of governing. According to some young, left-wing activists, it felt like the country was 'close to a social breakdown ... the Unions had been defeated, the Labour Party had rolled over and died, and much of the revolutionary Left was an embarrassment' (Anon 2018).[3] This led to a resurgence of interest in anarchism, which reflected a sense of disaffection with aspects of Thatcher's Britain in an era of rising unemployment, economic volatility, the Falklands War and perceived immanent nuclear war. This Anarchist resurgence was shaped not only in response to Thatcherism (The Bash Street Kids 1998), but also to questions among members of the radical left about the trajectory of state socialism and a perceived need to re-envision an emancipatory, Socialist society through less state-centric forms of politics (Beswick 2022).

The punk music of the late 1970s and 1980s is said to have catalysed and disseminated 1980s Anarchist ideology in Britain in many ways (Anon 2018; Beswick 2022; Cross 2014: 136). In particular, British bands Crass and Poison Girls worked collaboratively to promote anarcho-punk through their lyrics, activist acts and pedagogical album notes. As well as taking an anti-war and anti-nuclear stance, anarcho-punk's interests extended to: 'militant vegetarianism and animal liberation; civil liberties and opposition to police powers; struggles against wage slavery; feminism and struggles over gender equality; opposition to organized religion; and opposition to cuts and the reductions in the wider "social wage"' (Cross 2014: 137).

Do-it-Yourself (DIY) principles were key to their identity, and these revolved around values of non-profit making, autonomy, anti-commercialism, collaboration and anti-hierarchical organizing (ibid.). 'As a means of reapproaching power', Ben Holtzman et al. (2007: 44–5) suggest, 'DIY became a way of withdrawing support from capitalism and the state while constructing and experimenting with other forms of social organizing'. By creating 'counter-institutions' built around different values and structures, DIY attempted to create spaces of empowerment, solidarity and struggle.

Squatting was also common at this time. The population of London had almost halved in the 40-year period from 1941 to 1981. People moved out to new suburbs, leaving empty properties in, often, run-down areas. Many of these filled up with activists and artists, as well as other people on low incomes (Elms 2011). As a consequence, there were many overlaps between these different movements. Casas-Cortés et al. (2014: 460) suggest that squatting demonstrates 'tactical irreverence towards private property' by commoning market and state-run spaces so that they are removed from the possibility of real-estate speculation and property redevelopment by both private and public authorities'. This is significant in the context of an action such as that on the Pullens Estate, which took place in a borough where social housing was seen to be being mismanaged by the local authority, and in an era where social housing was being taken into private ownership through 'right to buy'.

By the 1980s, Southwark, where the Pullens Estate and Fareshares are located, had purportedly become the most squatted borough in London, 'largely due to the poor quality of the housing stock and the incompetence of the council' (mudlark121 2018). More than 60% of the council's empty properties in its immediate area – Walworth – were squatted by the mid-1980s (ibid.). The area where the Pullens Estate is also had a squatters' network, SNOW (Squatters' Network of Walworth), which included one of Fareshares' founding members, Martin Oddsocks – or to give him his full name, Martin OddsocksMcWeirdoeltuttifruttiMrfartohellohippopotamusbumIthinkwe-canallliveincooperationasfreeindividualswithouthurtingourfellowsentient-beingsbutwewillhavetoworkonittheworldisforsharing (undercurrentspaulo, 2010). This is a name he registered by deed poll in order to 'confound the forces of law and order' (as Martin explained to me) when he was regularly in police stations and courts of law. As Martin described it, SNOW was 'a large, squatting self-help group, a mutual aid group' and it was very active.

By all accounts, Martin had always had an interest in activism. When he left school in West London where he grew up, he jokingly told me, he had this 'quite simplistic masterplan of saving the world'. This involved living with his parents 'while doing this succession of menial, but well-paid jobs' so that he could save up enough money to buy his own home recording equipment and make a record that would sell 'several billion copies'. He planned to give the proceeds to the non-governmental organization Action Aid, which worked against poverty and injustice worldwide, and become 'the saviour of the world'. While the first part of the plan came together, the second part did not. Instead, he moved to East London and became involved with voluntary work doing odd jobs for older people as a pretext to talk to them and hear more about their lives. He then became a peace activist campaigning against the arms trade for several years. During that period, he started squatting, moved to south London and got involved with SNOW.

FARESHARES

By 1986, the council was attempting a crackdown on unlawful occupation in the borough of Southwark with plans to clear 800 squats (mudlark121 2018), including those on the Pullens Estate. While the Pullens eviction was not successful,[4] others were. These included the 'half knocked down street off the Old Kent Road' where Martin was living, which was demolished on 15 January 1988 with just 16 hours' notice. Martin had been running a buying group called Rabbit Food Co-op out of his flat there for a while, and Adina, who was squatting on the Pullens Estate at the time, mentioned to him that the shop next to her flat on Crampton Street was empty. It had been for around a decade. Adina was a North Londoner who had moved to a squat on the Pullens Estate around 1985 when she was in her twenties.

Adina and Martin started to discuss the idea of setting up a storefront food co-op there. When Martin's housing was knocked down, he moved into the back of the corner shop at 56 Crampton Street, and work started to turn the front into a food co-op. As Adina recalled:

> We knocked a hole through the back of our toilet [in the flat next door where Adina was living] . . . got through to the back of the workshop area and knocked a hole big enough to climb through. We went in and we started getting a bit of electricity in and we had a friend who was an electrician . . . Once we'd got water and electric in there, we un-boarded the front bit and there we were.

When they first got into the building it was filled with gravestones, old fireplaces and other bits of masonry, which the council were storing in the building. Reluctant to throw these out, they went to visit the council at their office on the nearby Walworth Road to ask if they wanted to pick everything up, or let the squatters get rid of it. A few days later, the council came by with a van to move the items elsewhere.[5] In terms of electricity, there were many people on the Pullens (as it is often called by locals) who knew how to adjust the meters. As Adina explained, 'what they did with the electricity meters is that they would just slow it down. So, it would go so slow that you were only paying like a penny a week for the electricity or something. So, it wasn't like you weren't paying anything at all. You were paying something, but it was much, much less'.

It took around three months to get the old corner shop ready – on Sunday 13 March 1988, Fareshares opened for 'non-business' as a vegan, wholefood co-op. Along the walls in the early days there were hand-written posters highlighting different aspects of the project's principles: fair conditions for food producers; welfare for animals; Fareshares 'not cheating anyone' as it was a non-profit project. Others dealt with practicalities – requesting users to donate when they could and to tidy up after themselves, and reminding them that all of the workers were volunteers. There was also a slogan that read 'nobody's business, everybody's business', presenting discourses of social anarchism, collective ownership, reconfigured economic relationships, and non-hierarchical organizing.

The food co-op reflected the Anarchist and punk structures of feeling at the time through its horizontalist, DIY approaches and its concerns around animal rights and environmentalism. It also connected to aspects of the food projects of the counterculture, including the same 'quiet' politics of participatory democracy, anti-consumerism and non-profit making (Belasco 2007: 89). Through these methods, the space of the co-op and the food it sold were reclaimed as common resources 'inflected with personal and communal meanings' (Ince and Kadirbeyoglu 2020: 38) and grounded on notions of sharing and fairness as the pun in Fareshares' name alludes. It was a 'propositional enactment of a different kind of politics and an alternative mode of organizing resources' (Casas-Cortés et al. 2014: 459) premised on producing 'collective and non-commodified' goods (Harvey 2012: 73 in Casas-Cortés et al. 2014: 455) and social relationships (Caffentzis and Federici 2014).

In the early days at Fareshares, there was very little shelving, so many of the goods were placed in crates and boxes on the floor. 'Kind of perversely, we didn't have too many things in sacks at the beginning because we couldn't afford it', Martin told me. 'It was a question of gradually, gradually building up the value of the stock. Particularly in the first few years, it was essentially built up with my dole money'.[6] He laughed, 'So, apart from a few porridge oats . . . everything would have been in five-kilogram bags, which would have been bagged down'. To build the stock further, Martin used to borrow four or five hundred pounds from his parents each November so Fareshares could buy extra goods. By buying in greater quantities, the food co-op was able to get a bigger discount on the stock, and the savings made could be invested into further items. Martin would then pay his parents back by Christmas.

There were many wholefood workers' co-ops around in those days, and Fareshares got the bulk of its goods from one in a nearby area called Loughborough Junction. To begin with, Martin would pick the goods up on his bike, but as the project grew, different delivery arrangements were made. Bread also came from a south London workers' co-op, while vegetables were initially bought from a woman called Oriel, who sourced them from a farm in Kent and sold them as part of a box scheme in Denmark Hill. From the beginning, there was always a desire to work with other cooperatives, which resonates with the classic Rochdale Principle of 'cooperation among cooperatives' (International Co-operative Alliance n.d.). It also highlights a common grassroots cooperative interest in scaling out rather than scaling up to create networks of cooperatives while resisting economies of scale and more conventional forms of Capitalist accumulation (Homs and Narotzky, 2019: 137).

'They were there', Martin explained, 'so it was possible'.[7] There were also various 'idiosyncratic one or two person businesses' that they bought from, which included vegan, sugar-free 'community cookies' made by a former 'hash cake maker by appointment to Jimmy Hendrix' the US rock guitar player. Many of the relationships with suppliers also seemed to be very personable. Martin knew a lot of information about the different enterprises he described, demonstrating more socially embedded relations (DuPuis and Goodman 2005), rather than simply transactional ones. With one, a wholefood, wholesale cooperative, which was an important supplier for a while, they had even talked about potentially merging the two projects when the wholesaler got into financial trouble. They could not work out the best way to do this though.

Rather than adhere to one strict organizational structure or alternative vision, many of the co-ops and collectives that started in this era had a DIY ethos, experimenting 'with different forms of cooperation', adapting as necessary to their own particular situations (Müller 1991: 33–4), while prefiguratively practising collective organizing, horizontalism and autonomy. When I asked Martin if there was anything else like Fareshares around at the time, his answer demonstrated the experimental aspect of such collectives and the flexibility of their structures. 'I didn't know of any quite like that', he told me, 'because it was never really a straight, legit food co-op as there was no membership. You became a member by using it'.[8] Again this alluded to a sense of a communally owned and managed resources evocative of a 'commons imaginary' whereby needs are managed and met collectively through more egalitarian structures and norms (Asara 2020: 15–16).

While there were plenty of other types of cooperative enterprises around, ranging from workers' co-ops to buying clubs, all the food co-ops Martin knew worked on a more 'conventional' consumer co-op model with official membership policies and, for some, profit making. He felt that Fareshares' less rigid or conventional model was one of the elements that made the co-op 'some sort of education tool' in relation to food, highlighting his interest, not only in non-hierarchical organizing methods, but also in the politics of food. Following Martin's own food politics, key components of Fareshares' ethos were veganism, local goods and the avoidance of so-called cash-crops such as tea, coffee and sugar. As Martin explained:

> I'd read a bunch of stuff in my late teens. Stuff about food politics and development and the ever-worsening terms of trade and the basic raw materials and the foodstuffs being continually drained away from places where most people were quite poor and having all the value added elsewhere. I was involved with a few people thinking how can you try to disengage with all that? Eschewing things like tea and coffee and

> sugar for political reasons and the whole vegan slant was always about fairness for human-animals as much as any other animals.

Martin was also aware of the ambivalences and inconsistencies of ethical consumption, however. He told me he found non-dairy milks (which in those days tended to be soya milk) particularly complicated due to the distance travelled, the use of non-recyclable and non-reusable Tetra Pak,[9] soya's connections to the cattle-feed industry, and the fact that it was not a particularly good food source in his opinion.

From the time of Rabbit Food Co-op onwards, the stock was an eclectic mix of what Martin could afford, what people wanted to buy and what he wanted people to buy. Others within the collective also saw the value of this kind of food politics though. 'Being a vegan was a very political statement' Adina explained, and there were not many of them around. She also identified the avoidance of 'third world cash crops' as a key political factor along with the co-op's choice to operate on a non-profit basis. The founder members attempted to keep the food co-op's range deliberately spartan – pulses and grains, dried fruits, sugar-free jams, nut and seed butters, soya milk, vinegars, oils and condiments, seaweeds, breads, organic fruit and veg, ecological cleaning products, toilet paper and the odd vegan treat like the 'community cookies'.

As more people started to use the project, making it less reliant on Martin's dole money, many goods started to be bought in bulk. As Adina recalled:

> Martin is a really dedicated nutter. He didn't want to create any waste, so they bought everything in massive containers and decanted it. There wasn't recycling like there is now with bins on the end of the street. They hadn't started any of that. Maybe there were bottle banks, sometimes near the supermarket. So, it was a recycling project as well. There were two massive sinks at the back where the Infoshop is now . . . somebody's awful job was cleaning all these jars in cold water and then filling them up with oil or washing up liquid or whatever we were doing in bulk.

For a time, paper and cardboard were also collected for recycling as there were no facilities for this in the area.

In the first few years, the project consistently made losses, which, according to a newsletter of theirs from 1989, was down to:

- An overgenerously slapdash approach to weighing out dry goods, veg etc.
- Failure to keep the shop prices in line with wholesale price rises.
- Periods of time when donations have not been remotely sufficient to meet running costs (heating, lighting, replacement of equipment, etc.).
- Occasional instances of suspected petty theft, and one of un-petty theft.
- Users' debts have not always been settled with the desired promptness(!)

To compensate for this, Martin regularly subsidized the project with his own money to begin with.

Following a meeting of 'friends and supporters', the co-op decided to add a small mark-up to the dried foods to account for this discrepancy. But everything else was to remain at cost price. As they acknowledged in the newsletter, however, even at cost price 'some of the things we provide (e.g. organically grown vegetables) are still not cheap'. Instead, they agreed to 'leave it to the user to decide to what extent s/he is able to contribute to the co-op's running costs' (i.e. how much of an additional donation to make on top of the cost price of goods in the food co-op). The newsletter added that, 'the fairness of this decision is based on the assumption that donations are made in proportion to each donor's ability to pay; a patently fallacious assumption. Oh well'. This again highlighted aspirations of mutuality through commons-based practices, as well as some of their challenges. Despite all this, in the 11 months to November 1989, Fareshares 'managed to turn over £20,000 worth of stock' (fareShares 1989).

As well as selling foods, the co-op soon set up a crèche in response to the fact that some of the people who were very involved with Fareshares had toddlers. So, when the co-op was open, you could bring your baby or toddler in too. While Adina did not have children herself at that point, she told me she really enjoyed running the crèche as the children were 'all so sweet'. As the co-op did not really have any shelves at that time, all the produce was piled in boxes in the middle of the floor, and 'as soon as the kids could walk, they spent their whole time emptying the boxes on the floor', Adina told me, which made the gated crèche area extra useful. There was also a library area in the corner for swapping and borrowing books and a self-help bike repair space. The floor above was squatted too and turned into workshops. Adina, who worked as a musician and a busker at the time, set up an instrument repair workshop with a giant lathe. A couple of years after Fareshares opened, Martin then moved into the flat next door, and by 1991, the space that he had been living in became the 56a Infoshop – an Anarchist social centre. People would come from all over Europe to visit.

In terms of regulation, the council took little interest in the early days. The crèche was visited once and deemed to fall between the cracks as it was neither a proper crèche nor a baby and toddler drop-in service. As such, the council representative told them no action was required. No one came to inspect how the food was being kept or handled as far as Martin could remember. 'There never was anything about licensing or food hygiene I don't think . . . That's a card they could have played', Martin acknowledged, 'but they never chose to. It puzzled me slightly'. Not long after the food co-op was in full operation, however, someone did visit them to discuss the payment of commercial rent. 'We couldn't do it', Martin explained, so legal action started. Luckily for them, the first set of court proceedings did not come to anything as the person dealing with their case left. 'We weren't causing too much of a problem and we didn't kick up a fuss, so it just got forgotten about.' The council made two further attempts at eviction, but eventually conceded, instead moving the project onto a 'peppercorn' (nominal) rent. As far as Adina remembers, this was around one pound a year. 'It was nothing', she recalls. 'But it was to make it official'. At this moment, therefore, they succumbed in some small ways to the 'bureaucratization of charisma' by taking on a more official status 'for the sake of their long-term reproduction' (Rakopoulos 2015: 96). Over time, the rent started to increase slowly, but even at the time of my fieldwork, it was reasonably low, and the building was entitled to business rate relief as all of its projects were non-profit making.

While Adina left the area in 1991, Martin stayed for seven years in total. Then, at the age of 35, he moved away. There were various reasons for him deciding to leave at that point. As well as wanting to move on to other things, he and others in the project felt that him stepping down would be the only way for Fareshares to become truly sustainable. At that point, he was still seen as the lynchpin of the project in many ways. People regularly deferred to him as they knew that it had been his baby to begin with. He still lived in the flat next door, so it also fell to him to cover shifts when others did not show up.[10] Having invested so much money in Fareshares over the years, before Martin left, they held a fundraiser so that they could try to pay him back, asking people who used Fareshares to buy 'shares' in the project in order to keep it running, but with a clear understanding that they would never get the money back. In the end, they were able to give Martin about half of what he had put in and he seemed happy enough with that. He continued to have some interaction with the collective for a couple of years before life circumstance meant that he lost touch with the co-op for around eight years. He has been in a handful of times since then. Every now and then on a significant anniversary, such as Fareshares' 25th or 30th birthday, he has also emailed to mark the date. In the 30th anniversary message, which was entitled 'Thirty (Glorious?) Years . . ', he sent 'greetings and congratulations' to the collective members 'for hanging on in there and staying so true to the original spirit, in the face of gentrification etc.', signing off with '[l]ove and solidarity and that kind of thing'.

NEW LABOUR AND ACTIVE COMMUNITIES

Just as the mid-1990s marked a period of change at Fareshares, in the country more broadly, the political mood was also changing. When Margaret

Thatcher reluctantly resigned from her position as the UK's longest serving Prime Minister of the twentieth century in 1990, politics was dogged by civil unrest in response to the newly implemented community charge known as the poll tax and party infighting about the European Economic Community (which was later incorporated into the European Union in 1993). Thatcher was succeeded by the former Chancellor of the Exchequer John Major, who had been a strong ally of hers.

Having turned 18 just two days before the 1 May 1997 general election, like many other young adults, I received a video cassette of a Labour Party political broadcast in the post. The video depicted a smartly dressed man in his early forties walking down a high street on the way to cast his vote – polling card tucked into his front pocket. His face was yet to be seen. On his way, a band of multicultural citizens engaging in a range of daily activities – having haircuts, selling flowers, and handing out balloons on roller skates – enthusiastically greeted this mysterious figure as he passed. They then followed him down the street in a Pied Piper-esque procession. After he had cast his vote, the man was finally revealed to be Tony Blair, the soon-to-be Prime Minister (1997–2007). All this was accompanied by the pop song *Things Can Only Get Better* by D:Ream (*'Labour's 1997 Party Political Broadcast – Things Can Only Get Better'* 1997).

By the mid-1990s, the Conservative Party was going through a rough patch. Reflecting his caricature in the puppet satire show *Spitting Image*, John Major was seen as a grey (dull) man who had struggled to move out of Margaret Thatcher's shadow. His cabinet was also mired in sexual scandals, infighting and alleged corruption. Many saw Blair as a refreshing alternative – young,[11] charismatic and filled with new ideas for the Labour Party, and the country. He and his party promised a 'new', clean politics, which promoted the idea of free trade, wealth creation and a healthy economy, as well as welfare provision that ensured a prospering NHS and education system ('From Bambi to Blair' 2007). On 1 May 1997, they won a landslide victory.

In Tony Blair's words, the mission for 'New' Labour, as they came to be known, was 'to promote and reconcile the four values which are essential to a just society which maximizes the freedom and potential of all our people – equal worth, opportunity for all, responsibility and community' (Blair 1998 in Rose 2000: 1397). This period came to be known for increased spending on services such as health and education; attempts at creating a more inclusive Britain, where more women were present in the cabinet, and where communities were more multicultural. In terms of this multiculturalism and the potential for civil unrest, New Labour's approach centred on the idea of community cohesion, in which relationships were fostered between people from different backgrounds, and where everyone should have similar life opportunities (Shukra et al. 2004: 188).

Tony Blair believed that the world was changing fast in relation to interconnection and globalization, both of which could be good things for his brand of politics. As a consequence, his party implemented a programme of managed migration, which saw the expansion of low and high-skilled worker schemes in the UK, the relaxation of work permit criteria, and the doubling of international students. Through this expansion, New Labour hoped to reap the positive economic benefits of global labour migration.

The means by which New Labour structured welfare and fostered community were clearly very different to those of Thatcher or Major, but, with the adoption of market models for some public services and increased citizen responsibilization, they still had a distinctly neoliberal flavour. As Stuart Hall (2005: 319) highlights, 'eighteen years of Thatcherite rule had radically altered the social, economic, and political terrain in British society'. In the run up to the 1997 election, the Labour Party had a decision to make about whether to stick with old left politics or adapt to the climate and rationalities that Thatcherism had created by subscribing to centrist politics and more neoliberal policy positions. They opted for the latter.

New Labour Home Secretary Jack Straw (1997–2001) described the 'Third Way' stance they adopted as 'a clear coherent route between the Right . . . and the old, neo-Marxist Left' (Straw, 1998 in Rose 2000: 1396). Like Margaret Thatcher, Straw, announced that 'there is no such "thing" as society' at a conference devoted to the Third Way (ibid.: 1395). While Thatcher's famous assertion suggested that it is neither the government nor society's job to solve people's problems as this led to a cycle of dependency that stopped them from taking responsibility for themselves, Straw packaged citizen responsibility in softer terms. As he put it, 'society in not a "thing" external to our experiences and responsibilities. It is us, *all of us*' (ibid., emphasis added), thus emphasizing collaboration, collectivity and citizen participation, as well as individual responsibility. The role of parliament, he suggested, was not only to share this belief, but also to mark it out (ibid.: 1396). In other words, while the state had to 'provide the conditions for a good life', which should be available to all in principle, its subjects 'must deserve to inhabit it by building strong communities and exercising active responsible citizenship' (ibid.: 1398). In New Labour's vision of citizenship, therefore, there was a shift from an Old Labour emphasis on rights (social citizenship) to a New Labour vision of duty and responsibility (active citizenship) (Goes 2018: 113). By couching it in discourses of community, however, he attempted to reassure the party that '"duty" was in fact a traditional Labour value' at the same time as differentiating New Labour from the 'more individualistic and market-driven Conservatives' (Ibid.: 112–13).

This focus on community (which included social cohesion and inclusion) also responded to an acknowledgement of diversity within society when it came to 'culture, values, and mores' and the need to build collectivity while acknowledging difference and enabling 'equal recognition in a single constitutional form' (Rose 2000: 1401). Given New Labour's celebration of a multicultural society, and the ways in which the party attempted to benefit from migrant labour, finding a means of creating cohesion, equality and citizen responsibility must have felt all the more pressing in that period.

The Third Way had a decidedly moral tone, emphasizing a 'framework of belief', or social imagination, that both citizens and parliament must conform to (Rose 2000: 1396). In line with this push towards greater citizen participation, the 'third sector', which comprises of non-governmental and non-profit-making organizations such as community and voluntary groups, charities and cooperatives, expanded rapidly. This project of 'welfare diversification' created a more professionalized and competitive third sector, which was expected to carry more of the weight of welfare provision (Lambie-Mumford 2017: 107).

Just as Straw highlighted the necessity for all citizens to take collective responsibility for themselves and their society in order to be deserving of inclusion in it, Tony Blair also wrote about the necessity for citizens 'to give as much as what they take' in order to build 'successful communities' (Blair, 1996 in Rose 2000: 1404). A key form of giving was through working. Indeed, Goes (2018: 112) suggests that for New Labour, the 'main duty in society was the duty to work'.

Volunteering was another key aspect of duty both as a form of welfare-to-work, and also as a means of active citizenship and community connection that everyone could participate in. As Jack Straw stated, voluntary activity was 'the essential act of citizenship' (in Rose 2000: 1404). In contrast to the kind of citizen who has expectation of the state providing a 'safety net' as part of the social contract, Hyatt argues (2002: 205) that this form of volunteer is 'a new kind of political subject, one who is deemed better adapted to the particular requirements' of 'neoliberal governance'. It is also one who should be accepting of state withdrawal and of the 'claim that the free market is the most cost effective and fairest way of delivering services to the poor and the nonpoor' (ibid.).

In relation to food, many third sector schemes in the UK took the form of local food projects, which were funded by statutory services, such as local Primary Care Trusts (Goodman et al. 2014: 83). This was a time of growing concern about food issues, ranging from food safety (thanks to food scares such as BSE and foot-and-mouth disease)[12] to anorexia, obesity and children's eating habits (Dowler and Caraher 2003: 57). This interest in food was reflected in the volume of food schemes set up in this era. The early 2000s also saw the launch of the government's 5-a-Day programme, which encouraged people to eat at least five portions of fruit and vegetables per day in order to improve nutritional health, while reducing the risk of cardiac diseases, cancer and diabetes (Policy Navigator 2003). Local food projects were well placed to promote this message. Many local and health authorities also seized on the idea of community-based food initiatives when 'charged with reducing inequalities, exclusion and poverty' seeing them 'as a means of solving what are perceived to be the particular food problems of those who are poor and lack skills and decent affordable shops nearby' (Dowler and Caraher 2003: 57).

These projects were certainly empowering for those participants who previously felt excluded or disenfranchised, and may have helped with food-based behaviour change in others. Nonetheless, food policy scholars Caraher and Dowler (ibid.) look at them with some negativity as these initiatives did not necessarily address wider structural issues. Neither did they necessarily always build on the energy they created in order to develop wider strategies for a community, or fully engage local people in that process. For many of those involved in community food projects in this period, however, the early 2000s still felt more positive than life under Thatcherism, or, indeed, the more recent era of Conservative government. There was funding available, local authorities were receptive to the needs and concerns of activists and community groups, and they were able to get more done.

ST HILDA'S

If Fareshares was formed at the height of Thatcherism, in a model of activism that fitted that era, then arguably St Hilda's East Food Co-op's form and structures are also reflective of the New Labour years, and some of the logics around community building and nutritional health apparent in local food projects of that time. Since the late 1990s, Tower Hamlets Cooperative Development Agency (CDA)[13] had been particularly active in relation to community food co-ops, setting up around 26 of them in the east London borough in a range of community centres, housing estates, religious buildings and schools. In line with the CDA's aim of enhancing health, wellbeing and economic conditions for the local community, they targeted areas 'where the population was at risk of poor-diet-related ill health such as Type 2 Diabetes, Cardio Vascular problems and Obesity' (Cohn 2015). These are all issues that are prevalent within Tower Hamlets and, in particular, within the Bangladeshi community[14] that has been in the area in significant numbers since at least the 1960s (Tower Hamlets JSNA Reference Group 2016).

When I interviewed Gregory, who worked for Tower Hamlets CDA at the time, and led the drive to set up food co-ops in the borough, he explained to me that the cooperative development model had been thriving up until around the year 2000, supporting people who were 'furthest from the employment market' by setting up different kinds of cooperatives. Due to changes in available funding for community projects, however, he decided to focus in on food. 'I thought it's sort of on mission in as much as it's food co-ops and it's addressing health and deprivation issues, and there's money so we can stay alive', Gregory explained, demonstrating his entrepreneurial skills as well as the precarity of the CDA movement at that time. Speaking to Abi, who worked in the Public Health Department of Tower Hamlets Council at the time of our conversation, she felt that Tower Hamlets CDA had been a strong force in relation to food projects in the area in the 2000s. She spoke positively about the food and community projects set up there and the work that the CDA did, suggesting that Tower Hamlets has been 'an area of social change and social justice'.

In line with the other food co-ops of this era, Gregory acknowledged that they 'weren't really co-ops' from his perspective, despite being facilitated by the CDA. When I pushed him on how they came to be called co-ops, he asked me 'well, what is a co-op?' He pointed out that in 'Britain there is no legal definition for a co-op', although to register as a limited company you would need to demonstrate what made you a cooperative (none of the Tower Hamlets CDA did register). He then turned to elements of the International Co-operative Alliance's definition, explaining that 'a co-op is controlled by the people who are involved with it . . . so in a food co-op, it would by definition be controlled by the volunteers'. He went on to reflect:

> the problem with food co-ops started by people like me who want to improve health in the community and community dynamics and cohesion, they're not started to make a *co-op*. Whereas with the worker co-ops [which had previously been the bread and butter of the CDA], you start the co-op to make the business. It's all intertwined. And the people who volunteer [at the food co-ops] are coming to *volunteer*. They're not coming to work in a co-op, and they probably don't know what it is. And most people in the street don't actually know what a co-op is, so it's called a co-op because it's what we've got used to.

He was not sure where the usage of the term 'food co-op' had come from for these kinds of food projects. No one else I spoke to seemed sure either, although many were perplexed about what made them co-ops.[15] Abi, who worked in Public Health in different London Boroughs throughout this period and became involved with supporting various food co-ops as part of health-related interventions, also found it confusing. The projects she had worked with in other boroughs tended to work a little differently to how they did in Tower Hamlets. In Fulham, for example, a group of parishioners had got together to self-organize bulk buying. At a local school in White City, the aim was to 'get people from the White City [housing] Estate to become members so you can actually control the purchasing power . . . so the community has some cooperative power'.[16] She said that they 'never quite managed it though'. Nonetheless, she 'went in thinking a cooperative is all about purchasing power and bulk buying' and member (i.e. consumer) decision-making, therefore, evoking many of the original logics of the Rochdale Pioneers. As a consequence, she was 'quite shocked' when she came across the Tower Hamlets model. To her, the Tower Hamlets food cooperatives seemed more 'structured around employment and enterprise' and 'felt a bit like a shop'.

Tower Hamlets CDA food co-ops generally operated as market stalls selling fresh fruit and vegetables once a week or so. Gregory explained that they would get grants of £5,000–15,000 to set up a food co-op. One of their staff members would then run the stall for a period of time, while training people at the venue on how it operated. This would often include a mixture of paid staff and volunteers, but there were no official cooperative decision-making mechanisms. While some of these food co-ops managed to last beyond the periods in which they were funded, Gregory acknowledged that many of them closed once the relevant grant had finished. From Abi's perspective, even if they did not last longer than a year, they could still be deemed a success due to the 'skills attained' by those involved, which she saw as an 'important part in terms of employment'.

The foundation of St Hilda's Food Co-op in 2005 very much built on the momentum within the borough. In 2005 the Bengali Elders' day centre, which had been hosted in the sports hall at St Hilda's Community Centre from Monday to Friday each week moved out to a bespoke site further east in Shadwell on the request of the local authority. It was not something that the community centre would have chosen to do because the day centre 'was really good in terms of multicultural contact between different groups'. Nonetheless, as Rupert, the community centre's white, British director at the time of my fieldwork told me, this loss did leave the hall free for other projects to move in.

A couple of other factors also helped to bring St Hilda's Food Co-op into being. Around that time, the community centre had received a report about local food co-ops from Tower Hamlets CDA who were looking for more sites for food co-ops. A local resident had also approached Lourdes, the volunteer coordinator at St Hilda's at the time, about setting up a food co-op at the centre. She had previously been involved with some in the US and was keen to continue with them in London. By 2005, Lourdes had been working in community development for several years, having started at a community centre in Bow, another area in east London, in the late 1990s when she was 20. Lourdes could see the potential in the idea, so she made a proposal to the centre's managerial board. 'Obviously we had to have some conversations about what it would involve and finances', Rupert told me. But, as the centre was in a better financial position compared to the challenges that many community projects face today, it was able to take the financial risk of starting the project. With the board's approval, Lourdes began to set things in motion for a stall every Thursday morning in the sports hall. This was to be open to everyone within the neighbourhood.

While the Bengali Elders' Project may have moved out, the room next door to the hall still housed the Older People's Project – a lunch club and weekday service for people aged 50 upwards which received some funding from the local council. The Older People's Project has been a significant customer base for the food co-op since the beginning, enabling people with potentially limited mobility to do their own shopping (with the support of food co-op volunteers), to be a little more active and to benefit from interacting with the project and its participants.

When I asked Rupert what the main aim of the food co-op was at that time, he answered honestly that when it started, it did not have one 'clear mission statement'. Like many of the centre's projects, it worked more organically, responding to emerging needs and opportunities:

> So, there wasn't a decision at the management board, or by us, that we want to do this because it's an anti-food-poverty initiative . . . But I think the reason . . . that was certainly in Lourdes' mind and my mind and other people's minds, was that (not necessarily in this order) it was a really good initiative for making people more aware of healthy food and particularly in an area where people have bad nutrition, low incomes etc. that was really important . . . It's affordable fresh food . . . It provided a lifeline (which is always the word we use) to people coming into the community centre who are housebound in the Older People's Project . . . And, it also fitted in with the volunteering ethos of the community centre, sort of encouraging people from the local community to get involved, but also providing informal experience, on-the-job experience, to people who can then use that when applying (especially younger people), when applying for jobs.

In the early days, Tower Hamlets CDA provided the fruit and vegetables, which they sourced from New Spitalfields Market in another area of East London called Leyton. The stall tried to take into consideration the diverse tastes of the community it was serving, providing a range of South Asian, Afro-Caribbean and seasonal British produce. To begin with, there was a lot of trial and error with some items, such as bulk bags of onions, selling very quickly while other produce went more slowly. Then there was the issue of pricing, 'although it's very trendy now, Shoreditch, when we set it up, it wasn't', Lourdes told me. 'It was really deprived. It still is really deprived, it's just hidden. But it wasn't a food desert and it isn't now, so people had a choice, they could go down the market and get a bowl of fruit for a pound or come and get some really nice fruit and veggies from us.'

As savvy shoppers, many of the Bangladeshi women in the area were well aware of produce prices in different shops and how much they were prepared to pay for each item; and while some things worked out cheaper at the food co-op, others did not. Instead, it focused on providing the freshest produce that the wholesale market had to offer, that lasted a lot longer than the kind of pound-a-bowl fruit and veg you might find at some of the local street markets. The co-op then sold these as cheaply as it could. Prices could also vary considerably from week to week depending on availability, harvests and markets, which customers did not always understand. 'I think they sometimes thought we made it up as we went along'. Lourdes commented wryly.

The weekly takings for the scheme could also vary wildly. 'We never ever made any money on it', Lourdes explained 'but that wasn't the point . . . It was like, if we made five pounds, we were really happy because usually we lost a little bit'. Rupert, who had been the director of the centre since 2001 when I interviewed him in 2017, was always very supportive of the scheme, and as he told me, 'once it was started, we could see the social value'. Between the two of them they were able to explain the value of the project to others in the centre, ensuring that it continued to 'carry' the project financially for some time without the trustees objecting.

Lourdes also had to ensure that there were enough people to run the stall:

> There was one time we would have people queuing up to get in. That was when I think a lot of the Bengali women had sussed that there were certain things that were really cheap with us. Then of course, it was really difficult to get volunteers, that sustainable flow of volunteers. So, we'd get a load of customers and then they'd be waiting ages at the tills, so it was really difficult to get it right. So, we'd get some of those, you know, more white, middle-class volunteers who'd come in for a bit and then they'd be off doing something else, and it was really hard to get that sustainable volunteer group in there. It was trial and error and working hard to get different volunteers in every week.

Lourdes acknowledged that the job was challenging in many ways. As volunteer coordinator for all of the projects in the community centre, it was a substantial amount of work to balance the food co-op's books, attempt to predict the weekly needs of the stall's customers, reiterate to the finance team that this was not intended as a profit-making project,[17] promote the food co-op and support its volunteers, all on top of her other work responsibilities as volunteer coordinator within the centre. Lourdes had no background in food, and she joked that her mum had said to her (mimicking her mum's South Asian accent) 'Oh my God, did you get your degree to work at a market?' She persevered though, working things out through trial and error, or picking up the phone to the people she thought might be able to help – asking questions and setting up connections. It was still hard to juggle everything necessary to keep the project going, however, and she admitted that at one point, she had needed to take a bit of time off from the food co-op as she was feeling worn out by the physical work involved as well as the challenges of keeping the project going.

In relation to funding Lourdes told me, 'it is hard when there's not a lot of funding around. It's really tough for these sorts of organizations [i.e. community centres], you know, sort of middle sized . . . you're squabbling around for that same sort of funding, and it's tough'.

Although these challenges continued for several years, in 2011, the food co-op started to become 'a vehicle for funding for St Hilda's' as Lourdes put it. This meant that Rupert and Lourdes were able to secure a Big Lottery grant as part of Local Food – a £59.8 million programme which attempted to make locally grown food more accessible and affordable to people. This distributed money to more than 500 projects across the UK (National Lottery Good Causes 2011). The funding, which lasted from August 2011 to March 2014, enabled the food co-op to provide accredited Social Enterprise Skills training to volunteers in order to 'increase their employability and entrepreneurial skills' (St Hilda's East Community Centre 2012). Rupert and Lourdes both saw this as a turning point for the food co-op. Through the funding, Lourdes was able to put more time into the food co-op and expand its activities further to include healthy living workshops, produce tastings, smoothie making and more networking with other organizations, such as the community centre's neighbour Women's Environmental Network, who take an interest in food, growing and environmental sustainability.

Not long before the funding commenced, the food co-op started supplementing the produce on the stall with organics from a farm just to the east of London in Essex called Sarah Green's Organics. At this point, therefore, it took on some of the logics of an alternative food network through directly interacting with a local farmer and stocking some local and sustainable foods (Goodman et al. 2014). By getting the foods straight from the farm, they were able to offer organic produce for much less than any of the well-to-do, local shops which stocked it. Some of these were surprised to see the prices at St Hilda's. 'We're just getting it straight from the farm', Lourdes explained, 'straight to the market for those low-income families to encourage them to really think about what they're eating where it's from, tasting it. It would taste a bit fresher, look a bit different . . . encouraging children as well'. Over the years the main supplier of (non-organic) fruit and vegetables also changed to Community Food Enterprise, a social enterprise based in Newington, east London, which provided good quality fruit and vegetables from Spitalfields Market at more affordable prices to community food projects for a small delivery fee. The stall also started to sell pulses, rice and other dried goods from a local cash and carry. These proved popular as the discounted, bulk prices meant the products could be sold very cheaply at the food co-op.

Lourdes left the project, and the community centre, in 2014, and there had been two subsequent coordinators by the time I arrived – Helen, who only stayed for a brief period before Jenny, who was coordinator during my fieldwork, took over. Of the 26 or so food co-ops set up in Tower Hamlets since the late 1990s, today only a handful are still open, and St Hilda's has to be one of the most successful. Nonetheless, the question of how much longer it will be able to keep going in a challenging funding environment is always on the minds of the centre's staff.

THE LOT OF FOOD CO-OPS

As for food co-ops more generally, as both the political and economic conditions in the UK have continued to change, so too has the situation for food co-ops. The four years after the food and financial crises of 2007–8 saw an upsurge in food co-op activity in Britain as many more people started to question the methods and values of the mainstream food and economic systems (Goodman et al. 2014: 120). Media coverage of food co-ops also increased, including a four-part TV programme on Channel 4 about a new, consumer food co-op called 'The People's Supermarket' set up in London in 2010. This was started by celebrity chef Arthur Potts Dawson to critique supermarkets and the mainstream global, industrial food system, while also improving access to 'good food' in an area with people on varying incomes ('The People's Supermarket' 2011). Then Prime Minister David Cameron even paid a visit to the People's Supermarket in its early days. This was part of the Conservative Party's bid to make cooperative values part of its Big Society initiative (Cameron 2007), which followed similar logics in relation to community and volunteerism as New Labour.[18]

During this period, the Conservative Party also set up the Conservative Cooperative Movement to promote cooperative enterprises as a means of tackling social problems and improving communities (Norman and Hunt 2008). The leader of the movement, Jesse Norman, asserted that there was nothing left-wing about the cooperative model, encouraging people to:

> look more closely at the Rochdale principles, to which all co-ops must adhere. They speak of voluntarism, personal responsibility, teamwork, shared ownership, independence, the importance of education and mutual support, and concern for the wider community.
>
> These are the active values of engaged citizens – to which we all subscribe, even if they are hard to abide by. And they are universal, not specific to a subgroup of society, religious creed or political party. (Norman 2008)

He goes on to argue that 'the energy, vision and entrepreneurship needed to make a co-op succeed are characteristic of capitalism at its best' (ibid. 2008). This Tory co-option of the cooperative was deeply unsettling for the traditional cooperative movement, which had always identified with left-wing politics (Norman and Hunt 2008; Roberts 2009). Interestingly, after the Conservative Cooperative Movement launched in 2007, the first publication it put out was *Nuts and Bolts: How to Start a Food Co-op* (Coyle 2007).

In 2007 a five-year project about food co-ops was also launched. This was headed by Sustain – the alliance for better food and farming – to promote food co-op activity in England, as part of a large Big Lottery-funded project, Making Local Food Work. In their final report, Sustain estimated that there were at least 1,000 food co-ops in operation across the UK at that time (Sustain 2012). Their figures took into account food access-based co-ops and co-ops seeking alternatives to the dominant agri-food system (i.e. alternative food networks).

As austerity started to bite, however, the funding landscape changed substantially, and this area of work seemed to be deprioritized. Milbourne and Cushman noted a shift within the voluntary sector, whereby the increasingly competitive funding environment created a competitive culture between third sector organizations that were 'previously allied locally as advocates for better services' (2015: 474). During my fieldwork, I heard various stories from organizations that supported and promoted food co-ops and other community food initiatives about how other organizations that they had previously collaborated and cooperated with had won funding in ways deemed a little devious in recent years. This included quietly submitting sole funding bids for ideas that had been worked on collectively. There were also frustrations about other organizations taking on work that they considered themselves better equipped to do. This has purportedly led to more individualized, competitive and more secretive working practices in some cases, although there is still a veneer of cooperation.

While there has been heterogeneity in each wave of food cooperatives discussed in the introduction to this book, from within, contemporary food co-op activities seem fragmented, and considerably diminished since their peak in the 2000s. Despite the significance of the Rochdale Pioneers to the broader history of the cooperative movement, twenty-first-century Britain has a 'smaller, weaker and more atomized' cooperative sector than in many other countries in the OECD (Organisation for Economic Co-operation and Developmen), with significantly fewer cooperatives and mutuals (Lawrence et al. 2018: 17). It also has less legislation to either support cooperative enterprise or enforce specific organizational forms, which goes some way to explaining the diversity of contemporary food co-ops in Britain.

Many food co-ops have also had to adapt and respond to the shifting objectives of state and civil society funding streams (Caraher and Dowler 2014: 10). Others have proved 'ephemeral', due to the constraints of the political-economic climate in which they operated, where funding was scarce and people were time poor. This ephemerality is a trend that Vargas-Cetina argues is increasingly common within contemporary cooperatives operating within the constraints and challenges of global capitalism and neoliberalism, where they attempt to adapt by changing form, size and structure or quickly cease operation due to the challenges of a changing political-economic climate (2005). Despite these changing times and conditions, however, Fareshares and St Hilda's still remain.

CONCLUSIONS

In many ways, St Hilda's and Fareshares food co-ops are both responses to specific political-economic moments, adopting rationalities, modes of activism and community building that are reflective of each era. Since Margaret Thatcher came to power in 1979, the country's welfare and economic policies have been on a distinctly neoliberal trajectory. This has clearly impacted the lives of everyday citizens in multiple ways. Since the late 1970s, neoliberal governmentality has been through many different phases in this country, corresponding to the ideologies of the parties and people in power as well as broader global political and economic events. Each new regime may have reframed or attempted to erase aspects of the one that went before, but the marks of each are still visible in mainstream politics, local communities and the lives of citizens.

Each food co-op's history also highlights aspects of the wider story of neoliberalization within the UK, the forms of governmentality that each successive political regime has adopted in relation to citizenship, welfare and community, and the impacts that this has had on notions of collectivity, individuality, entrepreneurialism[19] and personal responsibility, which all play out within the food co-ops. This social, cultural, political-economic and historical context is fundamental to how food co-ops operate, and how they operationalize the basic principles of cooperativism. As Nash and Hopkins suggest, the political environment in which a co-op is founded can influence its structures as much, if not more than 'adherence to cooperative rules and principles' (1976: 15). The social world and values of a cooperative cannot, therefore, be disentangled from those of their participants, broader society or, indeed, their histories. Cooperatives are always context specific and often changing (Vargas-Cetina 2005: 246–7).

With Jupp (2022: 2) I argue that '[a]t the centre of such changing forms of activism and changing relationships with the state are matters and practicalities of *care* [emphasis original]'. These raise questions about the forms of care that are being provided or withdrawn by the state, and the forms of caring practices that emerge within community action, all of which allude to different understandings and imaginaries of care and community (ibid.). Through the histories of Fareshares and St Hilda's East and the political regimes they have shaped themselves in relation to, it is possible to gain insights into the nature of food-based social and political action since the 1980s, the relationship this has to the state, the market and capital, and how the structures of feeling at the time have informed the food co-ops' activities, discourses and imaginaries. While cooperatives have been a presence in every era since the movement's foundation in Britain in the mid-nineteenth century, the issues they respond to, and therefore their countercultural qualities (Bauman 1976) are ever shifting. The neoliberal regimes of government seen during Thatcherism and the New Labour years also fostered both radical and more liberal imaginaries, practices and projects along with different understandings and mobilizations of community.

Hyatt (2012: 160) notes that during the Thatcherite Conservative years (1979–97), high levels of community activism emerged in the UK. These attempted to defend the communities that its welfare reforms were perceived to be failing. They were, therefore, clearly a site of struggle against the prevailing political economy (Caffentzis and Federici 2014). Hyatt argues that with the arrival of New Labour, however, the 'oppositional energy' of these activities 'was increasingly domesticated and harnessed'. Instead, activists 'were enmeshed into participating in a range of bureaucratic projects of self-governing', which were fundamental to the logics of the Third Way. Local communities were expected to help with the regeneration of local areas while participating in mutual contracts with local authority figures. While the language of New Labour spoke of 'enabling' communities, as with Thatcherism, embedded within this vision of an enabling state was an 'emphasis on entrepreneurialism and self-help as alternatives to what was alleged to have become a dispiriting dependency on public services among the poor' (Hyatt 2012: 161). These regimes, therefore, had the potential to foster very different subjectivities, social imaginations and structures of feeling. While one fomented the political from Hyatt's perspective, the other co-opted, bureaucratized and supressed it.

As Rozakou points out (2016: 83), it is necessary to study 'everyday life' within such volunteer projects as well as 'the participants' point of view' in order to better understand volunteers and third sector projects not simply 'as objects of processes of subjectification', but instead as agentive and 'creative constitutors of meanings'. It would be easy to binarize projects such as Fareshares and St Hilda's along lines of 'resistance' and neoliberal 'incorporation' (Cloke et al. 2017: 721; Jupp 2022: 4). Nonetheless, as Jupp and Cloke et al. argue, we can be 'ill-served' by such 'analytical binaries' (Cloke et al. 2017: 721), which run the risk of flattening our understandings of community action and everyday politics as well as the more transformative and hopeful qualities it might contain (Jupp 2022: 3). This raises questions about what other kinds of political energies and imaginations these structures of feeling produce within food co-ops, however messily they may be entangled with neoliberalism. In the next chapter, I therefore start to explore food cooperative imaginaries at Fareshares and St Hilda's East from the perspective of those involved.

NOTES

1. In 1980, Margaret Thatcher's Conservative government implemented the right for council tenants who had rented a property for at least three years (later reduced to two), to buy their council homes at much reduced rates (Boughton 2018: 170). 'Right to buy', as the policy is known, was seen as a positive move by many council tenants as it allowed them to access the housing market in a way that might never have been possible otherwise (and later to benefit substantially from the sale of their former council properties in some cases as housing prices have risen by more than 400% in the UK since 1980 (Sunlife 2016)). It also reduced the quantity of council housing stock, however, and meant that local authorities were unable to invest as much in the maintenance of remaining council properties due to reduced revenues (Tyler 2015: 1174).
2. This included a family allowance of 5s a week for each child after the first, unemployment and sick pay, benefits for people injured at work, and 'national assistance' for anyone in severe need.
3. Working with Anarchist and squatter history, I use a range of sources including some which would often be considered less 'authoritative', such as blogs, zines and activist materials in order to allow these movements to speak for themselves rather than simply refer to academic accounts about what they did and how that period felt for them.
4. As Adina put it, the council just gave up in the end and gave the residents (including her) tenancies.
5. An act that seems remarkably tolerant and facilitative when compared with the current situation for squatters in the UK, which generally sees them moved on very swiftly, and since 2012 has included the criminalization of squatting in residential properties.
6. State benefits paid to the unemployed.
7. It is worth noting that this was a time when cooperative development agencies were very active in the UK and had a lot of funding, as Rachel, one of the member-volunteers at Fareshares at the time of my fieldwork pointed out, which further contributed to the proliferation of cooperatives at this time.

8. As a consequence, I use the terms 'volunteer', 'volunteer-member' and 'member' interchangeably when discussing Fareshares.
9. This contrasted with his childhood, when liquids such as milk came in reusable glass bottles.
10. Holmström (1993: 114) notes that it is not uncommon for founder members of a co-op to end up with more rights and responsibilities due to the investments (both financial and in terms of labour) that they may have put into their cooperative. In the Spanish, industrial cooperatives he worked with, however, they seemed to see this as an entitlement, while Martin and others at Fareshares were trying to remove the hierarchy it produced.
11. At 43, Blair was the youngest leader to be elected since 1812 when he became Prime Minister in 1997. As a consequence the press nicknamed him 'Bambi' after the main character of the animated Disney film of the same name, who was a deer fawn ('From Bambi to Blair' 2007).
12. BSE (Bovine Spongiform Encephalopathy), or 'mad cow disease', is a fatal, neurodegenerative disease in cattle, which is also transmissible to humans as Creutzfeldt-Jakob disease. There was a serious BSE crisis in the UK in the late 1980s and 1990s, which led to the mass culling of contaminated cattle as well as the death of numerous people. Foot-and-mouth disease is a highly infectious virus affecting cloven-hooved animals. There was an outbreak in the UK in 2001. This led to a crisis in British agriculture and tourism, due to the risks that visiting rural areas could cause in terms of spreading the disease further.
13. Interestingly, the Cooperative Development Agency movement itself was a top-down initiative, which started after the Labour government set up the national Cooperative Development Agency in 1978 to promote worker cooperatives. This followed the 1976 Industrial Common Ownership Act, which 'provided £250,000 to promote cooperatives and establish a revolving loan fund' (Cornforth 1984).
14. 'Bengali' is the term that people with Bangladeshi backgrounds most commonly used to describe themselves and their community in Tower Hamlets during my fieldwork, whether they had grown up in the UK or Bangladesh. Many of the white, British people in the area referred to this group as 'Bangladeshi'. I never heard anyone refer to people with Bangladeshi backgrounds with terms such as 'British Asian'. Discussing the distinction between 'Bengali' and 'Bangladeshi' with different people with Bangladeshi backgrounds, I got different answers, ranging from one being a nationality and the other a language, to the two being interchangeable. None referred to the difference between ethnicity and nationality, and the people I spoke to about this were too young to have been born before the partition of India, which ultimately led to Bangladesh's formation. I therefore use the term 'Bangladeshi' for geographical specificity. I use the term 'community' with an understanding that this is not a homogenous or cohesive group.
15. Anecdotally, when I raised the issue at a British cooperative studies conference, one member of the audience felt sure that it had come from the NHS or Public Health in line with these food-based interventions, but this is not something I was able to substantiate.
16. This was set up as part of the Buywell Programme, a retail strand of the umbrella project Well London, which focused on 'communities working together for a healthier city' (see Well London n.d. for more information).
17. They only added enough of a mark-up to cover the delivery costs of the produce.

18. Successive political regimes have also maintained an interest in the voluntary sector, as evidenced in David Cameron's Conservative Party's 'Big Society', which proposed 'a new culture of voluntarism, philanthropy, social action' (Cameron 2010 in Espiet-Kilty 2018), and more recently, Theresa May's 'shared society'. This was proposed in response to Brexit and the forms of social division, inequality and resentment that the referendum highlighted. Within her vision of the shared society, May also highlighted the role that third sector organizations, such as charities, campaign groups and social enterprises, would play (May 2017). As with the active citizens of Thatcherism, active communities of New Labour, or Cameron's vision of Big Society, there was an emphasis within the conception of the 'shared society' on the duties and responsibilities of citizens, rather than their rights, or the government's obligations to them (Espiet-Kilty 2018).
19. Whereby individual citizens have to make choices about their lives and wellbeing and accept the risks associated with them (Masquelier 2017).

REFERENCES

Anon. 2018. 'Anarchism in the 1980s: An Interview with Another Ex-Member of Bristol Class War', *Bulletin of the Kate Sharpley Library* 95.

Asara, Viviana. 2020. 'Untangling the Radical Imaginaries of the Indignados' Movement: Commons, Autonomy and Ecologism', *Environmental Politics:* 1–25.

Barry, Andrew et al. (eds). 1996. *Foucault and Political Reason: Liberalism, Neo-liberalism, and Rationalities of Government* (2nd edition). Chicago: University of Chicago Press.

The Bash Street Kids. 1998. 'Nostalgia in the UK', *Uncarved (Original Smash Hits Issue 3)*. Retrieved 3 April 2021 from http://www.uncarved.org/music/apunk/nostalgia.html.

Bauman, Zygmunt. 1976. *Socialism: The Active Utopia.* Plymouth: Allen & Unwin.

Belasco, Warren. 2007. *Appetite for Change: How the Counterculture Took in the Food Industry.* Ithaca, NY: Cornell University Press.

Beswick, Spencer. 2022. 'From the Ashes of the Old: Anarchism Reborn in a Counterrevolutionary Age (1970s–1990s)', *Anarchist Studies* 30(2): 31–54.

Boughton, John. 2018. *Municipal Dreams: The Rise and Fall of Council Housing.* London; Brooklyn: Verso.

Brown, Derek. 2001, 14 March. '1945–51: Labour and the Creation of the Welfare State', *The Guardian.*

Caffentzis, George, and Silvia Federici. 2014. 'Commons Against and Beyond Capitalism', *Community Development Journal* 49: i92–105.

Cameron, David. 2007, 8 November. 'In Full: Cameron's Co-op Speech', *BBC.*

Caraher, M., and E. Dowler. 2014. 'Food for Poorer People: Conventional and "Alternative" Transgressions', in M. Goodman and C. Sage (eds), *Food Transgressions: Making Sense of Contemporary Food Politics.* Farnham, Surrey: Ashgate, pp. 227–46.

Casas-Cortés, Maribel et al. 2014. 'The Commons', in Donald Nonini (ed.), *A Handbook of Urban Anthropology.* London: Routledge, pp. 449–69.

Cloke, Paul et al. 2017. 'The Geographies of Food Banks in the Meantime', *Progress in Human Geography* 41(6): 703–26.

Cohn, Gregory. 2015. *Launching a New Food Co-op.* Seeds for Growth, p. 3.

Cornforth, Chris. 1984. 'The Role of Local Co-operative Development Agencies in Promoting Worker Co-operatives', *Annals of Public and Cooperative Economics* 55(3): 253–80.

Coyle, Alison. 2007. *Nuts & Bolts: How to Start a Food Co-op*. London: The Conservative Co-operative Movement.

Cross, Rich. 2014. 'British Anarchism in the Era of Thatcherism', *Against the Grain*, The British Far Left from 1956. Manchester: Manchester University Press, pp. 133–52.

Dowler, E., and M. Caraher. 2003. 'Local Food Projects: The New Philanthropy?', *The Political Quarterly* 74: 57–65.

DuPuis, E. Melanie, and David Goodman. 2005. 'Should We Go "Home" to Eat? Toward a Reflexive Politics of Localism', *Journal of Rural Studies* 21(3): 359–71.

Elms, Robert. 2011, 22 November. 'The Roots of Squatting in the UK', *BBC News*.

Espiet-Kilty, Raphaële. 2018. 'Cameron and Big Society. May and Shared Society. Same Party: Two Visions ?', *Observatoire de La Société Britannique* (21): 213–33.

Evans, Eric. 2004. 'Laissez-Faire and the Victorians', *BBC*. Retrieved 7 January 2024 from https://www.bbc.co.uk/history/trail/victorian_britain/education_health/laissez_faire_02.shtml.

fareShares. 1989, 16 November. 'fareShares News'.

'From Bambi to Blair'. 2007, 2 May. *The Economist*.

Goes, Eunice. 2018. 'The Third Way and the Politics of Community', in Sarah Hale et al. (eds), *The Third Way and Beyond: Criticisms, Futures, Alternatives*. Manchester: Manchester University Press, pp. 108–27. Retrieved 15 July 2024 from: https://www.manchesterhive.com/display/9781526137883/9781526137883.00013.xml.

Goodman, David et al. 2014. *Alternative Food Networks: Knowledge, Practice, and Politics*. Abingdon: Routledge.

Hall, Stuart. 2005. 'New Labour's Double-Shuffle', *Review of Education, Pedagogy, and Cultural Studies* 27(4): 319–35.

Harvey, David. 2007. *A Brief History of Neoliberalism* (New edition). Oxford: Oxford University Press.

Highmore, Ben. 2016. 'Formations of Feeling, Constellation of Things', *Cultural Studies Review* 22(1): 144–67.

Holmström, Mark. 1993. *Spain's New Social Economy: Workers' Self-Management in Catalonia*. Oxford; Providence, RI: Berg Publishers.

Holtzman, Ben et al. 2007. 'Do It Yourself . . . and the Movement Beyond Capitalism', in Stevphen Shukaitis et al. (eds), *Constituent Imagination: Militant Investigations, Collective Theorization*. Edinburgh: AK Press, pp. 44–61.

Homs, Patricia, and Susana Narotzky. 2019. 'Within and Beyond the Market System: Organic Food Cooperatives in Catalonia', in Valeria Siniscalchi and Krista Harper (eds), *Food Values in Europe*. London: Bloomsbury Academic, pp. 132–46.

Hyatt, Susan Brin. 2002. 'From Citizen to Volunteer: Neoliberal Governance and the Erasure of Poverty', in Judith G. Goode and Jeff Maskovsky (eds), *The New Poverty Studies: The Ethnography of Power, Politics and Impoverished People in the United States*. New York: NYU Press, pp. 201–35.

———. 2012. 'The Work of Being Governed: From the Welfare State to the "Big Society" in Britain', in Kendra Coulter and William R. Schumann (eds), *Governing Cultures: Anthropological Perspectives on Political Labor, Power, and Government*. New York: Palgrave Macmillan, pp. 159–81.

Ince, Ayça, and Zeynep Kadirbeyoglu. 2020. 'The Politics of Food: Commoning Practices in Alternative Food Networks in Istanbul', in Derya Özkan and Güldem Baykal Büyüksaraç (eds), *Commoning the City: Empirical Perspectives on Urban Ecology, Economics and Ethics*. London: Routledge, pp. 37–50.

International Co-operative Alliance. (n.d.). 'Cooperative Identity, Values & Principles | ICA', *International Co-operative Alliance*. Retrieved 4 March 2021 from https://www.ica.coop/en/cooperatives/cooperative-identity.

Jackson, Ben, and Robert Saunders (eds). 2012. *Making Thatcher's Britain*. Cambridge: Cambridge University Press.

Jupp, Eleanor. 2022. *Care, Crisis and Activism: The Politics of Everyday Life*. Bristol: Policy Press.

Kureishi, Hanif. 2008. *Something to Tell You*. London Faber & Faber.

Labour's 1997 Party Political Broadcast – Things Can Only Get Better. 1997.

Lambie-Mumford, Hannah. 2017. *Hungry Britain – The Rise of Food Charity*. Bristol: Policy Press.

Lawrence, Mathew et al. 2018. *Co-operatives Unleashed: Doubling the Size of the UK's Co-operative Sector*. London: New Economics Foundation.

'Margaret Thatcher: A Life in Quotes'. 2013, 8 April, *The Guardian*.

Masquelier, Charles. 2017. *Critique and Resistance in a Neoliberal Age: Towards a Narrative of Emancipation*. London: Palgrave Macmillan.

May, Theresa. 2017, 1 September. 'The Shared Society: Prime Minister's Speech at the Charity Commission Annual Meeting', *GOV.UK*. Retrieved 12 May 2019 from https://www.gov.uk/government/speeches/the-shared-society-prime-ministers-speech-at-the-charity-commission-annual-meeting.

Milbourne, Linda, and Mike Cushman. 2015. 'Complying, Transforming or Resisting in the New Austerity? Realigning Social Welfare and Independent Action among English Voluntary Organisations', *Journal of Social Policy* 44(3): 463–85.

mudlark121. 2018, 6 December. 'Today in London Housing History, 1986: Pullens Estate Squatters Resist Eviction, Walworth', *Past Tense*. Retrieved 7 January 2024 from https://pasttenseblog.wordpress.com/2018/06/10/today-in-london-housing-history-1986-pullens-estate-squatters-resist-eviction-walworth/.

Muehlebach, Andrea. 2012. *The Moral Neoliberal: Welfare and Citizenship in Italy*. Chicago: University of Chicago Press.

Müller, Birgit. 1991. *Toward an Alternative Culture of Work: Political Idealism and Economic Practices in West Berlin Collective Enterprises*. Boulder: Westview Press.

Nash, June, and Nicholas S. Hopkins. 1976. 'Anthropological Approaches to the Study of Cooperatives, Collectives, and Self-Management', in June Nash et al. (eds), *Popular Participation in Social Change: Cooperatives, Collectives, and Nationalized Industry*. The Hague; Paris: Mouton Publishers, pp. 3–32.

National Lottery Good Causes. 2011. 'St Hilda's East Food Co-op | National Lottery Good Causes'. Retrieved 28 September 2018 from project/st-hildas-east-food-co-op.

Norman, Jesse. 2008, 21 February. 'Co-ops Are Not Leftwing', *The Guardian*.

Norman, Jesse, and Peter Hunt. 2008, 18 January. 'Co-operative vs Co-operative'. *BBC News*.

'The People's Supermarket'. 2011, 6 February. *Channel Four*.

Policy Navigator. 2003. 'The Government's "5-a-Day" Campaign for Healthy Eating Was Launched in March 2003 | Policy Navigator', *Policy Navigator*. Retrieved 7 January 2024 from https://navigator.health.org.uk/theme/5-day-campaign.

Rakopoulos, Theodoros. 2015. 'Solidarity's Tensions: Informality, Sociality, and the Greek Crisis', *Social Analysis* 59(3): 85–104.

Roberts, Phillipa. 2009. 'Why the Conservatives Are No Friends of Co-operatives', *The Co-operative Party*. Retrieved 7 January 2024 from https://party.coop/2009/09/11/why-the-conservatives-are-no-friends-of-co-operatives/.

Rose, Nikolas. 2000. 'Community, Citizenship, and the Third Way', *American Behavioral Scientist* 43(9): 1395–411.

Rozakou, Katerina. 2016. 'Crafting the Volunteer: Voluntary Associations and the Reformation of Sociality', *Journal of Modern Greek Studies* 34(1): 79–102.

Shukra, Kalbir et al. 2004. 'Race, Social Cohesion and the Changing Politics of Citizenship', *London Review of Education* 2(3): 187–195.

SNOW (Squatters' Network of Walworth). Circa 1986. 'Pullens Estate'.

St Hilda's East Community Centre. 2012. *St Hilda's East Community Centre Annual Report 2011/12*. London: St Hilda's East.

Sunlife. 2016. 'The Only Way is Up: House Prices in Britain Then and Now', *Sunlife*. Retrieved 1 July 2022 from https://www.sunlife.co.uk/blogs-and-features/the-price-of-a-home-in-britain-then-and-now/.

Sustain. 2012. *Food Co-ops Final Report – Draft*. London: Sustain, unpublished.

Tower Hamlets JSNA Reference Group. 2016. *Joint Strategic Needs Assessment Summary Document: Life, Health, and Wellbeing in Tower Hamlets*.

Travis, Alan. 2013, 31 July. 'National Archives: Margaret Thatcher Wanted to Crush Power of Trade Unions', *The Guardian*.

Tyler, Katharine. 2015. 'Attachments and Connections: A "White Working-Class" English Family's Relationships with Their BrAsian "Pakistani" Neighbours', *Ethnic and Racial Studies* 38(7): 1169–84.

Undercurrentspaulo. 2010. 'OddSocks – Changing Your Name to Confuse the Police Computer', *YouTube*. Retrieved 11 July 2024 from https://www.youtube.com/watch?v=P7w1qmloaDo.

Vanke, Alexandrina. 2024. *The Urban Life of Workers in Post-Soviet Russia: Engaging in Everyday Struggle*. Manchester: Manchester University Press.

Vargas-Cetina, Gabriela. 2005. 'Anthropology and Cooperatives: From the Community Paradigm to the Ephemeral Association in Chiapas, Mexico', *Critique of Anthropology* 25(3): 229–51.

Well London. (n.d.). 'Well London – White City Food Co-op (Buywell)'. Retrieved 25 July 2024 from http://www.welllondon.org.uk/385/white-city-food-co-op-buywell.html.

Williams, Raymond. 2015. 'Structures of Feeling', in Devika Sharma and Frederik Tygstrup (eds), *Structures of Feeling: Affectivity and the Study of Culture*. Berlin: De Gruyter, pp. 20–5.

CHAPTER

2

FOOD COOPERATIVE IMAGINARIES

FIRST ENCOUNTERS

On my first visit to St Hilda's I met Jenny, the food co-op's coordinator, to find out more about the project, its practices and aims, and to discuss whether I would be able to volunteer there as a participant observer. We sat in the computer room at the centre as Jenny would be facilitating an online food hygiene training course for some of the food co-op's volunteers after our meeting. Coincidentally, Jenny had studied anthropology at university as a mature student, and she seemed enthusiastic about the idea of someone studying food co-ops. She had done her undergraduate dissertation on cooperativism and trade unionism, spurred on by her own interests and formative experiences within cooperatives, and a desire to reflect on them further. She seemed keen to have the chance to talk more about all things cooperative, which on that occasion included the Rochdale Pioneers, alternative food movements and her work at St Hilda's East Food Co-op. She had been there for around a year and a half at that point.

After we had been chatting for a while, Jenny looked at the clock and wondered where the volunteers who were coming to the food hygiene session had got to as it was passed the time that they were due to arrive. Before heading off to investigate, Jenny introduced me to Kim, the volunteer coordinator, who gave me a tour of the building. This was spread over four floors, each painted a different cheerful colour. There were various offices and project spaces on each level, ranging from recreational rooms for youth activities to an advice office, a kitchen, a small roof garden and office spaces rented out to other local organizations such as a support service for acid attack survivors. There was also a basement, which I was told on another occasion was a bit of a no go area due to all of the artifacts from past projects and ongoing activities that lived down there.

During the tour, Kim talked me through the different projects at the community centre and introduced me to various people such as project coordinators, reception and office staff. She then gave me a form to fill in with details ranging from age and ethnicity to work status, qualifications and referee contacts. All this felt welcoming and organized. After I joined, the induction was further enhanced with opportunities to practise on the till and learn the basic systems of the food co-op before being thrown into a busy Thursday session.

Volunteers were efficiently inducted, trained and given a clear point of contact for any support needs they might have. Volunteer attendance was taken weekly, and at regular intervals throughout my time there we filled out volunteer surveys, asking about why we came to volunteer, what difference volunteering had made to us, and if the experience had impacted on our food practices. The surveys also asked for feedback and suggestions. All this created an environment in which St Hilda's staff could support the volunteers to the best of their ability and facilitate their understanding of volunteers' interests and needs. The surveys also fed into trustee and managerial meetings at the centre, the annual report for St Hilda's, and monitoring reports for project funders.

These were all key elements of the organizational culture of the community centre, which speak to the professionalization of the third sector discussed in chapter 1. This is a world in which forms of governance are distilled down to the administrative tasks of measuring 'quality, efficiency' and 'organizational *effectiveness*' (Shore and Wright 2015: 422, emphasis original; see also Rozakou 2016), as means of assessing how best to support the local community and volunteers, and to maintain a competitive edge in terms of fundability. They also speak to aspects of the food co-op's imaginary, how it has been shaped by specific times and values, and how these translate into its practices and norms today (Taylor 2003: 27). Like many volunteer-orientated community projects, however, St Hilda's culture included a mixture of clear structures and processes combined with a layer of unpredictability. Common factors that feed into this unpredictability include staffing levels and organizational infrastructures (both of which can vary depending on scale, funding, organizational priorities and staff members' skills and values), and volunteers with very different needs, interests and capacities to attend regularly.

As for Fareshares, the first time I tried to visit, I checked the Saturday opening hours, travelled the hour or so south from where I lived in East London only to find the food co-op was closed. Round the side of the building, various people were mending bikes as part of the Bikespace project. Next to them was a green 'cycles' sign, in which the white circle at its centre, containing a bicycle, had been masked out to create the Anarchist symbol. I asked them if they knew what was going on with Fareshares and they told me that if it was not open, it probably meant none of the Saturday volunteers had turned up. I did not manage to go back again until I started fieldwork there a few months later.

Figure 2.1. Bikespace sign, 2016 © Celia Plender

Induction at Fareshares was very different to that of St Hilda's.[1] After a prospective volunteer had got in touch, they would be contacted by someone from the group of volunteer-members who dealt with volunteer enquiries. Sometimes this could take a little while depending on who was in the 'new volunteers' group and what capacity they had at the time. The group would then assign the new volunteer to a shift based on what was needed at Fareshares and what that person was interested in and able to do. Someone from the 'new volunteers' group would then let the shift that the volunteer was going to join know, at which point it was over to the shift team. What happened next was very much dependent on who a new volunteer worked with. While there had been various plans to put together shift guides for each of the different weekly activities, ranging from unpacking, to ordering or serving customers, only a few had actually been written, and even if a shift did have one, others on the shift might not necessarily know or remember to share it. Instead, what a volunteer got to know about how things worked tended to depend on who else was on the shift, how connected they were to the collective as a whole and, often, how long they had been involved. New volunteers could quickly be thrown in at the deep end to work alone if a shift was short of people, even though everyone acknowledged that this was not an ideal scenario. This is not an uncommon experience in horizontalist collective organizing where the pedagogical logic can include an element of finding out for yourself (Müller 1991: 150).

These experiences are representative of the very different structures, logics and ideologies of the two food co-ops. As discussed in the previous chapter, one set is more closely connected to ideals of community, care, employability and more institutionalized and systematic forms of volunteering (St Hilda's). The other (Fareshares) on 'alternative modes of relationality and on visions of laterality and egalitarianism' (Rozakou 2016: 80) with less formalized structures and bureaucracies. If such projects are 'laboratories' for the 'crafting' of certain kinds of citizens and subjectivities (Rozakou 2016), then this chapter begins to explore the kinds of social imaginations and actions that each space (re)produced. I start the chapter by looking at what both food co-ops were like during my fieldwork, providing context to their materialities and socialities. I then move onto how those involved with each food co-op understood it – what it was, what it did and what its politics were. In many ways food co-ops are an interface between the materiality of the spaces and the things within them as well as the practices and storytelling that surround these. These allude to real and desired social, political and economic relationships, highlighting the ways in which imaginaries are not only socially constructed, but also materially (Davoudi and Machen 2022). As Asara (2020: 3) points out, the 'idea of imaginaries highlights ways of understanding and giving meaning to the social world, enabling the (re)production of social institutions, practices, and social change'. Such an exploration, therefore, helps to understand the imaginations and values interwoven into both food co-ops, as well as the spaces of possibility that Wright (2010) and Gibson-Graham (2008) associate with emancipatory social scientific work.

A PLACE TO SHOP, CHAT AND MEET

During my time at St Hilda's the food co-op looked much the same as it had back in 2005. Every Thursday morning, an A-board on the street outside the centre announced that 'St Hilda's Food Co-op Here Today! Fresh, local & organic fruit & vegetables on sale!' Inside, foldable tables were set up in the hall each week. The wipeable tablecloths had been upgraded from black,

Figure 2.2. St Hilda's sign, 2017 © Celia Plender

white and gold to dark red with a swirling black pattern. These had been chosen at a local street market by Shirina, one of the longest running volunteers at the food co-op. Jenny knew she liked that market and thought she would enjoy making choices about how the food co-op looked, while also giving her a sense of ownership and agency within the project.

To the side of the hall, a noticeboard covered with colourful images of fruit and veg was one of the food co-op's only signs of existence at other times of the week. This held information about the nutritional qualities of various fruits and vegetables in line with the food co-op's aims around healthy eating. There were also details of how to volunteer. In terms of what it sold, as well as a wide range of fresh fruits and vegetables from Community Food Enterprise and a smaller quantity of organic produce from Sarah Green, the stall regularly stocked some tinned and dried goods from the cooperative wholefoods wholesaler Suma and a small range of Palestinian solidarity products such as dates, olive oil and almonds from an enterprise called Zaytoun, again connecting it to some of the imaginaries of 'good' or 'ethical' food apparent in alternative food networks. At Ramadan the offering from Zaytoun would be scaled up, with large boxes of dates for breaking fast and gifting to friends. The stall also had laminated signs (for easy care) with details of who the suppliers were with text and images. This enabled customers to know more about where the goods they were buying came from, how they reached the food co-op and, in the case of the local, organic fruit and veg and the Zaytoun goods, who made them and under what conditions. This pushed back against commodity fetishism by bringing the producers back into the transaction (Coles and Crang 2010: 89; De Neve et al. 2008: 8). The range of products therefore mixed biopolitical concerns around healthy eating with food ethics and more politicized imaginaries around solidarity with local farmers, retailers and more distant Palestinian producers.

Behind the tables, one corner of the hall housed a tea and coffee area with jugs of hot water, mismatched mugs and often a few biscuits. Nearby a folding table was surrounded by chairs for volunteers and customers to take a break and chat, which we often did when things started to slow down on the morning shift. While our conversations covered anything from information about our families to recent activities or what we had watched on TV lately, food was a typical 'linking theme' providing commonalities between us (Wessendorf 2014: 81) as we discussed the produce we liked best on the stall, what we had tried lately and how we cooked it. As well as light topics, some of us also had more intimate conversations about particular challenges we might be facing in our personal lives, whether these were work, health or family related, therefore expressing care and empathy for each other's situations.

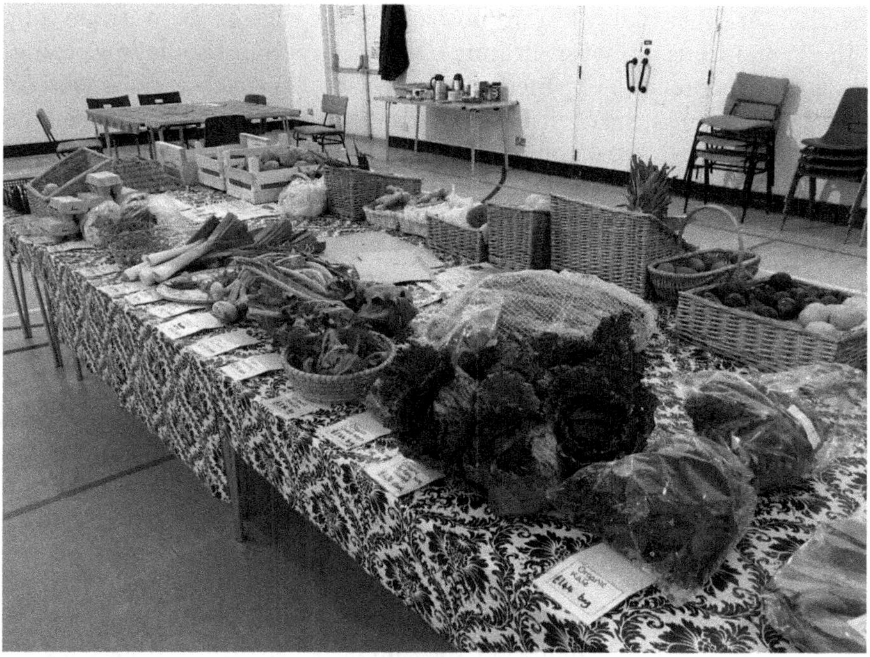

Figure 2.3. St Hilda's stall and tea and coffee area, 2016 © Celia Plender

The tea and coffee area was something that Jenny had implemented in order to give the food co-op a welcoming, friendly feel, which went beyond simply selling food. This correlated with the food co-op's aims to not only provide 'fresh fruit and vegetables at affordable prices to the local community' and to be 'a lifeline for housebound older people using the centre', but also 'a place to shop, chat and meet', where 'friendships are built across diverse cultural and social backgrounds and an interest in food is a common passion' (St Hilda's East Community Centre n.d.). This resonates with convivial ideals of fostering shared dispositions (in this case around friendliness and sociality) in order to cultivate a greater sense of community (Kavedžija 2021: 14–9) or 'convivial affect' (Passes and Overing 2000: 14), while also rendering diversity more commonplace (Wessendorf 2014: 45). As such, this was a means of encouraging a generous spirit and mutual respect as part of an active 'practice of collectivity' (Gibson-Graham 2003: 65).

As for the Older People's Project, this was still situated in the café next door to the food co-op, and as a morning shift got underway, the smells of cooking cabbage, chicken, gravy and other lunch offerings for the older people wafted through into the hall. When I walked past the café, I regularly saw Rupert, the director, sharing a chat and a cup of tea or meal with the older people, therefore expressing intergenerational solidarity and interconnection. At other times, I heard nostalgic music such as the wartime song 'The White Cliffs of Dover' drifting out of the room, or sometimes something more contemporary. There were often activities such as crafts, quizzes and gentle (sometimes chair-based) exercises, and every now and then the older people would be off on a daytrip. The food co-op always felt a lot quieter when they were not around. Daytrip locations ranged from Southend (a nearby seaside town) to the giant Asda supermarket on the Isle of Dogs in East London. When I expressed some surprise at the Asda trip, Jenny told me that that particular branch was pretty impressive to behold (I never got round to going to see it for myself though). Like many of the trips the older people took, the centre's minibus 'Ethel' also had strong links to the East End. It was bought with money donated from a fund set up after the death of the actress Gretchen Franklin who played 'Ethel' in the TV soap opera EastEnders for many years. The show focuses on the trials and tribulations of a working-class community in a fictional area of East London, therefore speaking to working-class imaginaries that are often connected to this area.

At its busiest times, the morning food co-op shift had as many as ten people volunteering; at its quietest (typically during holiday periods when volunteers might be away or have parenting responsibilities), one or two. For the majority of the volunteers, the shift began at 10am and started with unpacking fruit and veg, pricing produce and setting up the till. A handful of volunteers would come a little earlier to help put out the tables and start sorting through the orders. Some of the Bangladeshi mothers[2] would then leave early to get home to their families and domestic responsibilities. The first hour of opening from 11am until midday could often be very busy as the Older People's Project members, the chef of their lunch club and various regular customers all tended to arrive promptly – in the case of the older people, sometimes too promptly, as some would pop in as soon as they arrived on 'Ethel' so they could look for the choicest fruits and vegetables. We would have to politely tell them to come back once we had opened.

Jenny always tried to ensure that the most confident till users were ringing things through for the first half hour or so, and jumped in herself when needed, as the queues could get pretty long. While most of the customers were very patient, the odd one might get a little irritable, and no one wanted to keep the older people waiting in line for too long. Doing their own shopping, however, was seen as an important activity in terms of mobility and sociality, so they were encouraged to come through themselves, accompanied if needed, rather than simply give us a shopping list. Once the items had been selected, if there was likely to be a long wait, some might still head back next door to the lunch club and wait for us to bring their goods and change through once things had calmed down. By 12.15pm the food co-op had usually started to quieten, leaving more time for volunteers to catch up, have a cup of tea or do some chores as directed by Jenny, such as giving the fridge its monthly clean, bagging up nuts, grains and pulses or stock-taking. Volunteers would also do their shopping, with some spending no more than the £3.60 lunch allowance that most chose to spend on fruit and veg, while others would do more of a weekly shop. Once everyone had finished, these expenses were documented and each volunteer was reimbursed for £3.60 worth of their shopping, again representing the formalized processes, as well as the entitlements, of a voluntary project, along with some of its flexibilities in terms of the choice people made to spend the allowance on vegetables rather than lunch. We would then finish packing up the tables, cash up the till, and volunteers would start to dissipate.

When the food co-op started to have a second opening at 5–8pm (later adjusted to 5–7pm), I chose to do a double shift as this enabled me to become more involved with the food co-op and the centre itself. Sometimes I spent my break exploring the area around St Hilda's further; at others, I stayed in the centre, reading, studying or sharing lunch with some of the staff. In the evening, we then went through the same routine, setting up, serving customers, and packing down at the end of the evening, albeit with far fewer volunteers. Once we were done with this by about 8.30pm (or 7.30pm when the hours were adjusted), I would often head south to Elephant and Castle to do the weekly Infinity wholesale order at Fareshares before taking the one-hour tube[3] journey home with rather tired feet.

A COUNTER-CULTURAL FOOD SPACE

Fareshares also continues to operate in a similar vein to when it first started. As its website suggests, it aims 'to provide good food for the community at affordable prices in the belief that decent food is a basic necessity for health, regardless of means' (Fareshares, n.d.). It stocks 'simple unadulterated food (often called wholefoods) and related products', such as environmentally friendly cleaning goods and recycled toilet paper. As much of the stock as possible is 'organic, local and ethically sourced. All of it is animal product, sugar and GMO-free'. Many of Fareshares' suppliers are also cooperatives or 'collectives that work for the same aims' (ibid.). This privileging of like-minded projects and the enforcement of stronger connections between producers and consumers resonates with ideals of a solidarity economy and the ways in which it emphasizes the 'multiple social configurations of an economic system' (Rakopoulos 2014).

While I was at the co-op, the front of the building was a shiny dark green colour, framed by dark red pillars. 'fareshares food co-op [*sic*]' was written in yellow lettering above the door, and below that was a red and blue

Figure 2.4. Fareshares exterior, 2014 © Celia Plender

Lyon's Tea sign that looked like a remnant from the building's former life as a conventional corner shop. Opening times were listed on a wooden board attached to the shop front along with a range of flyers and posters for local events and more radical activities such as the anarchist bookfair or grassroots campaigns. Inside, the walls and window frames were painted turquoise, orange and yellow, with turquoise, deep pink and dark wood shelving housing much of the stock. Towards the back, the old wooden counter contained instructions about 'how to use Fareshares ' with illustrations of bags and containers to fill up, chits to fill in, scales to weigh goods and calculators to tally everything up. When I first arrived at Fareshares in 2014, there was also a second-hand till on the counter. Not everyone was a fan of what this represented in terms of Capitalist retail transactions though. By 2015, when I returned, the till had malfunctioned and only its drawer remained.

Although the crèche and book swap were gone, the Bikespace and Infoshop were still there, making up the 56a building collective. In the Infoshop, there was shelving up to the ceiling filled with radical books, pamphlets and ephemera from different movements, ideologies and specific campaigns and actions. During opening hours, whoever was on shift often sat on an old, battered sofa chatting to visitors and other members of the collective as they came in and out, directing those who were interested to specific aspects of the archive, selling the odd radical calendar or pack of Zapatista coffee, or just having a conversation. On a Wednesday, I often found myself stopping by for a chat about anything from the release of British social realist film director Ken Loach's film *I, Daniel Blake* (which came out at the time and engaged with austerity and the welfare system in Britain)[4] to the activities of Focus East 15 (a campaign group started by some mothers who were threatened with eviction from their emergency accommodation in Newham, East London in 2013. The group was very active at the time of my fieldwork).

Behind the Infoshop was a kitchen space and toilet. We still regularly cleaned out empty bottles that shoppers brought in and filled them with washing up liquid and laundry detergent from big bulk containers in the kitchen. This felt no more enjoyable than when Adina and Martin were doing it back in the early days. The kitchen was a hive of activity as a thoroughfare from the Bikespace and the Infoshop, making it another interesting place to chat. The kitchen also contained a range of practical activist information and memorabilia from various political events and movements, including a squatters' noticeboard and posters about Rojava (the de facto autonomous region of northeastern Syria). In the toilet hung a police shield from the

Figure 2.5. Fareshares interior, 2017 © Celia Plender

Brixton poll tax riots of the 1990s and on the inside of the toilet door was a sticker that stated 'I am a vegan and I poop three times a day'.

As for the food co-op, its aesthetic values were evocative of the crowded and more chaotic feel of punk or countercultural food spaces (see, for example, Belasco 2007; Clark 2004). Goods were placed simply into the vegetable racks, shelves or jars. The 25-kilogram sacks of grains, seeds and pulses were housed in black, heavy duty plastic rubbish bins with scoops for shoppers to portion out as much or as little as they wanted. All this created a distinctive visual and material culture that worked to differentiate Fareshares and its stock from industrial goods and retail spaces such as supermarkets, and from their values in relation to consumerism and profit.

Every shop shift had a slightly different feel to it. While Saturdays tended to attract shoppers who appeared to have comfortable enough incomes to buy a lot of their weekly groceries at Fareshares, Thursday and Friday evenings were often less conventional, and more sociable. If the Saturday shoppers were there to get their groceries and get home to families, friends and weekend activities, some of the Thursday and Friday evening regulars might stay for the whole evening, drifting between the food co-op, the Infoshop and the Bikespace before heading home with some carefully chosen purchases. The colourful chairs that used to be in the middle of the shop in the early days declaring the space's sociality were long gone by the time I arrived. But there was still a wooden chair where shoppers could sit, relax and chat with volunteers and other shoppers – some that they already knew and others not. Many also perched on the stepping stools used for reaching higher shelves.

On a Thursday and Friday evening there was often more of an alternative crowd, made up of lefties, hippies and conspiracy theorists, and the conversations that took place could be about anything from activism to the veracity of the moon landings or the values of 'Native American' wisdom. While I did not hear it myself, other members told me that they had also heard talk of lizard people. This is a classic conspiracy theory in which many of the rich and powerful people on planet earth (including the British Royal family and the US political dynasty the Bushes) are, in fact, shapeshifting reptilian aliens who are ruling the planet. Dietary practices were another popular topic on all the shifts, with the 'alkaline diet', in particular, much discussed during my time at Fareshares.[5]

I worked various shifts during my fieldwork. For the first four or five months, I worked a Thursday evening when the co-op was open to shoppers, and for the last five months or so I did one or two Saturdays a month. The shift I stayed with the longest, however, was unpacking deliveries on a Wednesday afternoon in preparation for opening on a Thursday as this shift needed additional help at the time. Work at Fareshares could be much more atomized than at St Hilda's as everyone worked on different shifts. Each person had responsibility for their shift, with one or two other people, and for specific jobs, at times individually and at times with a handful of others, which was the case with the ordering and Facebook page curation that I helped out with.[6]

For much of the sixteen months I worked on the Wednesday shift, it was often just Ed and me. Other volunteers would sometimes stop in from time to time though, especially when I first started. The shift had been short for a while, so people had begun trying to come by when they could so that Ed did not have to do it on his own. When we arrived at 4pm, the various deliveries would already be there, and over the months, Ed and I got into a quiet routine, taking it in turns to check off the dried goods or fruit and vegetables before putting aside any pre-orders, and then placing all of the goods on the co-op's shelves. As there were no shoppers to interact with, the shift gave Ed and me plenty of time to chat about our lives, our values and the workings of Fareshares, developing our own ways of working with and caring for each other. Ed was a quiet and thoughtful person, who, having lived in a housing cooperative for over thirty years, was also great to talk to about the ideals and realities of cooperation. Sadly, he is no longer with us as he died less than four months after I completed my fieldwork. I still miss him and think of him often.[7]

As these descriptions highlight, the material world and social practices of both co-ops reflected aspects of their origins, their ethos and their stance on issues such as care and community. One was premised on social inclusion, affordable, nutritious food and service to a local community, the other diverse economic practices and countercultural values. In the following sections I start to explore how those involved understood them, and what kinds of imaginations they produced.

GOOD FOOD AND ETHICAL SHOPPING

In 2017, I had the chance to interview Fareshares founder member Adina together with another long-running Fareshares member called Colomba. Colomba arrived on the Pullens Estate in the early 1990s from Chile and soon became a Fareshares visitor and then volunteer. She still lived on the Pullens Estate during my fieldwork (where the three of us met in her flat) and worked as a medical interpreter. Although she had had breaks from volunteering at the co-op over the years, she regularly did a Saturday shift during my time there. As for Adina, she lived in a new-build apartment across the road from Fareshares, having moved back to the area a few years earlier. She worked as a music teacher these days and still shopped at the food co-op regularly. At one point she had also considered starting to volunteer again, although in the end she decided not to.

When I asked Adina and Colomba what they thought Fareshares was for today, Adina suggested that 'people still come for the same reasons'. Colomba agreed that it was about 'the same old principle'. Colomba felt that a lot within society had changed, but the objective for Fareshares remained the same – 'to supply good, healthy, cheap goods to the community'. Adina mentioned that this was 'without the mark-up and also trying to avoid too much packaging, trying to avoid people making huge profits'. Her description, therefore, contained a mixture of environmental and alter-Capitalist concerns as well as a communitarian ethos, which all resonate with practices of commoning and diverse economies (Asara 2020; Gibson-Graham 2008).

Adina and Colomba both felt that Fareshares was 'unique' and that people went there for lots of different reasons both social and ideological. 'There is the political side as well', Adina added, 'it's the kind of grassroots, doing it for yourself. And it's also knowing that the people that do the orders there . . . there's really strict principles in place'. Adina thought that working with wholefood, wholesale cooperatives such as Suma and Infinity also meant that those involved knew they were working with good organizations who did not have 'big directors who are having massive bonuses'. Both of them appreciated these things, and how they facilitated more ethical and political shopping practices.

For many members of the collective, food was a core aspect of their motivation for being involved with Fareshares. They could access more affordable foods, while also promoting certain forms of consumption perceived to be more ethical and environmentally sustainable. Anna, for example, told me, 'I always try to find the most ethically produced, healthiest thing to buy'. At the time of our interview in 2017, she had been at Fareshares for around two years working on the Thursday afternoon shift. She acknowledged that buying ethical foods could be expensive and that 'her attitude' towards food buying was 'incredibly privileged'. She went on to explain, 'I think it's great for an organization to try to give people access to affordable, healthy, ethical food'. She considered this to be Fareshares' 'brief'. While she questioned whether Fareshares did always manage to fulfil the brief, she told me that this brief 'is one of the reasons I love Fareshares'.

Anna had previously been a member of a buying club in Canada, where she moved to from England in 1991 while in her twenties. When she came across Fareshares, she told me she was 'delighted' to find it. 'It was instantly recognizable to me. The bulk buying and the bins of food', she explained. 'And it was such a relief because I hadn't found anywhere where I could get stuff [staple foods such as lentils] loose that wasn't in stupid small expensive packages'. She was also keen to get involved with the local community, so she started volunteering there straight away.

Like Anna, Rachel, who did the vegetable ordering, also mentioned access. She told me that the 'whole idea of trying to provide these resources, making them as accessible as we can is a political idea'. After joining the Thursday afternoon shift around 2006, she found she really liked the project, the 'kind of engagement you had with customers . . . the decisions you had on stock and stuff like that'. Rachel was born in Scotland in the 1960s and became involved with the punk and anarchist scene in her youth. After moving to London, she had also spent time living in a short-life housing co-op[8] and worked with various activist projects, such as rape crisis, where less hierarchical organizing was part of the makeup. She told me that, to her, cooperation 'really makes sense as a way of doing things'. She also valued healthy food and the logics of non-profit making, so many aspects of Fareshares worked for her.

For many members of the food co-op, vegetarianism and veganism were another important draw.[9] Kell (they/them) told me that they were 'attracted to it [Fareshares] because it was a vegan project'. Kell is a queer, non-binary, trans woman and a vegan. They had been at Fareshares for around 11 years at the time of my fieldwork and volunteered on a Friday evening. They liked the fact that Fareshares was trying 'to provide vegan organic food that's affordable to people'. As a benefit recipient due to ill health, they acknowledged that 'people on the dole can't afford to buy much organic vegan food' necessarily, but Kell suggested that foods such as beans, grains, rice and nuts were more affordable at the co-op.

Now in their early fifties, Kell had been an activist since their teenage years. They had started off by engaging with local CND (the Campaign for Nuclear Disarmament) action in the Midlands where they grew up. Later they became very active with different LGBTQ rights issues, including the Spanner campaign in the 1990s (which demanded recognition of sadomasochism as a legitimate sexual practice in response to police investigation and prosecutions of various homosexual men who practised it). By the time they arrived at Fareshares, they were very burned out from their previous activism, and it felt nice to find a 'quieter' form of political work that was done through cooperative mechanisms of consensus decision-making and through food. Others also spoke of Fareshares' politics as 'quiet' or less overt, but they still had the sense that the project *was* political due to the kinds of food it sold, their attempts to make them accessible and the cooperative mechanisms by which the project operated (which I discuss further in the following chapter). The lack of profit was also a key component of their understanding. This was not simply a means of making food more accessible, but also a way of pushing back against capitalism through alternative economic practices.

NEW SOCIAL AND FINANCIAL RELATIONSHIPS

One thing that particularly struck me on my first shift at Fareshares was the difference between the transactions that took place at the co-op and those of a 'normal' shop. The volunteer who I was shadowing sat back on a stool for much of the shift, talking to shoppers when he felt like it, but without the formalized efforts and expected 'emotional labour' of a standard, commoditized service arrangement (Hochschild 2003). He was not unfriendly, but nor did he make a particular effort to help shoppers or appear congenial as he took the money for their purchases. This is something that led me to reflect on how I wished to be in the space, and whether I wanted to unlearn some of the service practices that I had been socialized into in previous retail work. Each volunteer seemed to make slightly different choices on how to be in the space based on anything from ideals and previous experiences to personalities.

Petra, who had volunteered at Fareshares for several years, explained that she strongly objected to the idea of 'service' in a place like Fareshares. Everyone who was involved should find a way to pull their weight. If they were not volunteering, then they should make a donation as well as shopping; and if they objected to there being unpacked goods in the shop that volunteers had not had time to deal with yet, then they should step up and unpack them themselves. In this way, she articulated a vision of the cooperative in which the labour as well as the space and its goods were part of a commons which people could contribute towards in different ways (Akbulut 2020). Petra also mentioned the shop's original slogan as we spoke: 'Not a shop, an experiment in community', again reframing those who interacted with Fareshares as part of a communality rather than a service arrangement, in which those who shopped there were 'pushed beyond the boundaries of being consumers motivated by self-interest and summoned into being subjects who share a concern for the well-being' of the project (ibid.: 199).

When I asked Anna about who the 'customers' at Fareshares were, she pushed back against my language use telling me 'I try and call them "users", just to remind both them and me that actually this is a collective and we are volunteers and there isn't a hierarchical system here. Because sometimes people seem to think they are in a shop and behave towards volunteers like they are in a shop and they're not'.

This and the co-op's slogan exemplify Gibson-Graham's understanding that within 'diverse economies', language (as well as practices) can be used to 'explore the multidimensional nature of economic existence and the possibilities this creates for political acts of economic transformation' (Gibson-Graham 2006: 77; see also Butler 2011, 2016 on performativity and the resignification of norms). Food, therefore, started to become 'a pivot around which social and economic relationships' could be 'rewoven' at Fareshares (Grasseni 2013: 5).

According to Kell, 'it's about trying to create spaces and places and relationships which are breaking and disrupting those state/capital mechanisms'. Along with the co-op's non-profit model, a rejection of wage labour, and the forms of non-hierarchical organizing within the project, the promotion of more sociable and less consumerist or service orientated shopping experiences was one of the ways in which this was done. Kell went on to tell me that Fareshares was a community which disrupted the idea that everyone within society is a consumer and, therefore, the culture of consumption itself. No one within the collective would try to make shoppers buy more than they wanted, but volunteers might try to have a chat.

Similarly, Nuala, an Irish member of the collective who had been volunteering for around a year at the time we spoke, suggested that when people came through the door at Fareshares, they tended to slow down. They did not treat the volunteers as shop assistants and they knew they needed to pull their weight by cleaning up after themselves as they selected and weighed out their goods. Even if they did not pick up on the co-op's 'alternativeness' the first time they visited, by the second time, she observed, they would have started to behave in line with the food co-op's ethos. As such, rather than 'customers' or 'consumers', visitors to the co-op became community members who felt involved with the project, even if this meant just bagging their own goods and treating transactions differently, rather than becoming fully active in running the project.

In his research with a workers' cooperative café in Istanbul, Akbulut saw similar dynamics between the workers and 'customers', who were expected to become active choice makers within the café in relation to pricing, and often also pitched in with aspects of the cooking and serving. Akbulut (2020: 198) argues that the 'the Collective [*sic*] does not position itself as a producer of only (or primarily) a particular service, but also – and more importantly – a certain type of relationship'. This is a relationship that 'transcends the duality of customers vs. the collective' (ibid.). Such an approach speaks to a desire for social interdependencies to be acknowledged and fostered through 'economic being-in-common' (Gibson-Graham 2006: 165). All those who participate in such a project are, therefore, implicated in the 'care-work' involved in maintaining and reproducing the commons that is created through these actions (Caffentzis and Federici 2014: 91).

Colomba told me, 'people go there and share ideas, talk, discuss things, so it's not just the provision of goods, but also the provision of a social space for interactions'. This too was political from Anna's perspective. As she explained, 'I think that any venue that encourages community is political because it makes people strong, because you're strong as a group and so people talk and make connections. And yeah, it makes people stronger and that is political'. This, again, resonates with Gibson-Graham's vision of community capacity building and Federici's understanding of the strength and potential of social cooperation, mutuality and collective responsibility (Federici 2012; Gibson-Graham 2003). Fareshares is, therefore, a social and physical space for action, which is relational and political (Jupp 2022: 23).

THE THING OF BRINGING PEOPLE TOGETHER

At St Hilda's, I also asked Jenny to describe what the food co-op was and what it did on various occasions. She did not find it the easiest thing to describe or define due to the variety of functions it served for different volunteers and customers as well as the different meanings that those involved derived from it. As she explained on one occasion:

> I think it's . . . that's a question that I'm still finding hard because I kind of think it's a community service, but I don't like the word 'service', but I can't think of a better word because I don't think it's a business. Community would definitely be in there somewhere. Run by volunteers . . . I think it's sometimes led by volunteers, but I'd like it to be more led by volunteers. For the volunteers, I think it's about lots of different things depending on the volunteer, and I guess that's a big part of my role. That's probably why it's quite hard to define because for some volunteers, it's an opportunity for them to get work experience within a community setting, but then you've got the business side because they're learning customer service and things you'd learn in a shop: ordering, stock-taking, food hygiene, all of those practical skills that are really useful if they're going on to work in a business. So, I suppose I'd change my definition depending on which audience I'm approaching. Then from the customer side, I guess it's about the health aspect. Sometimes I have a visual in my head . . . when I was doing my figures of the amount of fruit and vegetables that we'd bought and sold in the last year, I thought I would love to see what that actually looked like as a pile of fruit and vegetables, and to think of that all circulating locally in terms of health and balance.

Jenny's description highlights many of the objectives common to voluntary sector food projects discussed in the previous chapter. This ranged from skills for employability to providing a source of healthy and affordable food, and a space of social inclusion. Like other community centres started in the late nineteenth century as part of the British settlement movement, at St Hilda's East's very foundation was an ideal around the benefits of interactions between people of different backgrounds (Scheuer 2011). So too was a set of charitable objectives. As such, it was premised on ideals of service to the local community. Yet, in Jenny's discomfort with the word 'service' (whose discursive power implies a hierarchy of givers and receivers), she both accepted and contested aspects of 'stratified' third sector sociality (Rozakou

2016: 88). While other projects within the community centre would describe those who participated in them as 'service users' Jenny would never use that term either. Baines and Hardill (2008: 308) suggest that in the UK, voluntary action has two roots, one drawn from a philanthropic tradition, the other from mutual aid. In Jenny's understanding of the role of volunteers within the co-op as active, decision-making leaders, rather than simply recipients, she also pushed at some of these boundaries (as I discuss further in the following chapter). This worked to create more 'caring and solidaristic relationships' between Jenny and the volunteers (Jupp 2022: 26), and a sense of 'co-ownership, co-production and co-management of social goods and spaces', which, again, resonates with notions of a cooperative commons (Arbell et al. 2020: 59).

Jenny continued:

> I think . . . again, it's an area I would like to develop more, but the thing of bringing people together. We can have a queue of customers where there's such a wide range of ages, backgrounds, abilities, both in the team but also the people using the co-op. But I'd like to do more about coming together if they want to, some people don't want to, some people don't need that, others do. So, I'd like to make it, if that's what people would benefit from, more opportunities for them to have that. I guess that would be through workshops and things like that. I am trying to define it [the food co-op], but I think that's the key elements in its definition. And the intergenerational stuff I think it's really good.

An ethos of inclusion and diversity had been an important part of the food co-op since it started. For example, Lourdes, the original coordinator, talked about a British-Bangladeshi volunteer called Arpan who had learning differences. She explained that other voluntary organizations had not wanted to take Arpan on, as he had higher support needs than some volunteer projects felt they could manage. 'But it's really worked here' she told me. 'He says to other people "I'm going to work" on a Thursday morning. "I'm going to my work at St Hilda's". So, it was a real sense of pride for him and he was given certain jobs and it was really interesting'.

As such, there was a sense that his 'work' as a volunteer created opportunities for Arpan as an 'active citizen' who gained value and meaning from what he did at St Hilda's (Baines and Hardill 2008; Hyatt 2002). Like Arpan, for many of the volunteers at St Hilda's and at Fareshares, it could be a means of keeping busy, building structure into one's week, feeling useful and more visible (Malkki 2015; Muehlebach 2012).

Arpan continued to be an integral part of the food co-op team while I was there, building connections with many other volunteers as we all learned to work together and understand each other's varying backgrounds, boundaries, interests and vulnerabilities. He still took pride in his work with the food co-op. As he told me during a volunteer interview for the newsletter, he felt 'so happy' when he came to the food co-op. He also enjoyed helping the customers.

At Fareshares, too, some of the volunteers who were not working due to physical and mental health issues acknowledged that they found the routine that volunteering with the collective gave to their week was something they valued. It meant that they knew for at least one day of the week, people would be expecting them and notice if they did not show up, and this felt reassuring. To create a greater sense of purpose, structure and belonging for themselves, these volunteers engaged in activities which involved routine and social contact. In doing so, they not only attended to the needs of the project or the others involved, but also to themselves, enacting forms of 'care of the self' (Foucault 1988; Malkki 2015: 10).

In that first encounter with Jenny in the computer room at St Hilda's she told me:

> I think the beauty of the [St Hilda's food] co-op is there's so many different kinds of roles that people can do. So, it lends itself to whatever your ability is, you can get involved. So . . . there's, people who I think would find it difficult in other volunteer roles who feel very much a part . . . and I think the volunteers, especially the long-term volunteers, feel very much like they own the co-op.

This sense of ownership (which I return to in chapter 3), again spoke to something more than a service relationship, evoking a sense of social cooperation and mutuality (Federici 2012). As well as continuing to work with Arpan, and ensuring that he was supported and working well with others, in line with recommendations from support workers at his assisted accommodation, Jenny also worked with another volunteer whose mental health issues made it too challenging for her to come in on a Thursday when so many people were around. Instead, she came on a Monday to help Jenny with admin jobs for the food co-op, or practise using the till and scales. In both of these cases, the project coordinators went beyond the remit of the project as a fruit and vegetable stall to ensure those who could otherwise feel excluded were able to be part of what the project was and what it did.

The co-op's diversity and vision of inclusion took many other forms, too, ranging from income level to work experience, and identity. While some volunteers were fluent in English, others were working on their language skills and the co-op provided a space to practise and build confidence while (in many cases) also working on employability. This was the case for Jasmine, for example, a Bangladeshi single mother of four young children who joined the project through a collaboration between the food co-op and a local social housing provider to give employability and volunteer opportunities to their residents. Jasmine explained that although she still had work to do, volunteering had given her a lot more confidence in her English when she went to the bank, for example, or spoke to council officials. It had also given her work skills, which she appreciated. When she came to the centre it felt like 'family', she told me, again emphasizing the importance of affective qualities in fostering conviviality as a set of amiable and intimate relationships premised on living or working together well (Kavedžija 2021: 14–15; Passes and Overing 2000: 14).

This combination of a welcoming environment and a place to develop new skills came through in my conversations with many of the women who came to volunteer at the community centre from the Bangladeshi community. For some, this was their first experience of work. For others, it was the first time working in the UK. Alisa who joined the food co-op as part of a link up with the ESOL (English for Speakers of Other Languages) classes at the centre told me that despite her nerves, when she arrived at the food co-op, she found her experience there very positive. Alisa was always a strong communicator, but over the months she spent at the food co-op it was clear that her language skills and confidence were growing. While she worked on the morning shift, she often popped by in the evening with her husband to drop off samosas, curries and other delicious snacks for Jenny and the evening volunteers, further reinforcing convivial relations. She stayed with the food co-op long beyond her placement, only stopping when she moved away from London. Rather than following the logics of 'activating' employment skills among volunteers who were then moved on into the job market, there was a strong sense at the food co-op (as well as many other projects at the centre) that anyone who wanted to, could be a part of the St Hilda's community for as long as they wanted. The food co-op, therefore, fulfilled 'productive purposes' through the provision of nutritious and affordable foods and employability skills, but also 'pedagogic, convivial functions' (Asara 2020: 14), which promoted social integration for anyone who wanted to be a part of the community, including migrants and those with learning differences. It is 'a place of sociality and communality, and a micro-environment that defines a range of social possibilities, contacts, relations and experiences' (Vanke 2024: 61).

NOT LIKE A SUPERMARKET

When I asked volunteers what the food co-op was and what it did, as with Fareshares, healthy food was a common theme within their answers, as were affordability and access to good/healthy food for people in the area who needed it. Ideas of who these people were included those on low incomes and members of the Older People's Project, some of whom had mobility issues.

As long-term volunteer Teressa defined it in a focus group I held for food co-op volunteers in 2017, 'I think [the food co-op's about] sourcing foods from different places, it's about healthy food and bringing it to a community mainly for people who can't get out or are on a smaller budget'. Teressa was a Londoner who had previously worked in the civil service and now ran a mobile hairdressing and beauty business, including home visits to elderly people. Despite living in southwest London, she travelled to St Hilda's every week to volunteer at the food co-op. She had first found out about the project by visiting the centre with her sister and her nephew who used to live in the area and went to a children's group at the community centre. When Teressa found herself with a bit of time on her hands, she decided it would be a good place to volunteer. These logics, therefore, spoke of wanting to make a positive contribution to the centre and the local area, in line with common understandings of the motivation to volunteer (Muehlebach 2012). Teressa had been with the food co-op for around two years at this point and enjoyed working with all the volunteers. She felt it was a friendly place and a good team and that she had made new friends there.

Many of the volunteers at both food co-ops were keen to contribute something to the local community, to support people perceived to be less privileged than themselves, or, at St Hilda's, to support the older people who shopped at the food co-op. In interviews that I conducted for the newsletter at St Hilda's, helping the older people often came up as one of the aspects of the project that people enjoyed, and which, no doubt, made them feel that they were doing something tangibly useful and beneficial to others. By helping the older people with their shopping, we were giving them access and enabling them to choose what they wanted to buy and eat, while benefitting from the sensorial experience of assessing the produce and picking the items they liked the look of. This was also a potential bonding experience for both the volunteers and the older people.

Lots of the volunteers valued the fact that you could learn about different produce and how to cook it from other volunteers and customers. Anita, a Caribbean volunteer who came to the food co-op through the same scheme as Jasmine, told me, 'you meet different people, different ages, and they all have something to tell you'. This included the customers as well as the volunteers and community centre staff. She mentioned that they sometimes explained how to cook with some of the less familiar vegetables she had come across on the stall. This added to her sense of connection to the food co-op and the centre.

When Anita first started at the food co-op, she was unsure of what a food co-op actually was and how it differed from a regular market. She soon came to appreciate its sociable and supportive qualities, however, as well as its food. For Anita, the idea of a food co-op was fundamentally tied up with notions of community, as well as food. During the focus group she told me, 'to me, when you hear co-op, that's about the community, isn't it? And it's a way of introducing foods that you wouldn't normally see, because coming here that's what happened with me. I got to know about the different organics, the different foods. It's an education in food – that's how I see it'.

Sophie, who was on a short placement at St Hilda's from an American University (another official route to volunteering at the centre), also enjoyed the food co-op's sociality. As she explained, 'because it's volunteer run it's a lot friendlier and everyone is within the community, because people who come by are generally people who live around the area. You're more likely to talk to them because you're not just staff in a supermarket. I think that's nice, and it's nice to see how the co-op is run'.

As with Fareshares, these forms of exchange, which Sophie framed in terms of sociability and connectedness, were put into contrast with less personal forms of economic activity, such as buying from the supermarket. In the focus group, others also contrasted St Hilda's with the supermarket, both in terms of the quality and freshness of the produce, and the unscrupulousness that some associated with the profit-making model that supermarkets use. As such, the visions of community that volunteers articulated moved beyond neoliberal notions of active community (Goes 2018), fostering consciousness and critique in terms of the negative qualities of food retail within large multiples such as supermarkets, and the values of more community-based food and economic practices. They identified and valued the co-op's alternative economic credentials and their feeling of trust in the project and its produce, which were the opposite of the deep mistrust they seemed to feel for the supermarket's methods and foods.[10] Gibson-Graham (2006: 69) also discuss the forms of alternative economic subjectivation that can happen in community contexts through being and doing in common, suggesting that everyday diverse economic activities such as those of the co-op can awaken a 'yearning for a communal (noncapitalist) economy' along with less capitalocentric imaginations. These processes of 'resubjectivation', they argue, are inherently political (Gibson-Graham 2003: 55).

Teressa explained to me that 'we know it [the organic food] comes from the farm. We've been to the farm as well, so you can trust it compared to the supermarket . . . With the food co-op, we have the facts of where the food comes from and a bit of history on the food, how it's grown and so on. But when you go to the supermarket you don't know where it's from'. The farm visit Teressa mentioned catalysed much discussion of the time, care and effort that went into growing Sarah Green's organic produce. As Anita put it, the vegetables there were 'grown with love'. The week after the farm visit, as we sat and drank tea at the end of the morning shift, some of the volunteers were still thinking about the trip. Vanessa, an East Londoner who had heard about the project from Teressa and felt that it was a nice opportunity to get out into the community while her children were at school and nursery, told us about a TV programme she had seen recently. The show highlighted the impact of supermarket ordering systems on farmers if orders were changed at the last minute and income and stock were lost. Teressa suggested that the government should be held more accountable for these things, for allowing the system to become this way and not intervening sufficiently. Vanessa agreed.

The conversations about food transactions and production methods highlights the food co-op's role in creating space for education, experimentation and deliberation in relation to food (all important components of a more radical imagination (Haiven and Khasnabish 2014)). The direct relationship between the food co-op and Sarah Green also attempted to foster a more collaborative and socially embedded relationship between consumers and producers, subverting aspects of commodity fetishism by making the producers and their labour more visible (Homs and Narotzky 2019: 136). In less overtly or uniformly politicized food co-ops, such as St Hilda's, such processes of 'politicization' often 'emerge organically from collective practices rather than as an *a priori* abstract ideological framework' (Homs and Narotzky 2019: 137) as these activities suggest.

Guthman (2008: 1175) argues that people often call for better knowledge of how their food is produced rather than tighter regulations of the food system, therefore, propelling them 'to make reflexive, ethical food decisions' as responsibilized citizens. While food co-op volunteers valued this knowledge, the trust that the direct supply created between producers and consumer, and the new appreciation of farm labour that the visit to Sarah Green fostered, on this occasion, evoked a social democratic social contract in which the state had a responsibility for solving the problem, rather than simply responsibilized or ethical citizenship.

At St Hilda's the relationship to ethical consumption was less pronounced than at Fareshares. While some customers would come purely for the organic and fairly-traded goods, others would avoid them. Although many of the Bangladeshi families who regularly shopped at the food co-op focused on price and quality, some always bought organic goods as they felt that these were healthier. With the members of the Older People's Project, most focused on the cheaper non-organic goods, at times feeling suspicious of the organics and why they were generally more expensive. Some, who were more physically capable of cooking and interested in different kinds of food, mixed and matched between the organics and non-organics though, based on what they liked the look of. Many volunteers also mixed and matched, feeling that their budgets would not stretch to exclusively organic produce, but they were still keen to add some into theirs and their families' diets, often for health reasons.

While Fareshares' volunteers talked explicitly about the politics of food, perhaps not unsurprisingly, cooperativism and diverse economies did not come up so organically in my conversations at St Hilda's. When I went back in 2020, however, I asked people more directly about the project's politics. Among St Hilda's volunteers, some acknowledged that they had never really thought of the food co-op's activities in political terms, instead framing the project in relation to community, access to food and low-cost shopping. Others did see these things *as* political, however, mentioning community, solidarity and reconfiguring social and economic relations.

Alice, for example, had not reflected on St Hilda's as a political space before, but she felt its very existence and approach to inclusivity and community spirit were politically resonant in some ways. She was a retired art teacher, who was born and raised in Sri Lanka (where her father was from) before moving to England (where her mother was from) at around 11 or 12. She did lots of volunteering including for a charity shop and a homeless charity. She joined St Hilda's as she loved 'good food' and 'just thought it would be a nice place to work'. By the time of our interview she had been volunteering at St Hilda's for about three years. Alice told me, 'I think that just the way that it is, *is* a different way of approaching . . . serving the community, you know, with basic needs really, and I think just by doing that it's a kind of standard for how things can be', she told me. 'But I don't think it's got aspirations to try to change anything else . . . but it must have had aspirations just to become what it is'. While she questioned its wider transformative power, she still saw prefigurative potential in how social reproduction was envisioned and how social relations and understandings of care and responsibility were enacted along more collective and mutual lines. In sum, the food co-op still *felt* political to her. This chimes with Gibson-Graham's notion of capacity building, in which understanding the 'contingency' of the world as it is creates 'political possibility' for it to be otherwise (Gibson-Graham 2003: 53).

As for Jenny, she also saw the alternative economics of St Hilda's Food Co-op's practices as political. The 'food co-op is an alternative system of buying and selling food which I think is political with a small "p"', she explained. 'It's not in the mainstream', she continued and 'it's trying to do things differently' and more 'fairly' in order to make 'better quality' foods more accessible to 'everyone'. Such an ethos, therefore, resonated with the original values of the first wave food co-ops. Jenny saw the non-profit model the co-op worked by as an important part of its work as a diverse economy, and one that was deeply connected to its ethos of accessibility. Within the food co-op, therefore, the 'use value and general interest prevailed' above 'exchange value and individual interest' (Aernouts and Ryckewaert 2018: 6 in Arbell et al. 2020: 58) unlike in a typical Capitalist enterprise.

James also saw St Hilda's in political terms. He had been involved with many different kinds of activism over the years, ranging from the anti-poll tax movement to support for vulnerable migrants. James was a Londoner who lived on the nearby Boundary Estate. He had been a customer throughout my time as a volunteer at St Hilda's. After retiring from his administrative job[11] in the NHS at the age of 60, however, he decided to make the transition from customer to volunteer in 2020. When I asked James if he saw his work at St Hilda's as part of his activism, he told me, 'I think politics always starts from where you are and what needs doing, if possible. So yeah, I'm now not in a trade union, I'm not in other organizations like that. So, this is . . . yeah, this makes sense as part of my activism'. I went on to ask him how he would describe the political work that the food co-op and shop and drop (a shopping service set up by the food co-op for vulnerable people during the pandemic) did, and he told me:

> It's encouraging a sense of community, it's encouraging solidarity, it's all about solidarity with others, and encouraging a relationship with how we do things. So, we have a relationship with the farm that the organic stuff comes from. You know, we are related to how things are grown, which is political. Even if it is only half of what we're doing, so . . . and yeah, I think community . . . doing stuff in the community is political.

For James, therefore, the work of St Hilda's food co-op was about solidarity rather than more top-down 'service provision' (Asara 2020: 16), alluding to a vision of more equitable place-based forms of food and care provision, and an 'ethics of collaboration' (Krasny 2020: 177).

CONCLUSIONS

Food co-op practices and relationships shed light on how certain 'people relate to each other through the medium of things, the cultural ideas they bring to bear on that relationship, and the social processes and politics that surround it' (De Neve et al. 2008: 5). This relates not only to preferences for certain kinds of foods and retail transactions, but also to what the social interactions within the food co-ops mean to those involved, the personal, political and economic values embedded within them as well as their affective qualities.

Food itself was the 'medium' (Davoudi and Machen 2022) through which many aspects of the food co-ops' imaginaries were fostered. As well as the conviviality of the spaces, this related to stocking and buying foods perceived to be 'good', whether defined through notions of quality, healthfulness, ethics or politics. Many different values were interwoven into how 'good food' was articulated in each space, drawing together many different interests and concerns for selves and others (Miller 2001: 123). For both food co-ops, however, accessibility and affordability were important components of the formulation of 'good food', mirroring a classic concern within the food cooperative imaginary. At Fareshares, this was about making certain kinds of ethical goods more affordable through non-profit and bulk buying, while at St Hilda's it related more broadly to affordably priced, healthy food. But it was also about having the *option* to buy goods that were organic, fairly-traded or cooperatively sourced for those who wanted to, irrespective of income.

On first appearances, the logics and experiences of both projects would seem to conform to Hyatt's understanding of something more activist and oppositional (Fareshares) and something non-political (St Hilda's). As Rozakou points out (2016), however, the division between more activist and charitable voluntary projects is not always as straightforward as it may seem. For this reason, it is imperative to try to understand such projects from the ground up, taking into account the perceptions and experiences of those involved. At Fareshares many of those who volunteered were draw in from activist backgrounds and strong stances on the politics of food. They were articulate about the politics of food, non-hierarchical organizing and of community. At St Hilda's, many of the volunteers came in through more official routes, such as placements to promote 'active' forms of citizenship (Hyatt 2002), or a desire to do something good for the community (Muehlebach 2012). They were typically less forthcoming in their articulations of the politics of food, diverse economies or community, yet they still experienced the project as alternative to mainstream food and economic transactions due to its communality and mutuality. In their articulations of the importance of accessible food, they also spoke to more equitable visions of society.

More socially orientated settings such as food co-ops resonate with Gibson-Graham's notion of diverse economies, in which they propose the 'community economy' as a performative set of practices and ideas that destabilize 'the economy as it is usually known and performed' (i.e. Capitalist) (Gibson-Graham 2006: 79). Like many alternative economic movements and conceptualizations,[12] Gibson-Graham's community economy emphasizes the resocialization of economic relations. This is premised on interdependence as well as ethical decision-making. In relation to cooperativism (and in particular the Mondragon cooperators of the Basque region of Spain), they argue that its principles can act as a form of cultural commons. Their enactment contributes to a process of subjectivation around 'distinctive economic ways of being', while constituting cooperators as 'communal subjects' (Gibson-Graham 2006: 105). In Federici's terms, these acts 'reproduce our lives in ways that strengthen mutual bonds and set limits to capital accumulation' (Federici 2019: 166). As Rakopoulos points out in his work on the anti-middleman movement in austerity Greece, such informal networks premised on kin, friendship and feelings of affinity also have the potential to be powerful sites of mobilization in times of need (2015: 96).

At Fareshares and St Hilda's, their attempts to resocialize the economy on values of trust, conviviality and community speak to the ways in which practice and deliberation can open up spaces for different forms of alternative economic and political imaginaries (Siniscalchi and Harper 2019: 2), as well as the possibilities inherent in notions of social and radical imaginations (Haiven and Khasnabish 2014; Taylor 2003). The latter of which, Haiven and Khasnabish (2014) argue are situated in specific places, building out of alternative practices of social reproduction and cooperation. As such, both food co-ops had elements of a 'counter-space' which is 'occupied by the symbolic and the imaginary' (Lefebvre 1991: 366 in Goldstein 2017: 1456) working to de-commodify elements of everyday life (Goldstein 2017: 1456–7) through food-based economic practices. By creating certain kinds of spaces and forms of social reproduction within them, 'the space itself' is implicated in the creation and recreation of 'individual subjectivities' (Akbulut 2020: 199).

Asara suggests (2020: 4) that '[c]reating a critical distance between the instituted society and the horizon of potential otherness is the precondition for shaping and reshaping alternative social imaginary significations'. Building on Castoriadis and Appadurai, she suggests that within these imaginaries can be found the 'germ' of autonomy that can 'turn into the fuel for action'. From Goldstein's perspective (2017), the power of such counter-spaces relates to the forms of 'quiet' activism that Kell mentioned. Rather than 'turn things upside down in an instant' they start to open up 'cracks' or possibilities within the Capitalist system and the status quo by providing opportunities for critique of the world as it currently is, and opportunities to prefigure something different. Returning to Wright (2010) and the discussion of emancipatory politics in the introduction, this facilitates capacities to imagine and to hope, which have been fundamental to the cooperative imaginary since its inception. This highlights, therefore, the ways in which 'meantime' activities such as community food provision that are premised on care and welfare, such as St Hida's, are still 'capable of opening out rather more progressive and hopeful spaces of political conscientization, invention and reorientation' even if they do not necessarily seem to be overtly political or resistive on first impressions (Cloke et al. 2017: 721). While this chapter has focused on how each food co-op was experienced by those involved and what possibilities lie within these experiences and practices, in the following chapter, I move on to consider the impacts of the two food co-ops' differing structures on notions of autonomy, ownership and experiences of alienation.

NOTES

1. I should acknowledge that before re-joining, I was invited to one of Fareshares' monthly meetings, which was held on a Sunday afternoon. This was a chance to tell the collective about my project, seek their consent to my return and discuss any conditions they might have. The only condition they requested was the blanket usage of pseudonyms in my work unless I had specific consent from a member to use their name. This was included in the meeting's minutes meaning anyone who was not in attendance also got to hear about what I was doing, and feed back if they had any concerns or conditions. This aspect of my reintroduction seemed to run smoothly and efficiently. As this was a weekend meeting, some members also prepared food, so we all had a chance to eat and socialize together. In keeping with the food co-ops' policies in terms of stock, I brought vegan, sugar-free cocoa, date and almond balls, which seemed to go down well.
2. While I do not identify markers such as class, race or ethnicity every time I introduce someone within the ethnography, I try to give some context to people's identity to give a sense of who is and was involved in each project. I try to do this by including details that are relevant to the discussion. I then give further details as and when relevant in order to offer insights into how community and diversity are envisioned and enacted within these food co-ops in a superdiverse city, which I look at most explicitly in chapter 5. I acknowledge that this is not a perfect practice.
3. Underground train.
4. Some of the Infoshop and Fareshares' members that day felt that Loach has a tendency to over romanticize the working classes as a category.
5. This is based on the theory that you can change the pH of your body through the foods that you eat. The theory has not been substantiated scientifically (Torrens 2018).
6. Due to the shifts I worked, the duties I took on and the people this led me to interact with more, what this ethnography represents of the food co-op is inevitably partial in some ways.
7. Unfortunately, many of the members of the Older People's Project at St Hilda's who I knew well and often helped with their shopping are also gone now due to old-age-related illness. I have many fond memories of our time together. Covid-19 also took Anita who started volunteering at St Hilda's Food Co-op just a few weeks before I did. We spent a lot of time sitting together in the tea and coffee area of the food co-op, sharing details of our lives and experiences with each other. I really valued my connection with Anita and the time we had together and think of her often too.
8. A short-life housing co-op is a property that has typically been borrowed from the owner (often social housing providers) to provide short-term accommodation.
9. This is something that often came up quickly in conversations with the various people I worked with at the food co-op, and could feel a little as if one was being ethically sized-up. This was a test I failed as I am not currently a vegetarian despite eating a low-meat diet. I often felt compelled to share this piece of information with people, along with the fact that I had previously been a vegetarian for 11 years. This compulsion probably says as much about my desire to integrate into the collective as it does the judgements that members may or may not have been making of my eating choices.

10. Nonetheless, many also acknowledged that they did regularly shop at supermarkets often for convenience, as did various members at Fareshares.
11. James told me that having left school at 16, he was 'not really qualified for much except office work'.
12. See, for example, Polanyi 2001 and those who use his work to explore subjects such as food system localization and Fair Trade including Hinrichs (2003) and Raynolds (2012).

REFERENCES

Akbulut, Bengi. 2020. 'Cooperative Economies as Commons', in Derya Özkan and Güldem Baykal Büyüksaraç (eds), *Commoning the City: Empirical Perspectives on Urban Ecology, Economics and Ethics*. London: Routledge, pp. 193–206.

Arbell, Yael et al. 2020. 'Contested Subjectivities in a UK Housing Cooperative: Old Hippies and Thatcher's Children Negotiating the Commons', *Geoforum* 110: 58–66.

Asara, Viviana. 2020. 'Untangling the Radical Imaginaries of the Indignados' Movement: Commons, Autonomy and Ecologism', *Environmental Politics*: 1–25.

Baines, Susan, and Irene Hardill. 2008. '"At Least I Can Do Something": The Work of Volunteering in a Community Beset by Worklessness', *Social Policy and Society* 7(3): 307–17.

Belasco, Warren. 2007. *Appetite for Change: How the Counterculture Took On the Food Industry*. Ithaca, NY: Cornell University Press.

Butler, Judith. 2011. *Bodies That Matter: On the Discursive Limits of 'Sex'*. Abingdon, Oxon; New York: Routledge.

———. 2016. 'Rethinking Vulnerability and Resistance', in Judith Butler et al. (eds), *Vulnerability in Resistance*. Durham, NC: Duke University Press Books, pp. 12–27.

Caffentzis, George, and Silvia Federici. 2014. 'Commons Against and Beyond Capitalism', *Community Development Journal* 49: i92–105.

Clark, Dylan. 2004. 'The Raw and the Rotten: Punk Cuisine', *Ethnology* 43(1): 19–31.

Cloke, Paul et al. 2017. 'The Geographies of Food Banks in the Meantime', *Progress in Human Geography* 41(6): 703–26.

Coles, Benjamin F., and Philip Crang. 2010. *Placing Alternative Consumption: Commodity Fetishism in Borough Fine Foods Market, London*. University of Leicester. Retrieved 20 September 2023 from https://figshare.le.ac.uk/articles/chapter/Placing_alternative_consumption_commodity_fetishism_in_Borough_Fine_Foods_Market_London/10107038/1.

Davoudi, Simin, and Ruth Machen. 2022. 'Climate Imaginaries and the Mattering of the Medium', *Geoforum* 137: 203–12.

De Neve, Geert et al. (eds). 2008. *Hidden Hands in the Market: Ethnographies of Fair Trade, Ethical Consumption and Corporate Social Responsibility*. Bingley, UK: Emerald Group Publishing Limited.

Fareshares. (n.d.). 'Welcome to Fareshares'. Retrieved 13 September 2022 from https://fareshares.org.uk/front-page.

Federici, Silvia. 2012. 'Feminism and the Politics of the Common in an Era of Primitive Accumulation', in Silvia Federici, *Revolution at Point Zero: Housework, Reproduction, and Feminist Struggle*. Oakland, CA; Brooklyn: London: PM Press, pp. 138–48.

———. 2019. *Re-enchanting the World: Feminism and the Politics of the Commons*. Oakland: PM Press.

Foucault, Michel. 1988. *The Care of the Self. Vol. 3 of History of Sexuality* (Reprint edition). New York: Vintage Books USA.

Gibson-Graham, J. K. 2003. 'An Ethics of the Local', *Rethinking Marxism* 15(1): 49–74.

———. 2006. *A Postcapitalist Politics*. Minneapolis, MN; London: University of Minnesota Press.

———. 2008. 'Diverse Economies: Performative Practices for "Other Worlds"', *Progress in Human Geography* 32(5): 613–32.

Goes, Eunice. 2018. 'The Third Way and the Politics of Community', in Sarah Hale et al. (eds), *The Third Way and Beyond: Criticisms, Futures, Alternatives*. Manchester: Manchester University Press, pp. 108–27. Retrieved 13 July 2024 from: https://www.manchesterhive.com/display/9781526137883/9781526137883.00013.xml.

Goldstein, Piotr. 2017. 'Post-Yugoslav Everyday Activism(s): A Different Form of Activist Citizenship?', *Europe-Asia Studies* 69(9): 1455–72.

Grasseni, Cristina. 2013. *Beyond Alternative Food Networks: Italy's Solidarity Purchase*. London: Bloomsbury Academic.

Guthman, Julie. 2008. 'Neoliberalism and the Making of Food Politics in California', *Geoforum* 39(3): 1171–83.

Haiven, Max, and Alex Khasnabish. 2014. *The Radical Imagination: Social Movement Research in the Age of Austerity*. Halifax; Winnipeg; London: Zed Books Ltd.

Hinrichs, C. Clare. 2003. 'The Practice and Politics of Food System Localization', *Journal of Rural Studies* 19(1): 33–45.

Hochschild, Arlie Russell. 2003. *The Managed Heart: Commercialization of Human Feeling* (2nd edition). Berkeley; London: University of California Press.

Homs, Patricia, and Susana Narotzky. 2019. 'Within and Beyond the Market System: Organic Food Cooperatives in Catalonia', in Valeria Siniscalchi and Krista Harper (eds), *Food Values in Europe*. London: Bloomsbury Publishing, pp. 132–46.

Hyatt, Susan Brin. 2002. 'From Citizen to Volunteer: Neoliberal Governance and the Erasure of Poverty', in Judith G. Goode and Jeff Maskovsky (eds), *The New Poverty Studies: The Ethnography of Power, Politics and Impoverished People in the United States*. New York: NYU Press, pp. 201–35.

Jupp, Eleanor. 2022. *Care, Crisis and Activism: The Politics of Everyday Life*. Bristol: Policy Press.

Kavedžija, Iza. 2021, December. 'The Process of Wellbeing: Conviviality, Care, Creativity', *Cambridge Core*. Retrieved 31 July 2023 from https://www.cambridge.org/core/books/process-of-wellbeing/2B13755C28A5F785C47C70795AA509ED.

Krasny, Elke. 2020. 'Precarious Commons: An Urban Garden for Uncertain Times', in Derya Özkan and Güldem Baykal Büyüksaraç (eds), *Commoning the City: Empirical Perspectives on Urban Ecology, Economics and Ethics*. London: Routledge, pp. 177–92.

Malkki, Liisa. 2015. *The Need to Help: The Domestic Arts of International Humanitarianism*. Durham, NC: Duke University Press.

Miller, Daniel. 2001. *The Dialectics of Shopping*. Chicago: University of Chicago Press.

Muehlebach, Andrea. 2012. *The Moral Neoliberal: Welfare and Citizenship in Italy*. Chicago: University of Chicago Press.

Müller, Birgit. 1991. *Toward an Alternative Culture of Work: Political Idealism and Economic Practices in West Berlin Collective Enterprises*. Boulder: Westview Press.

Passes, Joanna, and Alan Overing (eds). 2000. *The Anthropology of Love and Anger: The Aesthetics of Conviviality in Native Amazonia*. London: Routledge.

Polanyi, Karl. 2001. *The Great Transformation: The Political and Economic Origins of Our Time* (2nd edition). Massachusetts: Beacon Press.

Rakopoulos, Theodoros. 2014. 'The Crisis Seen From Below, Within, and Against: From Solidarity Economy to Food Distribution Cooperatives in Greece', *Dialectical Anthropology* 38(2): 189–207.

———. 2015. 'Solidarity's Tensions: Informality, Sociality, and the Greek Crisis', *Social Analysis* 59(3): 85–104.

Raynolds, Laura T. 2012. 'Fair Trade: Social Regulation in Global Food Markets', *Journal of Rural Studies* 28(3): 276–87.

Rozakou, Katerina. 2016. 'Crafting the Volunteer: Voluntary Associations and the Reformation of Sociality', *Journal of Modern Greek Studies* 34(1): 79–102.

Scheuer, Jeffrey. 2011. 'Origins of the Settlement House Movement: Social Welfare History Project'. Retrieved 23 July 2024 from https://socialwelfare.library.vcu.edu/settlement-houses/origins-of-the-settlement-house-movement.

Shore, Cris, and Susan Wright. 2015. 'Audit Culture Revisited: Rankings, Ratings, and the Reassembling of Society', *Current Anthropology* 56(3): 421–44.

Siniscalchi, Valeria, and Krista Harper. 2019. *Food Values in Europe*. London Bloomsbury Publishing.

St Hilda's East Community Centre. (n.d.). 'Food Co-op Project'. Retrieved 15 July 2023 from http://sthildas.org.uk/projects/food-coop/.

Taylor, Charles. 2003. *Modern Social Imaginaries*. Durham, NC: Duke University Press.

Torrens, Kerry. 2018. 'What is the Alkaline Diet?', *BBC Good Food*. Retrieved 20 June 2019 from https://www.bbcgoodfood.com/howto/guide/what-alkaline-diet.

Vanke, Alexandrina. 2024. *The Urban Life of Workers in Post-Soviet Russia: Engaging in Everyday Struggle*. Manchester: Manchester University Press.

Wessendorf, Susanne. 2014. *Commonplace Diversity: Social Relations in a Super-Diverse Context*. Basingstoke: AIAA.

Wright, Erik Olin. 2010. *Envisioning Real Utopias*. London; New York: Verso.

CHAPTER

3

STRUCTURE AND STRUCTURELESSNESS

A FAMILIAR FEELING

A few months into my fieldwork, Jenny from St Hilda's asked me if she and her niece's seven-year-old son might be able to come to visit one of my shifts at Fareshares. Jenny had known about the co-op for some time, but had not previously had the chance to visit. As her niece's son, who she often looked after, had done odd jobs around the food co-op at St Hilda's before and enjoyed it, she thought he might enjoy visiting Fareshares too. After checking with my shiftmate Ed that he was happy for them to join our Wednesday afternoon unpacking shift for an hour or so (which he was, only mentioning jokingly that he would have to watch his 'effing and jeffing'),[1] I invited them along the following week. As soon as Jenny walked in, she enthusiastically told us that she thought the shop was 'beautiful'. I joked that it looked very much like something from a particular era, and she suggested that this was no bad thing. Fareshares looked and felt very familiar to Jenny from her time working at a workers' co-op in Newcastle in the early 1990s when she was in her twenties. The Red Herring, where she had worked, operated as a wholefood shop, bakery and café, and Jenny had many fond memories of her time there.

When Jenny first arrived in Newcastle in 1991 at the age of 21, she worked as a dinner lady at an agricultural college and had a second job at a pizza restaurant in a cinema complex. She lived in the same area as the Red Herring though, and found herself thinking that it looked like somewhere she 'would like to be'. When Jenny had first come across the Red Herring, it reminded her of Frome in the southwest of England which has been a hub of alternative living since the 1970s (Dyckhoff 2017). Jenny had spent time there as a teenager visiting her sister, who lived there. Jenny's sister was also very involved with Greenham Common Women's Peace Camp and its campaign against the storage of nuclear missiles at RAF Greenham Common. These teenage years were a significant period of political awakening in Jenny's life. She learned a lot about CND, feminism, alternative lifestyles and wholefoods. She explained that she had come from quite a 'traditional' family with Irish catholic roots, and it was very influential to see people finding 'politicized' and 'alternative' ways of living and working. The Red Herring was also a highly politicized environment in which one of its founder members went to prison twice for his protest actions. The first time was for paying his taxes in bread (made at the cooperative) in protest against the use of tax revenue in the funding of arms, and the second was for refusing to pay the newly implemented 'poll tax'[2] (see Red Herring Workers' Co-operative 1996 for more on the Red Herring).

'I didn't really understand before the Red Herring what a co-op really was', Jenny explained, 'and I completely bought into the idea, really. I just thought, "Why doesn't everywhere run like this?" . . . I was very big on co-ops, and very big in other co-ops. I got very interested in what they were doing'. Jenny told me that her time at the Red Herring had really 'formed her', teaching her about work practices as well as food and cooking. It also gave her a strong sense of what it felt like to be part of an autonomous collective, along with the challenges and rewards that came with it. This is reflective of the potential pedagogical power of the alternative forms of sociality reproduced at cooperatives such as the Red Herring and Fareshares, and the radical imaginations that can be fostered through collective practice and deliberation (Haiven and Khasnabish 2014: 9). Jenny explained:

> The Red Herring was the most directly influential job in my life. I think it changed everything for me in terms of how I work. But I'm really glad I didn't do it to start with because I think part of its power was having the comparison to working in very hierarchical . . . at the bottom of the hierarchy as well, very profit driven . . . some pretty nasty environments at times in terms of how managers were . . . It was just kind of very exploitative. So, I'm really glad I'd had that before because I don't think I would have appreciated the Red Herring as much.

While she has not worked as extensively with cooperatives since, she told me 'I took a lot of the workers' co-op with me, wherever I've gone'.

Nash and Hopkins (1976: 10) suggest the 'basic meaning of the word' cooperative 'refers to the organization of work; in principle it refers to an organizational structure in which all are equally workers and managers, and so exploitation is absent'. Cooperatives have, therefore, been seen as a solution to alienated labour as well as conflicts between labour and capital (Holmström 1993: 1) as workers own the means of production and employ mechanisms of self-determination. Through these environments of social ownership and collective decision-making, there is also said to be scope for self-actualization (Bryer 2010; Kasmir 2004) and the development of more political subjectivities (Sitrin 2012). In the case of two non-profit, volunteer-led food co-ops with very different organizational structures, this raises questions about the meaning of work, horizontalism and social ownership in these projects. These questions form the basis of this chapter. I start by discussing the types of politics and sociality expressed at Fareshares through its modes of horizontal organizing. This highlights the kind of radical imagination and visions of society embedded within Fareshares' everyday politics, as well as the kinds of structures that had informed Jenny's cooperative imagination at the Red Herring. I then turn to some of the forms of authority and uncomfortable power dynamics that have developed at Fareshares over the years as a consequence of tensions around how labour is valorized and knowledge instrumentalized. I then move onto St Hilda's, engaging with the ways in which horizontalist cooperative values fared within a more top-down, charitable organization with an ethos of support and care provision. Finally, I look at the changing meaning of volunteering and the forms of contestation Jenny enacted in relation to the more punitive approach to people without jobs that surfaced in austerity Britain.

COOPERATIVISM, REVOLUTION AND RADICAL CARE

Although unwaged, the structures and practices of Fareshares most closely resemble those of a workers' co-op. It is the volunteer-members who make the decisions, choose the stock and worry about the food co-op's survival (and here the two most common concerns while I was a member were volunteer numbers and finances). As a consequence, at its very core are questions about the structures of society, community and of work. It is an environment in which '[t]he "traditional" separation between administrators, planners, and coordinators on the one hand and executors on the other must be replaced by "the collective," which both takes the decisions and executes them' (Müller 1991: 100).

Within the ethos of an autonomous, DIY-style space, it is up to the individuals involved with Fareshares to collectively decide how things should be done. As Müller notes, such groups 'do not have a formal head, so any member can assume the role of de facto decision-maker' as and when needed (1991: 120). This works in the Anarchist spirit of spontaneous order, whereby a group of people with a common need will 'by trial and error, by improvisation and experiment, evolve order out of the situation – this order being more durable and more closely related to their needs than any kind of externally imposed authority could provide' (Ward 2008: 39). Here, there is an emphasis on political power of non-hierarchical organizing rather than modernist rationalities of efficiency. These methods, therefore, not only contribute to the collective's prefigurative power, but also to the potential 'chaos of collective organisation' (Müller 1991: 120).

Not always knowing who else they could ask, and often having a fierce sense of autonomy and independence, volunteers at Fareshares often developed their own ideas and systems for running a shift. These were based on what they may have seen from other members, their own life and work experiences, and the clues they found around the co-op about how things were meant to be done – such as the list of instructions on the daily takings and cashing up sheets, which were one of the food co-op's concessions to more rational-legal systems.

Here my own experience acts as a good illustration of the destabilizing feelings this less structured induction can foster, as well as the feelings of autonomy that may follow. After re-joining the collective in November 2015, by my third Thursday evening, I was left to run the 6–8pm shift alone as the other Thursday 'shifties' were unavailable. Although I had been shown some of the basics about shutting up and cashing up, there was still plenty to figure out as I went along. This was an anxiety-inducing experience as Thursday had the longest opening hours of the week, with many different people taking money and noting down sales throughout the day as they chatted to the customers and each other. By the time the money was cashed up, the numbers could often be different to what had been expected – at times substantially so. Doing the Thursday evening alone was also a point at which I started to feel more ownership of the shift and the space, however, because I was the only one there to make decisions. Not long afterwards, as other new volunteers joined, I was the one showing them how the shift ran as a self-actualized worker.

Fareshares is as much an ideological project as a space where food is sold, and much of the work that goes on relates to the social structures and bonds that the group attempts to build and reproduce. Among the more Anarchist and Leftist members that I spoke to, there was a clear connection between counterpower and the co-op's organizational form. This was a means of practically critiquing aspects of contemporary society through the creation of new structures and associations in terms of work, economic exchange and forms of sociality (Graeber 2004: 24; Shepard and Burghardt 2015: 2). Tina, a Portuguese former member-volunteer and an Anarchist told me:

> All these little spaces, whether they're social spaces or food co-ops, or all these little dynamics that go on, that is actually the revolution. The revolution is not overturning the government. The revolution is not the big coup. The revolution is fundamentally changing the way people interact on a small day-to-day level and doing that all over the place, and that's ongoing.

The day-to-day interactions that Tina referred to, therefore, became a pedagogical tool that helped to foster new forms of egalitarian relationships while opening people's imaginations to the idea of a state- and leader-less society. This resonates with Federici and Ticktin's vision of a feminist commons and collective care (Moraes and Brant 2016; Ticktin in Woodly et al. 2021). In Marina Sitrin's work with Argentina's horizontalist movement of the early 2000s, she also described such actions as revolutionary (2012: 87). She argues that the ways in which people came together after the financial crash (recovering factories, neighbourhood assemblies etc.), fostered a transformation in their 'ways of thinking, doing, being and feeling'. This form of revolution and the subjectivities it produced was both 'affective and relational'. As for anarchism itself, Heckert argues that it is 'an ethics of relationships' and of care which involve connecting 'directly, intersubjectively and warmly' (Heckert 2011: 187), while acknowledging that 'we will never cease creating new relations among ourselves' (Proudhon 1930 in Heckert 2011).

At Fareshares, this idea of an affective, more caring working environment was significant. Zoe told me that at Fareshares, volunteer-members could be mindful of each other's 'moods and temporary or permanent frailties', checking in with other members that people knew were struggling. She noted that she had never been in a working environment where such issues were spoken about 'so matter-of-factly, without stigmatizing or being scared of not knowing how to help'. As such, vulnerabilities had the potential to be expressed and acknowledged, not as forms of weakness, but as relational, social (Butler et al. 2016: 4) and integral to the human experience (O'Neill 2018).

For Zoe, these more affective and equal relationships in which people could bring their whole selves could also lead to a greater sense of connection to other members of the co-op and greater satisfaction in the work that she did with the collective (see also Akbulut 2020 on the creative energy and satisfaction that autonomous working can produce). In Marxist terms, this created the possibility for members to feel like themselves *in* as well as outside of the workplace, to work voluntarily rather than through coercion and to create solidarity and connection with other members rather than competition (Marx in 1844 Marx and Engels 2009: 69–84).[3] In principle, such practices could foster a less alienating work environment through social ownership and the removal of some of the emotional labour inherent in performing certain kinds of selves in the workplace (Hochschild 2003), instead producing an environment in which personal feelings could be expressed.

BUREAUCRATIZATION AND LABOUR

In the spirit of horizontality, rules, policies and other types of formal administrative structures were also contested at Fareshares.[4] Within a project with Anarchist roots, these could have the oppressive, hierarchical feel of Weber's Iron Cage (2012 [1905]). The language of bureaucracy could also be seen to have performative power – whereby discourses produced the phenomena that they regulated and constrained (Butler 2011). While discussing amendments to the new members 'policy', for example, the issue of naming came up, and there was almost as much discomfort with the term 'policy' (which according to Graeber 'assumes a state or governing apparatus which imposes its will on others' (2004: 9)) as there was with the proposed guidelines for when someone would become an 'official' member of the co-op. Breaking with such 'citational chains', therefore, was a means of relaxing the 'coercive hold' of the norms of such governing apparatus (Butler 2016: 18).

The membership guidelines were devised by a working group (including myself), following a suggestion at a meeting that a new process might be needed. This was in order to ensure a good supply of member-volunteers; enough support for non-shift jobs such as finances and ordering; and a better flow of information within the food co-op via better meeting attendance. Membership had previously been loose, with anyone who started to volunteer being treated as a member and therefore being added to the email list serve[5] and invited to participate in monthly meetings. Attendance of meetings was variable, however, with some member-volunteers coming regularly, others not coming at all, and many only coming when there were specific agenda items of interest to them (Holmström (1993: 74) noted a similar phenomenon in Spain).

The policy proposed that volunteers should have done a certain number of shifts and attended a meeting in order to 'officially' join. This was seen as a means of ensuring that everyone would contribute to the self-management of the co-op, not just its daily retail tasks. As such, membership was to become more connected to 'labor contribution' (Rakopoulos 2019: 154) and the commitment to self-management that attending meetings demonstrated. Through its approach, the policy therefore differentiated between the simple act of volunteering and more politicized forms of cooperative *labour*, that is, their governance and administration.

The policy proposal was, in part, a response to the fact that the same people tended to go to meetings and therefore signed up to do more jobs out of a sense of responsibility. This could lead to forms of self-exploitation as well as burn-out. At times, it was only when a member-volunteer left and certain jobs were no longer being done that people realized quite how much that member had been doing. These kinds of uneven division of labour not only put an unequal weight of responsibility on the shoulders of those who attended meetings, but also had the potential to produce an imbalance in power as those with more jobs could also end up with more permanent forms of authority.

Choosing not to attend meetings did not necessarily seem to relate to how committed someone was to the idea of cooperativism, however, or to Fareshares itself. Anna, for example, was drawn to Fareshares in part because of its non-hierarchical cooperative structure. She told me 'I think the meetings are really important', but she also admitted 'I don't go to enough of them'. She went on to explain:

> I think we all need to go to the meetings, or be encouraged to go to the meetings, as much as possible so that everybody's voice is heard. What can happen is that you get people who are really good and diligent who do go to the meetings so the decisions are made and the people who don't go to the meetings feel like they've been excluded from the decision. But they've self-excluded because they didn't go to the meeting.

This was something she acknowledged that she had experienced. In essence, meeting attendance or non-attendance, therefore, had the potential to start to reproduce the forms of class-based stratification others have documented between managers and non-managers within cooperatives and the feelings of disenfranchisement these can create (see, for example, Bryer 2010; Holmström 1989; Kasmir 1996).

Another member, Louise, also spoke favourably about cooperatives, the empowerment that could be gained from making your own decisions and deciding what jobs you wanted to do (she put this into contrast with working somewhere like a bar where there were few opportunities for self-actualization). She thought it was amazing that a group of volunteers managed to work together in this way to keep a project like Fareshares going for so many years. Louise had never been involved with a co-op before and happened to work on a shift that was seen as something of an outlier by those who did attend meetings as no one from the shift attended regularly. Louise told me that she had not fully understood the importance of the meetings to begin with and did not attend for the first year that she was at Fareshares. When she did finally go to one, she discovered all the work that went on within them. Despite this, she still did not attend regularly afterwards.

Louise suggested that co-ops were hard work, at times 'tedious' and 'frustrating' as well as time consuming – especially the meetings. For Anna, non-attendance also seemed to be an issue of time. 'I know I could have gone to the meeting . . . should have gone to the meeting', she told me. 'The trouble is, the meetings take so long sometimes that it's off putting. You don't want to necessarily sit there for two or three hours'. The system only worked, however, if enough people were willing to attend meetings and 'give up the necessary time and energy' to do so (Holmström 1993: 74).

As for the membership policy, its development showed the 'Weberian bureaucratization of charisma', in which 'informal activities' such as the work of a grassroots co-op, can become bureaucratized 'for the sake of their long-term reproduction' (Rakopoulos 2015: 96; see also Arbell et al. 2020 on tensions between fairness and efficiency, and fears of hierarchy and coercion in UK housing co-ops). Nonetheless, it also showed the ways in which these things can be contested. The proposed 'policy' was seen to be overly prescriptive and inflexible to the needs of potential members and the kinds of contributions they might be able to make, therefore working to 'valorize' some labour more than others (Rakopoulos 2019: 154).[6] As such, it had the potential to create disenchantment through the rigidity of rationalization (Weber 2012 [1905]), while excluding those who were only able to *volunteer* rather than entering fully into cooperative *labour*. The rejection of the policy, therefore, attempted to contravene the bureaucratization of the co-op, while ensuring that all labour within the cooperative continued to be part of its commons (Akbulut 2020), to which people could contribute as and how they felt able.

THE TYRANNY OF STRUCTURELESSNESS

When I first started working with Fareshares in 2014, the co-op was still reeling from the departure of a co-op member who had acquired the role of unofficial leader (Hannah). During most of the interviews I conducted with members who had been a part of the collective during this period, the situation with Hannah came up.[7] The rawness of her recent departure and the sense of relief that she had finally gone were palpable in those conversations. Hannah had been at Fareshares for well over a decade, and along with a handful of other key members, she had also helped to reopen Fareshares after a period of closure in the late 1990s, which was brought on by a mixture of more stringent food hygiene checks by the local authority[8] and financial/organizational issues. This meant that she helped to create many new processes at the co-op, and took on various responsibilities. As such, she was instrumental in shaping Fareshares' discourses as well as the norms and forms of knowledge of which they were constituted (Foucault 2002: 53; Rose 2012: 52). This established her with the authority that came of knowing the rules and having been around the longest. For several years she was also seen as someone efficient who got things done. As one member told me, Hannah 'is a very intelligent person and she was able to control everything. She had a mind for everything. I used to admire her because she was really capable'. As a consequence, people were prepared to accept her role as a charismatic leader until the balance of power had tipped too far (Weber 1978 [1922]).[9]

As Kate explained to me, by 2011 they had reached a point where there were some seriously 'entrenched dynamics around ownership, so people felt disempowered'. This, therefore, created a form of class consciousness (Kasmir 2004) between them – the workers – and Hannah – the unofficial boss – which required action. After considering strike action, and attempting mediation, they made the exceptional decision to take a majority vote on whether to ask Hannah to leave (rather than work by consensus). Of the 16 members who voted, 14 agreed to this action, while two abstained. A letter was then sent to Hannah asking her to step back from the co-op.

Through the overthrow and exclusion of their unofficial leader, Fareshares was able to reinstitute and reinforce values of non-hierarchical organizing; and while much of the imbalance of power within the co-op was attributed to Hannah,[10] this situation also offered the collective an opportunity to reflect on its internal workings, and how best to stop such situations reoccurring. As Francesca reflected:

> We like to be really flat and we like to not have hierarchies and too much bureaucracy, but that's when you understand the value of bureaucracy in a way. It takes away the personal and in cases like that, that's what you need. It's not between you and me, it's these are the rules . . . So, I think that's when as a group we really understand the value of that.

In this situation, the hierarchy of bureaucracy clearly felt more acceptable than the authority of an unappointed leader.

It was these 'rules' in the form of disciplinary and grievance procedures that the collective drew on when it was discovered a couple of years later that verbally abusive behaviour had been taking place on one of the shifts at Fareshares. Here, the combination of atomized working arrangements and DIY organizing may well have contributed to the abusive situation. Dave (the perpetrator) was well established on the shift where it took place. This meant he was responsible for producing the discourses around how the shift operated. In doing so, he was also able to control these discourses to some extent (Foucault 2002: 53). It was up to him how much he shared about the processes that were in place and the logics behind them with new members when they joined. While this gave him authority and a strong sense of ownership as a self-actualized worker on his shift, it also meant that the other members on the shift who were newer did not necessarily know the processes for running the shift; what the collective's stance was in terms of acceptable behaviour; or who to turn to if they wanted to discuss what was happening with Dave, leading to feelings of disenfranchisement.

After the issue had been discovered, it was brought to a meeting to be resolved. Turnout for the meeting was unusually high that day. There was an atmosphere of solidarity with those who had been personally affected by the incident. Many of us had not heard the full details of what had taken place before, and even newer members who had not necessarily met Dave or been aware of what had caused him to leave, showed support to those involved. There seemed to be consensus among all who were present about how to deal with the situation. It was agreed that it would be best to respond through an official grievance procedure 'in order to protect the collective and make the process less personal' as the meeting minutes noted. Two members, therefore, agreed to draft a letter to Dave based on this decision. In this moment, Fareshares showed unity, and an ability to follow formalized procedures. While this was not always the case within the co-op, on this occasion, the collective had a strong sense of how important it was to resolve the problem as quickly and efficiently as possible in order to protect those who had been affected by Dave's actions, and to demonstrate that such behaviour would not be tolerated.

When reflecting on all that had happened with Dave, Finn told me:

> At that time there were quite a few of us that had been through the whole process [with Hannah] and we discovered that people had been bullied. We were appalled because we'd been through this huge process of throwing somebody out of the project and trying to create a new, fairer, safer environment and it turned out that two people were actually being bullied . . . That's not what you do radical cooperative politics for. You think you are creating a new radical environment. You don't think you're creating a space for somebody to get bullied.

When discussing the dynamics at Fareshares and some of the conflicts that had occurred, more than one member of the collective put them down to the 'tyranny of structurelessness', a reference to Jo Freeman's classic activist text (1972) of the same name. In it, Freeman examines the issues she encountered within the women's liberation movement in the US in the 1960s and 1970s. She saw problems arising from informal structures, arguing that an ideal of structurelessness can often become a way of masking power, rather than genuinely eliminating it. As Bill explained:

> There is a bit of resistance to there being structures, but I think one of her [Freeman's] points is that there are always going to be structures . . . [There are] things that have gone on [at Fareshares] partly because people don't want to seem too rigid or formal about stuff. People want to think the best of each other and it's as if, if you have an identifiable process to deal with when people aren't acting responsibly it's somehow a bit not Fareshares-y enough.

The combination of this resistance to 'rules' or 'processes', and the fact that most volunteer-members already gave a lot of time and energy to keeping the project running, meant that it was not always easy to find the time and headspace to work on issues pre-emptively, instead reacting as situations arose.

Negotiating structures and power are classic concerns within grassroots activism (Freeman 1972; Gautney 2010; Kadir 2016; Polletta 2012) and cooperative organizing (Bryer 2010; Holmström 1989; Kasmir 1996; Müller 1991; Nash and Hopkins 1976: 10). This, along with personal and collective ideologies, and the instrumental concerns of keeping the project running, are mutually constitutive in shaping the social practices, rationalities and structures of each social group. While they can help produce more radical cooperative imaginations and caring practices, when unofficial leaders emerged at Fareshares, this led to stratification and a revalorization of labour in alienating ways. As such, members navigated different imaginaries when needed: one relating to the caring, relational, unalienated, non-hierarchical environment Fareshares attempted to reproduce, the other to more distant and rational-legal processes, which were seen to have their uses when leaders did emerge, despite the perceived hierarchies within bureaucracy.

A CO-OP IN SPIRIT?

Notions of hierarchy and authority also caused their tensions at St Hilda's. When Lourdes first started the food co-op, she had hoped that it would become a fully community-organized cooperative. In this spirit, she arranged meetings and encouraged volunteers to make decisions with the aim that St Hilda's East Community Centre would simply host the food co-op, while the members ran it. As was the case for Abi in White City (as discussed in chapter 1), however, this never happened. As she explained:

> I think you need to have some driving forces . . . You need really key personalities who want to take on that role, because it's huge, it's massive and you know you need that ethical drive almost like this is part of my way I want to live, so unless you've got that it's very hard.

While potentially rewarding and transformative in terms of radical imaginaries and practices, collective ownership and non-hierarchical organizing can be time consuming and emotionally taxing. To commit to collective ownership of the food co-op would, therefore, require a clear interest in, and understanding of, the benefits of cooperative methods. Having a paid position potentially also gave Lourdes 'more time available to devote to cooperative duties and ends' (Ulin 1996: 173) than the volunteers might have felt they had.

Within the pre-existing vertical structures of the community centre, there were also clear discourses around 'service provision' and support (as discussed in chapter 1 and 2), which McLaughlin suggests can differentiate between providers and recipients, reinforcing the hierarchies contained within these roles, while setting expectations on both sides (2009). Arguably, it would have required substantial work and a strong collective desire from participants in the food co-op to break with the forms of 'bureaucratized and stratified' third sector sociality of the community centre (Rozakou 2016: 88), in which those who provided support (paid workers) and those who received support (volunteers, community centre project service users and food co-op customers) were more clearly defined.

Lourdes told me that the centre itself seemed like another barrier to community ownership. 'I tried. I really tried to think round it, tried to give ownership over, but it was really hard because the premises was St Hilda's.' The community centre, therefore, wanted to have some kind of say in what was going on. The activities of the food co-op also required monitoring within the bureaucracies of the community centre. In essence, Lourdes and the community centre's authority was effectively already 'routinized' (Rakopoulos 2015: 96; Weber 1978 [1922]: 249–51) despite her best attempts to push back against it. This was then further reinforced by her labour, knowledge and decision-making power, and the needs of the community centre's own bureaucratic processes within a professionalized third sector. St Hilda's Food Co-op has continued with a more vertical structure ever since. As such, it is the community centre, rather than the volunteers, who own the means of production within the food co-op.

Both Jenny and Rupert, the community centre's director, were acutely aware of the fact that St Hilda's Food Co-op was not fully cooperative in structure. As Jenny recounted:

> For the first year or something that I was here, I couldn't work out why it was called a food co-op, and I was like really? Am I missing something? But then I thought, 'it's a co-op in spirit', that's what it is . . . rather than on paper. And I think probably one of the challenges is just how you keep that spirit. The big thing is the ownership, that's the big thing; that people feel it's theirs.

Often mentioned by cooperators, cooperative spirit is a concept that is rarely defined. At times, it refers to knowing how to behave as a cooperator – how cooperative practices, structures and values are enacted and how successfully; at others, it reflects on the inclination towards cooperation, or the structure of feeling within a place and time and how cooperative this is perceived to be (see, for example, Hall 2018: 211; Kasmir 1996: 188; Masquelier 2017: 60; Ulin 1996: 171). Clearly these are not unconnected, and within them are commons-based notions of collaboration, collectivity and egalitarianism.

After taking over as the coordinator at St Hilda's Food co-op, in many ways Jenny attempted to draw on the cooperative spirit that she had learned from the Red Herring. She regularly attempted to foster more egalitarian processes and a sense of social ownership by encouraging volunteer collaboration and autonomous decision making. Day-to-day decisions could range from the way the produce was laid out on the tables to volunteers choosing which jobs they wanted to do each session or making suggestions about the overall running of the food co-op and what it should stock. While some of the longer-running volunteers were very vocal about most aspects of the project, the jobs they wanted to do, or how it should run, some, typically newer, volunteers tended to defer to Jenny. To counter this, she tried to find ways of encouraging people to be confident in their own decision-making skills and other abilities as a means of fostering self-actualization. She therefore created situations in which volunteers would support and teach each other various jobs in order to 'foster positive leadership' and collaborative participation (Levkoe 2006: 95). From Levkoe's perspective, such activities are valuable forms of democratic learning and citizenship, which renders them powerful steps towards social transformation (ibid.).

In their descriptions of what the food co-op was, volunteers often used terms such as 'community', 'friendliness' and 'family', as discussed in chapter 2. This highlights the ways in which the project successfully fostered feelings of collectivity, collaboration and care, all of which have the potential to create social power (Wright 2010) and feelings of solidarity (Jupp 2022). Volunteers rarely spoke of the co-op's more egalitarian or democratic qualities, however, and there seemed to be considerable uncertainty and ambivalence around the food co-op's structures of governance or ownership. I was keen to explore these issues further when I went back to the food co-op in 2020. During interviews conducted at that time, I asked various volunteers about who owned the food co-op and what their own role was in decision making. Their responses were mixed. For many, it did not seem to be a question that they had reflected on much before.

Long-term volunteer Alice told me that she thought the community centre probably owned the co-op. As a former art teacher, she had used her artistic skills to make 'signs, painted boxes and goodness knows what' for the food co-op (as she put it), which she enjoyed. 'Jenny's quite good at sort of finding out what your skillset is and then kind of creating opportunities', she explained. Alice saw Jenny as the 'major organizer' within the food co-op and did not feel like she was a decision maker herself. 'But I think I could [make decisions]' she told me, and she saw this potential as 'a very important part of the co-op'.

Claire, a Hongkonger who had lived in the UK for over 20 years also saw Jenny as the organizer. Claire used to work for a charity supporting vulnerable older people to live independently. More recently she had been volunteering in a local children's centre as well as starting her own business making craft items, which she sold at a nearby market a couple of days a week. She first started volunteering at the food co-op after Jenny had run a pop-up food co-op at a children's centre where she was involved.[11] At the time of our interview, she had been with the food co-op for around four years. She knew the practices and organization of the project well and had quickly become a regular and dependable volunteer who often took on extra responsibilities, including occasionally coordinating a session if Jenny was off work. Claire suggested that the project was run by the volunteers, that 'it is everyone's food co-op', therefore invoking a sense of social ownership or commons. Despite this, she felt that she gave 'suggestions' rather than making 'decisions', therefore articulating something quite different to notions of shared management and decision making. This did not seem to cause her any concerns or feelings of disenfranchisement, though, within the structures and logics of the community centre.

While Alice and Claire had been drawn to the food co-op more out of an interest in food and community, James and Mark (who had both been customers for several years before becoming volunteers at the beginning of the pandemic), had started interacting with the project, in part, out of an interest in cooperativism. James defined the co-op as a 'community project where we, through the coordinator, come together to buy in bulk and distribute it [food] among ourselves'. On first impressions, he suggested, 'it feels a bit more like a shop . . . You don't necessarily feel that you are part of a cooperative. But yeah, in a way we all are'. While he acknowledged that if he was asked to design his own idea of a co-op, 'that wouldn't be it', he had a feeling that 'people made suggestions', 'people turned out as part of the community' and that they were part of a 'collectivity' in which they could have a say. As such, it was an empowering and intimate form of sociality born of community connections and cooperation (Rakopoulos 2015).

Mark, another English resident of the Boundary Estate, worked as a lecturer at an art school. He had been keen to get involved with some form of mutual aid during the pandemic so he started with the food co-op and its shop and drop service. He was 'keen on cooperatives' having spent time living in housing cooperatives in his younger years and still choosing to bank cooperatively. Although familiar with the idea that members *should* 'have a say in the governance and structure and organization' within a co-op, he acknowledged that at St Hilda's he only really thought of Jenny due to her 'facilitative position' and had never actually spoken to anyone about the co-op's governance. This made him unsure of how things worked. 'I see there are other people involved but I don't really know how they work together.' As a consequence, he concluded that things worked much more informally than in a traditional cooperative, although he did feel that Jenny wanted 'to get other people involved with decision making and thinking about how it's running'.

In a way, the volunteers expressed a form of '*citizen* subjectivity' through their 'sense of belonging to a larger entity . . . which comes with rights and responsibilities' (Arbell et al. 2020: 60 emphasis original) – in this case, the act of making suggestions and the perceived right to make decisions should they choose to. Nonetheless, there seemed to be a distinction for many between suggestions and decisions and who made which, highlighting a mixture of collaboration and stratification within the co-op. In relation to 'sovereignty and control' as 'producers' (Arbell et al. 2020: 60) things were, therefore, more ambivalent. While volunteers had individual control over many of their choices and aspects of their work, they did not necessarily have full control over the food co-op's systems.

As the volunteers' comments highlight, at St Hilda's cooperativism was more inferred than it was verbally articulated. This inference was seen in the name of the project and in the kinds of practices that were modelled and fostered. By contrast, within the grassroots collectives of austerity Greece, talking about cooperativism and its aims as well as working with cooperative mechanisms were both important aspects of the development of political subjectivities (Rakopoulos 2014). The lack of articulation at St Hilda's left volunteers to come to their own understanding of what a food co-op was, what it was for and, in prefigurative terms, what it could do.

In Jenny's case, her own values around grassroots action and egalitarianism made her feel that it was not her place to impose more formalized cooperative structures. If these were to be put in place, then they should come from the volunteers, not from her. Without the spaces for deliberation to complement the attempts at alternative forms of social reproduction, however, there were arguably less opportunities for the development of a fully cooperative imagination (or spirit).

STRUCTURES OF CARE

Since leaving the Red Herring, much of the work Jenny has done has involved food, community building, care and a desire to help others. As many of these jobs have been within the third sector, she is very familiar with the methods and logics of volunteer coordination. As a consequence, she attempted to negotiate the logics of cooperativism and a professionalized third sector at St Hilda's, which, at times, could be conflicting. On more than one occasion, I heard volunteers identify Jenny as 'the boss' of the food co-op, to which she would reply, 'we're all the boss', feeling uncomfortable with this authoritative role.[12]

Despite the tensions that this hierarchy created for Jenny, she also felt that imposing structure, was a way to provide a more supportive environment, in line with the community centre's ideals and her experiences in the voluntary sector:

> I think one of the things about having a paid position, whether it's me or whoever it is, is about the support for people . . . paid workers, you know, they're contracted to be there and it means that the co-op can be more inclusive, it can support more people, you have that guaranteed continuity, you have that guaranteed support there.

Volunteers knew how things worked and what they were required to do, which, Jenny pointed out, was particularly important for some of the volunteers with learning differences. Equally, no one was expected to take on levels of responsibility that felt incompatible with their skills or the demands of their lives. As she saw it, the reliability of a paid coordinator, whose job included 'care work' (Alber and Drotbohm 2015), as well as practical management of the project, was the best way to offer the support and emotional labour (Hochschild 2003) deemed necessary. This helped to ensure a more inclusive environment, in which there were volunteers with diverse support needs, interests and identities.

Jenny, the paid employee and representative of the centre, was the key provider of support and care. Care was a key component of the community centre and the food co-op's organizational ethos and its staff's responsibilities. Practices of inclusion and care imprinted the centre with strong ideals around the nature and shape of a 'good', or 'caring society' (Thelen 2015: 499), while also informing the ways in which its projects and social practices were structured. Jenny tried to be attuned to different volunteers' needs, interests and vulnerabilities. She attended diligently to her pastoral duties, often sitting and listening to details of the problems volunteers were dealing with in their lives or concerns they had. She offered a friendly face and a sympathetic ear.

Care was also 'realized in physical acts' that communicated 'affect, attention, empathy, and copresence – a touch on the arm, a tenderness in tone of voice, a hug' (Black 2018: 82). In doing so, Jenny imprinted the space with a certain set of ethics and values – both hers and the centre's, and with the affective forms of sociality discussed in the previous chapter. In doing so, Jenny created 'caring and solidaristic relationships' with project participants (Jupp 2022: 26), who reciprocated this care towards Jenny as well as each other. This, therefore, encouraged 'mutual support' and opportunities for connection 'by creating social networks' among volunteers, but also between volunteers and staff members (Levkoe 2006: 96). As such, it produced an infrastructure of sociality and care, which Arbell et al. suggest is pivotal to a cooperative commons (2020: 60).

Support also came in many other forms, from the training opportunities that Jenny facilitated for volunteers to the giving of certificates to celebrate their contribution to the centre or the use of other established volunteer support practices, which are part of a 'more bureaucratized' and 'stratified' sociality' (Rozakou 2016: 88). This kind of 'formalization and officialization' (Rakopoulos 2015: 87), therefore, created a sense of support and inclusion at St Hilda's, rather than rousing suspicion as it did at Fareshares.

In almost all cases, volunteers seemed to see the care they received from Jenny and the community centre, as well as from each other, in a positive light. People regularly discussed how lovely or how supportive Jenny was. And at times of difficulty, it was often this care and how Jenny accommodated different practical and emotional needs that kept volunteers coming back for a long time (often years). As such, this care work was part of what fostered a sense of social belonging and unalienated labour for those involved (Muehlebach 2012: 48).

THE WORK OF VOLUNTEERING

Jenny told me she had concerns about the ways in which the voluntary sector had changed during her time doing this kind of work, and what this meant in terms of the meaning of volunteering and its relationship to paid work and state structures in austerity Britain. As she explained to me: 'I'm very conscious of volunteering and exploitation really and I think there have been big changes in paid roles becoming volunteer roles and what that means in terms of exploitation and in terms of what people need really.' From the state's perspective, labour, whether paid or not, is seen as a significant aspect of citizenship. It is a means of demonstrating a good work ethic as well as deservingness for state welfare. This is highlighted in the language of successive regimes ranging from Thatcher's active citizens to Labour's active communities and Cameron's Big Society.

Much emphasis has been put on making the transition from 'economic inactivity to paid employment' in recent years (Patrick 2017: 4), along with an imperative to demonstrate the ways in which citizens are attempting to take responsibility for their own lives, needs and communities (as discussed in chapter 1). Nonetheless, McKenzie suggests (2015: 13) that 'work and employment have not been the route "out of poverty" that the last two governments insisted it' would be, and that people on '[l]ow pay, no pay, zero-hours contracts, and low-grade self-employed work' often end up oscillating between short contracts and periods of benefit receipt. As a consequence, she suggests that this has 'left families in extremely precarious positions in recent years'.

Many of the volunteers at St Hilda's who were out of work during my fieldwork were very keen to get into employment, and, in some cases, were also being pressurized to do so from the Jobcentres they attended. A significant number of them did not make it into this rotation between benefits and short contracts, however, as they were not even able to get into these precarious forms of work. Several of them faced obstacles to entering the job market, ranging from language barriers to mental health issues, learning differences or caring responsibilities for young children or relatives with additional support needs.

Jenny was also worried about the 'pressure on people in terms of their benefits and the welfare to work programme and where unpaid work crosses over with volunteering'. As she explained to me:

> There's a very thin line and if people are feeling they have to do volunteering for their benefits, then it's not volunteering, it's sort of coercion. Volunteering is, it's in the name, it's about freedom and wanting to give time to something. It's not about feeling you won't have any money if you don't, you'll have the very bare minimum. It, sort of, turns into coercion then. It's been a worrying trend, I think.

This form of volunteering can feel more like a duty than a choice, reflective of state interests in mobilizing so-called inactive or dependent populations (Muehlebach 2012: 139). This highlights the ways in which the voluntary sector has become embroiled with the punitive measures apparent in welfare reform, as I discuss further in the following chapter. It is also another aspect of precarious labour regimes where people are channelled into low-pay or no-pay internships and volunteer positions (Standing 2014: 27). In the context of 'welfare to workfare' ideologies (Koch and James 2022: 5), therefore, citizenship itself can become contingent, meaning people have to continually work to attain and retain it (Muehlebach 2012: 138).

Despite the values Jenny saw in the more professionalized aspects of St Hilda's Food Co-op and Community Centre and the structures that came with it, she was, also resistant to the 'policy regime' in which she was working, finding smalls ways to 'exert' her own sense of 'citizenship and agency' (Jupp 2022: 28). In this vein, she always made it clear that whatever a volunteer chose to contribute to the project on any given week would be appreciated. As she explained to me one day, this went against the standard volunteer coordinator protocol, in which enforcing time management was an important part of employability training. From her perspective, it was important to respect the challenges people faced in their lives and the gift of time they were choosing to give to the food co-op without creating situations in which this free labour could be taken for granted, or in any way exploited, therefore becoming a form of alienated unpaid work.

Jenny went on to describe some of the situations that she had witnessed as both an ESOL teacher and a staff member of an east London volunteer centre:

> and now, this is quite anecdotal, I haven't done the research to back this up, it's anecdotal and what I see and hear. But how it feels to me as an ESOL teacher, it's gone from people being stopped from coming to ESOL classes because of their benefits – they need to be ready for work, they can't go to classes – or being pulled out of classes to go to Jobcentre classes. To now, actually volunteering isn't enough. There was a point where, you know, you're not work ready, so you have to get a volunteer placement. And now I feel . . . it's kind of like, I'm hearing some volunteers saying I'm not allowed to volunteer because I've got to go and do this for the Jobcentre. So, it's kind of like, you're trying to help people into work because they want work. From various reasons from childcare to language skills to other skills to other family commitments . . . there's a whole array of reasons that might be barriers and you're trying to work with people to try to help them overcome those barriers, but then the Jobcentre seems to want to pull people into their way. So, I don't know . . . and obviously in terms of disability, and ESA [Employment and Support Allowance], and the kind of assessments that people have had to go under for those . . . I'm continuously worried basically. I really worry about that in terms of members of my own family, in terms of volunteers at the food co-op. In terms of how we live, how we treat each other as a community, as a society because I think they are inhumane . . . more when I was doing enrolment and stuff like that. There were times when there were people who were so unwell, so unwell, just being forced basically to sign up for courses or come to do job search and it's just like just so not what you need now. I feel for . . . I wouldn't want to work in a Jobcentre. I feel for their staff. I don't know how they are managing really. Where that's going especially after another Tory [Conservative] government, I really worry. And I think if at the food co-op, I feel quite confident that the volunteers overall are there because they want to be there, and I'd find it difficult if that changed.

This again highlights the emphasis on getting people into any work available, however precarious or inappropriate, rather than jobs that may involve stability, satisfaction or career progression (Patrick 2017: 13). This impacts on people's relationship to time, and their ability to look beyond the present and plan for the future, as much as it does their sense of self (Patrick 2017: 3). This, then, has the potential to lead to even greater forms of alienation, frustration and anomie (Standing 2014: 33). The affective environment and caring practices of the food co-op attempted to push back against these forms of alienation and disenfranchisement, by valuing people and their labour differently.

As Jenny's actions at St Hilda's show, while those working within third sector spaces may become 'brokers of the civil society project' they often still navigate different values, interests and ideologies within their work, drawing from various political traditions and possibilities (Rozakou 2016: 92). Through her approach to volunteer coordination in the context of austerity Britain, Jenny 'interpretively intervened and conceptually redefined' processes of subjectification of volunteers, 'introducing a subversive element to conventional discourses' and practices associated with the professionalization of volunteerism (ibid.), which drew on feelings of solidarity and experiences of politicized cooperativism.

CONCLUSIONS

Fareshares and St Hilda's are both historically and socially constituted within specific visions of community and of work and volunteerism, along with established discourses of structure and hierarchy. In both food co-ops notions of community and care were entwined with the creation of a (non-) workplace in which it was acceptable to bring one's whole, affective and vulnerable self, and to feel safe in doing so. In opposition to a Capitalist work arrangement in which '*social* relationships were based on exploitation, regularization, alienation, and commodification', these relationships could be more 'empathetic', 'cooperative' and 'meaningful' (Heller 1999: 93 emphasis original). Each food co-op chose to go about this in different ways, with one emphasizing structure, the other structurelessness, and each approach had its consequences on the dynamics of the project.

At Fareshares, members attempted to enact their political values around non-hierarchical organizing, affective relations of care and anti-capitalism through 'everyday organizational practices . . . "learning how to organize the world differently" through experimentation and direct action' (Land and King 2014: 929). Through collective ownership and decision making about the management of a shared asset or sector, cooperatives such as Fareshares aim to promote horizontal relations and egalitarian values among their members. From Wright's (2010) perspective, such practices have the potential to be powerful models of democratic egalitarianism and social ownership, both of which have significant potential in terms of emancipatory politics and pathways to a post-Capitalist society. Inevitably, 'all social systems are a tangle of contradictions', however, and these contradictions can lead to practical and ideological tensions about the structures, practices and balance of power within a system (Graeber 2004: 34). By resisting structures, Freeman (1972: 4) suggests, rather than abolishing power, a group simply 'abdicate[s] the right to demand that those who do exercise power and influence be responsible for it'. This allowed some members at Fareshares to act in certain ways without a sense of accountability to the collective as a whole, which led to forms of alienation, resistance and decisive action to reset the balance. Here, the coldness of bureaucratic processes felt helpful in taking the affective charge out of these situations.

Following the publication of Freeman's paper on structurelessness (1972), many activists (mis-)understood it to be a call for the necessity of hierarchy and how to institutionalize those that already existed by making them more formal and visible (Graeber 2015:202). As such, it was seen as a criticism of the Anarchist ideal of spontaneous order and non-hierarchy. Instead, it was believed to promote a mass organization with strong, centralized control, which required rules, policies and other bureaucratic forms, which come with the modernist rationality of being governed (Graeber 2015, pp. 202–5). As Anarchist thinker, Malatesta (1897) suggests however, 'organization, far from creating authority, is the only cure for it and the only means whereby each one of us will get used to taking an active and conscious part in the collective work, and cease being passive instruments in the hands of leaders'. People have to have the time, energy and commitment to put this order in place, however.

At St Hilda's, more professionalized and bureaucratic practices were clearly part of the logics of the centre and its structures. While these helped to create care, solidarity and an unalienated volunteer experience for those involved, Jenny also drew on her own past cooperative experience to foster feelings of autonomy, ownership and egalitarianism among the volunteers. Jenny and I often talked about the structures of St Hilda's and of Fareshares and the difference between the two in terms of practices, social make-up and affective relations. On one occasion I explained to her:

> I know coming here [to St Hilda's] each week, it's all doing what it needs to anyway irrespective of whether I'm here. So, everyone does their jobs, but sometimes it's nice to have someone to defer to, or not to have the weight of that responsibility for making sure it keeps going.

'Is that at the cost of ownership do you think?', she replied highlighting the ongoing dilemma she faced as a voluntary sector coordinator on one hand, and a cooperator on the other. While Jenny tried to enact mutual and agentive practices in an attempt to create 'a field of fluid and open sociality that contravenes the professionalization of volunteerism' (Rozakou 2016: 95), she was still seen as an authority figure within the project, due in part to the top-down logics of the voluntary sector and the distinction between a paid staff member and the volunteers within the project. In many ways this highlighted the tension between the two value systems she attempted to work by as a cooperator with an interest in autonomy and social ownership, and a coordinator with a role of support and facilitation.

While thinkers such a Karl Marx and Adam Smith devalued unwaged labour, seeing it as distinct from so called 'productive' labour (Muehlebach 2012: 38), within contemporary society and within food co-ops, voluntary labour has taken on a different status. From a statutory perspective, volunteering has become an area of increasing interest not only as part of a neoliberal reconfiguration of the welfare state in which the third sector has a greater part to play (Koch and James 2022; Muehlebach 2012), but also as a component of a punitive, austerity policy focus on welfare to work, as Jenny's concerns over the meaning and experience of volunteering for those out of work highlight. Her actions attempted to push back against some of the more coercive and alienating qualities that might come with this. At Fareshares, too, unwaged work was a key component in creating a more agentive and caring environment less mediated by the market. As such, in some ways it was a means of gaining '[a]utonomy from capital . . . entailing the satisfaction of basic needs through the solidarity economy and the redefinition of work' (Asara 2020: 7). In both co-ops there was a distinction between notions of volunteering and labour. At Fareshares, the ideal was for everyone to become involved with cooperative labour, not just to be volunteers. At St Hilda's the aim was for everyone to be a volunteer, rather than do unwaged labour in order to avoid feelings of alienation as a consequences of punitive government policy. As Muehlebach points out (2012: 49), 'like wage labor, unwaged labor is a complex composite of exploitation and salvation, exclusion and utopia, alienation and new forms of unalienated sociality'. This complexity is clearly evident in both food co-op's relationship to work, the wider context in which it takes place and the organizational structures in which it happens.

Arguably, affective spaces such as St Hilda's and Fareshares become all the more important in the face of changing welfare and working conditions. Such conditions can compel people to seek out spaces of community and connection where they might feel supported and/or empowered. Nonetheless, the work of non-hierarchical organizing, consensus decision-making and member-ownership all take time, effort and conscious reflection on processes. While this chapter has started to engage with the impacts of austerity Britain, in the next chapter I address it more squarely, exploring how its structures of feeling were felt and experienced within the food co-ops and the country.

NOTES

1. 'effing and jeffing' = swearing. Not that I noticed Ed swearing very often.
2. The poll tax was a per-person household charge, which replaced a system of rates based on the rental value of a property. This was implemented by the Conservative government of Margaret Thatcher between 1989 and 1990. Its unpopularity led to widespread riots in the UK in 1990.
3. While Marx refers to waged work, such arguments are still relevant here as the co-op acted most similarly to a workers' co-op, although unwaged as I discuss further in this chapter.
4. Some systems did exist, however, although some were adhered to more closely than others. For example, everyone filled out the cashing up sheets, but few put their name on the weekly rota, as each group of volunteers was in charge of maintaining the needs of their own shifts, and tended to communicate with each other independently in order to ensure each shift was covered. This could make things a little confusing for the volunteers dealing with new volunteer enquiries at times, as they were not always sure who to tell that someone new would be shadowing a shift.

5. The time it took for this to happen could vary a little depending on how quickly the member who managed the list serve became aware of their existence. In Nuala's case, for example, it took some months, which meant she did not feel that she knew many people in the co-op outside of her shift and also had not had the chance to go to meetings as the details (date, time and agenda items) were generally shared on the list serve.
6. Here it is worth noting that while researchers such as Holmström (1993: 75) noticed a gendered division of labour in relation to meeting attendance and decision-making, as a project where there were many women, those who attended meetings at Fareshares included women and also mothers.
7. Although Hannah was not always directly named in these discussions due to the sensitivity of the topic. Here, I use pseudonyms for everyone discussing the issues with Hannah and Dave due to their sensitive nature. Hannah and Dave are also pseudonyms.
8. Food hygiene regulation became significantly more stringent during the 1990s and 2000s with substantial input from the EU. The bureaucracies involved clearly did not sit comfortably with the collective's values. This was an area of governance to which they were obliged to conform, however, in order to continue their activities.
9. Although I did not have a chance to discuss these events with Hannah, in other ethnographic accounts, scholars have noted that unofficial leaders can often feel 'pushed into the role by the pressure of circumstance' rather than deliberately attempting to seize authority. Once there, it is not always easy to step down from it (Müller 1991: 116).
10. This is not uncommon in social groups attempting to work by egalitarian structures as a means of avoiding the tensions and contradictions that could come with attempts to reintegrate them into the group as an equal (Barth 1965; Müller 1991).
11. I should acknowledge that the children's centre was run by a friend of mine. Jenny and he had met socially through me, but then arranged the pop-up food co-op between themselves.
12. If one volunteer had done a lot to support and train someone new, this might also mean that they were deferred to at times by this volunteer. As with Fareshares, their knowledge and labour contribution could potentially lead to forms of stratification. In my own case, for example, an evening volunteer who I had been helping to train up referred to Jenny as 'the boss' and me as the 'mini boss'. Like Jenny, I did not feel particularly comfortable with the title although it was also funny. Inevitably as an ethnographer there to study the project, I was very committed. This meant I contributed considerable amounts of labour to the co-op (as I also did at Fareshares) and I was also knowledgeable about its practices and processes. This labour contribution and knowledge no doubt played a part in the inadvertent authority that I took on.

REFERENCES

Akbulut, Bengi. 2020. 'Cooperative Economies as Commons', in Derya Özkan and Güldem Baykal Büyüksaraç (eds), *Commoning the City: Empirical Perspectives on Urban Ecology, Economics and Ethics*. London: Routledge, pp. 193–206.

Alber, Erdmute, and Heike Drotbohm (eds). 2015. *Anthropological Perspectives on Care – Work, Kinship, and the Life-Course*. New York: Palgrave Macmillan.

Arbell, Yael et al. 2020. 'Contested Subjectivities in a UK Housing Cooperative: Old Hippies and Thatcher's Children Negotiating the Commons', *Geoforum* 110: 58–66.

Asara, Viviana. 2020. 'Untangling the Radical Imaginaries of the Indignados' Movement: Commons, Autonomy and Ecologism', *Environmental Politics*: 1–25.

Barth, Fredrik. 1965. *Political Leadership among Swat Pathans*. London: Berg Publishers.

Black, Steven P. 2018. 'The Ethics and Aesthetics of Care', *Annual Review of Anthropology* 47(1): 79–95.

Bryer, Alice. 2010. 'Beyond Bureaucracies? The Struggle for Social Responsibility in the Argentine Workers' Cooperatives', *Critique of Anthropology* 30(1): 41–61.

Butler, Judith. 2011. *Bodies That Matter: On the Discursive Limits of 'Sex'*. Abingdon, Oxon; New York: Routledge.

———. 2016. 'Rethinking Vulnerability and Resistance', in Judith Butler et al. (eds), *Vulnerability in Resistance*. Durham, NC: Duke University Press, pp. 12–27.

Butler, Judith et al. (eds). 2016. *Vulnerability in Resistance*. Durham, NC: Duke University Press.

Dyckhoff, Tom. 2017, 10 November. 'Let's Move to Frome, Somerset: "You Want Community? You Got It"', *The Guardian*.

Foucault, Michel. 2002. *Archaeology of Knowledge* (2nd edition). London; New York: Routledge.

Freeman, Jo. 1972. 'The Tyranny of Structurelessness'. Retrieved 10 December 2023 from http://www.jofreeman.com/joreen/tyranny.htm.

Gautney, Heather. 2010. 'Antiauthoritarian Social Movements', in Heather Gautney, *Protest and Organization in the Alternative Globalization Era: NGOs, Social Movements, and Political Parties*. New York: Palgrave Macmillan, pp. 111–39.

Graeber, David. 2004. *Fragments of an Anarchist Anthropology*. Chicago: Prickly Paradigm Press: Distributed by University of Chicago Press.

Graeber, David. 2015. *The Utopia of Rules: On Technology, Stupidity, and the Secret Joys of Bureaucracy*. New York: Melville House Printing.

Haiven, Max, and Alex Khasnabish. 2014. *The Radical Imagination: Social Movement Research in the Age of Austerity*. Halifax; Winnipeg; London: Zed Books Ltd.

Hall, Alison Sánchez. 2018. *All or None: Cooperation and Sustainability in Italy's Red Belt*. New York: Berghahn Books.

Heckert, Jamie. 2011. 'Listening, Caring, Becoming: Anarchism as an Ethics of Direct Relationships', in Benjamin Franks and Matthew Wilson (eds), *Anarchism and Moral Philosophy*. Basingstoke: Palgrave, pp. 186–207.

Heller, Chaia. 1999. *Ecology of Everyday Life: Rethinking the Desire for Nature*. Montreal; New York; London: Black Rose Books.

Hochschild, Arlie Russell. 2003. *The Managed Heart: Commercialization of Human Feeling* (2nd edition). Berkeley; London: University of California Press.

Holmström, Mark. 1989. *Industrial Democracy in Italy: Workers' Co-ops and the Self-Management Debate*. Aldershot: Avebury.

———. 1993. *Spain's New Social Economy: Workers' Self-Management in Catalonia*. Oxford; Providence, RI: Berg Publishers.

Jupp, Eleanor. 2022. *Care, Crisis and Activism: The Politics of Everyday Life*. Bristol: Policy Press.

Kadir, Nazima. 2016. *The Autonomous Life? Paradoxes of Hierarchy and Authority in the Squatters Movement in Amsterdam*. Manchester: Manchester University Press.

Kasmir, Sharryn. 1996. *The Myth of Mondragon: Cooperatives, Politics, and Working-Class Life in a Basque Town*. New York: State University of New York Press.

———. 2004. 'Activism and Class Identity: The Saturn Auto Factory Case', in June Nash (ed.), *Social Movements: An Anthropological Reader*. Malden, MA: John Wiley & Sons, pp. 78–95.

Koch, Insa, and Deborah James. 2022. 'The State of the Welfare State: Advice, Governance and Care in Settings of Austerity', *Ethnos* 87(1): 1–21.

Land, Christopher, and Daniel King. 2014. 'Organizing Otherwise: Translating Anarchism in a Voluntary Sector Organization', *Ephemera* 14: 923–50.

Levkoe, Charles Z. 2006. 'Learning Democracy Through Food Justice Movements', *Agriculture and Human Values* 23(1): 89–98.

Marx, Karl, and Friedrich Engels. 2009. *The Economic and Philosophic Manuscripts of 1844 and the Communist Manifesto*. Prometheus Books.

Masquelier, Charles. 2017. 'Beyond Co-optation: Revisiting the Transformative Function of "Workers' Self-Directed Enterprises"', *Socialism and Democracy* 31(2): 53–72.

McKenzie, Lisa. 2015. *Getting By: Estates, Class and Culture in Austerity Britain*. Bristol; Chicago: Policy Press.

McLaughlin, Hugh. 2009. 'What's in a Name: "Client", "Patient", "Customer", "Consumer", "Expert by Experience", "Service User" – What's Next?', *The British Journal of Social Work* 39(6): 1101–17.

Moraes, Alana, and Maria A. C. Brant. 2016. 'SILVIA FEDERICI: "Our Struggle Will Not Succeed Unless We Rebuild Society": An Interview with Silvia Federici', *Sur – International Journal on Human Rights* 13(23): 203–13.

Muehlebach, Andrea. 2012. *The Moral Neoliberal: Welfare and Citizenship in Italy*. Chicago: University of Chicago Press.

Müller, Birgit. 1991. *Toward an Alternative Culture of Work: Political Idealism and Economic Practices in West Berlin Collective Enterprises*. Boulder: Westview Press.

Nash, June, and Nicholas S. Hopkins. 1976. 'Anthropological Approaches to the Study of Cooperatives, Collectives, and Self-Management', in June Nash et al. (eds), *Popular Participation in Social Change: Cooperatives, Collectives, and Nationalized Industry*. The Hague; Paris: Mouton Publishers, pp. 3–32.

O'Neill, John. 2018. 'Food, Needs and Commons', in Jose Luis Vivero-Pol et al. (eds), *Routledge Handbook of Food as a Commons*. Abingdon, Oxon; New York: Routledge, pp. 103–20.

Patrick, Ruth. 2017. *For Whose Benefit? The Everyday Realities of Welfare Reform*. Bristol: Policy Press.

Polletta, Francesca. 2012. *Freedom is an Endless Meeting*. Chicago: University of Chicago Press.

Rakopoulos, Theodoros. 2014. 'The Crisis Seen From Below, Within, and Against: From Solidarity Economy to Food Distribution Cooperatives in Greece', *Dialectical Anthropology* 38(2): 189–207.

———. 2015. 'Solidarity's Tensions: Informality, Sociality, and the Greek Crisis', *Social Analysis* 59(3): 85–104.

———. 2019. 'Seventy Percent Zapatista? Solidarity "Ecosystems" and the Troubles of Valuing Labor in Food Cooperatives', in Valeria Siniscalchi and Krista Harper (eds), *Food Values in Europe*. London: Bloomsbury Academic, pp. 145–60.

Red Herring Workers' Co-operative. 1996. *Cordon Rouge: Vegetarian and Vegan Recipes from the Red Herring*. Earthright Publications.

Rose, Nikolas. 2012. *Powers of Freedom: Reframing Political Thought*. Cambridge: Cambridge University Press.

Rozakou, Katerina. 2016. 'Crafting the Volunteer: Voluntary Associations and the Reformation of Sociality', *Journal of Modern Greek Studies* 34(1): 79–102.

Shepard, Benjamin, and Steve Burghardt. 2015. *Community Projects as Social Activism: From Direct Action to Direct Services*. London: SAGE Publications, Ltd.

Sitrin, Marina A. 2012. *Everyday Revolutions: Horizontalism and Autonomy in Argentina*. London; New York: Zed Books Ltd.

Standing, Guy. 2014. *The Precariat: The New Dangerous Class* (Revised edition). London; New York: Bloomsbury Academic.

Thelen, Tatjana. 2015. 'Care as Social Organization: Creating, Maintaining and Dissolving Significant Relations', *Anthropological Theory* 15(4): 497–515.

Ulin, Robert C. 1996. *Vintages and Traditions: Ethnohistory of Southwest French Wine Cooperatives*. Washington, DC: Smithsonian Books.

Ward, Colin. 2008. *Anarchy in Action*. London: Freedom Press.

Weber, Max. 1978 [1922]. *Economy and Society: An Outline of Interpretive Sociology*. Berkeley: University of California Press.

———. 2012 [1905]. *The Protestant Ethic and the Spirit of Capitalism*. US: Renaissance Classics.

Woodly, Deva et al. 2021. 'The Politics of Care', *Contemporary Political Theory* 20(4): 890–925.

Wright, Erik Olin. 2010. *Envisioning Real Utopias*. London; New York: Verso.

CHAPTER

4

CHANGING TIMES, CHANGING POLITICS

ODDSOCKS

In the summer of 2017, I met Fareshares founder member Martin Oddsocks to find out more about the food co-op's early history. True to form, he was wearing odd socks. Towards the end of the interview, a parcel delivery person knocked on the door, and when they asked for Martin's name for their paperwork, it elicited some surprise. Martin reassured the delivery worker that 'Oddsocks' really was his name, to which the worker replied that he had never heard that surname before, and in his line of work he heard a lot. Within such a mundane and everyday interaction, the name felt incongruous. The delivery person seemed to see it as nothing more than an interesting quirk, unaware of the name's subversive qualities and history. Much like Martin's name, Fareshares also has the feel of something from another era with its colourful walls, bulk grain bins, and low-tech systems. The food co-op's history is also very much still a part of its make-up, as seen in its structures, stock and stated ideals. When I asked Martin if it felt like it had changed much on the occasions he had been back, he told me 'so much of whenever you return to old haunts, what's peculiar is the mixture of things which seem exactly the same and things which seem completely different'.

Within the country itself, some things are also the same and inevitably others different. During my fieldwork, newspaper headlines were filled with talk of austerity, climate change and the complex relationship between

Brexit, migration and populism. Shops and supermarkets were stocked with the kinds of wholefoods, alternative milks, organic and fairly-traded goods that have been Fareshares' mainstay since the 1980s; and at times, the supermarkets sold them at lower prices. Veganism was also a rapidly growing trend, seen by some as an important form of food politics, animal welfare, or environmental action, and by others as 'lifestylism' or the latest fad diet (Hancox 2018).

When I asked Martin what he thought Fareshares was for today, he replied that he had also been wondering about this. 'People say that everything is of its time', he suggested, 'but it wouldn't still be going if it was just a few hobbyists maintaining a tradition. So, it's obviously serving . . . addressing a need of some sort. I'm interested to know who values it now, because obviously lots of people do'.

Undoubtedly, as Martin said, many people do still value Fareshares and for all sorts of different reasons, as discussed in chapter 2. There could, nonetheless, be mixed feelings among its members about its purpose and its methods in austerity Britain.

In this chapter, I engage with the impacts of change on public moods, values and discourses in Britain. In doing so, I explore the structures of feeling of austerity Britain, what its affective, social and material infrastructures might be (Sharma and Tygstrup 2015: 2) as well as their impacts on the co-ops and their participants. Jupp suggests (2022: 28) that along with 'material and financial constraints, the context of austerity has been seen to produce a kind of deadening of political energy and horizons' as well as a 'wearying, exhausting set of dynamics among those encountering, coping or seeking to resist it'. This raises questions about what such structures of feeling do to the everyday politics of Fareshares and St Hilda's and their ability to imagine and do political work. The following three chapters pick up on this question, exploring experiences of political-economic change at Fareshares and St Hilda's from different perspectives, and asking how neoliberalization and austerity were experienced and what they did within the co-ops and the country during this period.

In this chapter, I focus on the interaction between politics and the political in austerity Britain as they played out within the food co-ops and the country. The chapter starts by engaging with Fareshares and St Hilda's East's relationships and responses to changing times, needs and interests. I focus, in particular, on changing attitudes towards time, political action, and collective and cooperative organizing at Fareshares. I then look at the impacts of changing state agendas around food insecurity and welfare at St Hilda's. In both sections I also explore what these changes did to imaginations and moods. I then look at austerity more directly. This is seen by many as a 'deepening and intensification of the neoliberal turn' in relation to welfare reform, inequality and precarity (Powers 2022: 464). I explore how austerity was implemented in the UK and the wider attitudes, discourses and affects that came with it. I then detail some of St Hilda's and Fareshares' members' personal experiences of austerity. Like Hitchen, I understand austerity as a multiplicity, which goes beyond policy or economics due to the ways in which it is 'always and already multiple as it is lived' (2016: 103; 2021: 297), shaping sites, spaces, relationships, temporalities, subjectivities and feelings. It is this multiplicity and its structures of feeling that I refer to when discussing austerity Britain within this book – austerity Britain's complex, amorphous and multifarious 'affective present'. A present that is shared and felt among diverse phenomena, but also lived and related to differentially (Anderson 2016: 747).

CHANGING SKILLS AND VALUES

Adina and Colomba, who had both been involved with Fareshares in the early days, felt that things were pretty tough in Britain these days. Adina explained that around the time that Fareshares was founded, rent had been cheap, dole money was more accessible and education was free, so people did not have to work 'all the hours'. 'If your rent was only £20 a week or you were squatting', she told me, 'even if you weren't squatting, the rent was cheap, so you didn't have to work so hard'. She continued:

> Now I think, for me, the reason why I'm not involved in Fareshares and I'm not involved in the local community that much is because in order to live it seems that I have to work incredibly hard. Rent goes up and up and up, and it seems to me that everyone I know is so busy, and so struggling to just make it . . . make everything work . . . It seemed to me that things were very different [when Fareshares was founded], that people didn't have to kill themselves to just manage . . . ['Just manage' Colomba echoed] and that things were cheaper and people helped each other a lot more. And that's partly why there was more community, maybe people just had a bit more time.

Just as the structures of feeling in the country at the time of each food co-ops' foundation left their mark on the food co-op's organizational models, logics, ethics and relationship to community action, the social, political and economic conditions of post-financial crisis, austerity Britain did too, as Adina's words highlight.

While Adina acknowledged that those involved with the 'Pullens'[1] at the time of the squatting action and Fareshares' foundation were mostly young, and that her life had changed considerably since then, her words speak to the 'affective elements of consciousness and relationships' (Williams 2015: 23) that the experience of a particular 'lived present' can create (Sharma and

Tygstrup 2015: 1). In the case of the post-Fordist era of flexibilization of the labour market in which risks and insecurities are transferred from the state or the employer onto workers and their families (Standing 2014: 1), this is a shift which is often perceived to have been accompanied by precarious lives and subjectivities. This, Molé (2010) suggests, can lead to enhanced feelings of anxiety, marginality and apprehension. In combination with the precariousness of social protection and residency that come with the state withdrawal of care and the commoditization of the housing market (Standing 2014: 5), precarity can also impact on people's relationship to time as Adina's words suggest. Sugarman and Thrift describe this as a temporal malaise, suggesting that a neoliberal socio-political and economic order is negatively reshaping understandings and experiences of time, leaving people feeling constantly busy (2020: 809). Arguably such structures of feelings have the capacity to 'enclose' imaginations (Asara 2020) in ways that might contribute to the 'deadening of political energy and horizons' that Jupp described (Jupp 2022: 28).

Many other members at Fareshares also spoke about feelings of precarious time. Rachel, for example, felt that people used to spend more time socializing at Fareshares than they did today. That 'people had a little bit more time available to hang out here. Whereas now it feels like it's really hard for people to spend two hours here'. She also connected this to the economic situation. Nina, a newer, younger member also suggested that people had very limited time and had to spend a lot of it working. To her this seemed to be particularly acute in London where housing costs were so high. This experience of busyness meant that it had taken her some time to feel as if she could commit to volunteering at Fareshares regularly.

When I asked her what Fareshares was for today, she raised questions about how the food co-op could adapt to changing times and changing needs. Steve wondered what needs it was meeting locally and whether it was more of a low packing, no waste shop (a trend that was developing at the time in response to climate change), or a 'community shop'. Adam also had concerns. He worried that the meaning of the co-op was changing. He suggested that it should be about people from the community coming together and providing something for themselves out of mutual aid (as it had been from the start). As the demographic within the area changed, however (as I discuss further in the following chapter) he worried that it might be an amusing oddity for more affluent people with the added perk of lower prices. He also worried that for some of the newer volunteers there might be the sense that they were working in a charity shop where they could express more 'liberal' forms of care for the poor through their volunteering (Woodly et al. 2021), rather than engage in the forms of cooperative labour discussed in the previous chapter. (I explore the tensions between mutual aid and charity further in chapter 6.) Either way, he felt concerned that Fareshares might be losing its political energy. Rachel also felt that the project was less anarchist than it used to be, and that its politics were 'more under the surface'.

Only a few of Fareshares' members would identify as anarchists these days and others feel no great connection or commitment to some of the DIY or Cooperativist elements of the project, such as collective decision making. More than Fareshares' left-wing politics, many of the more recent (often younger) members who were there during my fieldwork seemed to be drawn to the project because of its ready supply of more affordable organic, fairly-traded and (for some) vegan foods. They also appreciated the co-ops' environmental stance in terms of the goods it stocked and its position on packaging, which required customers to bring their own shopping bags and containers to decant bulk goods into. This was also the site of much of their political action, whether based on individual acts of consumption (choosing local, organic, unpackaged or vegan goods, for example), entrepreneurialism in relation to ethical goods, or the choice of environmentally focused jobs of one sort or another. Where many of the older members were highly articulate about their political ideology, for the younger members, their politics was more often framed around specific issues – typically climate change, and, for some, growing inequality. The assertion of Fareshares anti- or alter-Capitalist qualities was also often something that was kept vague in people's articulations and assessments of the project, although many appreciated such qualities and identified them as an important part of Fareshares' politics (as discussed in chapter 2).

For some, the organizational structures of the cooperative could feel frustrating – too slow, labour intensive or inefficient. Frictions over changing times and members' values often became most evident in meetings or on the email list. If newer members did not fully see the logic or know the history of certain long-standing systems or if they felt that there was resistance to an idea that they put forward for what they saw as the benefit of the co-op, they could feel frustrated. For longer-running members, frustrations could be felt if they had the impression that something was being done impetuously without fully following consensual processes, showing a cooperative spirit or working out all the practicalities before taking action.

One meeting in which these generational tensions came to the surface, related to a new organic vegetable supplier. Hughes, the producer that Fareshares had been working with for many years, was no longer able to provide the co-op with as much fruit and veg as it used to, so, some work had been done to look into alternative options. As one newer member already had a relationship with a reliable company called Brockman's, they offered to take on the responsibility for this order along with another newer volunteer. More than one member of the co-op then wrote an email with relevant information about what steps might need to be taken in order to set up a new supplier – ranging from details of how to get them added to Fareshares' payment system; how the delivery would be received (by a person or by giving the business a set of keys); and the schedule for when the other veg orders came in and got unpacked so that the produce could be checked off properly and refrigerated in good time.

Before the payment system was fully set up, or some of the other issues around how and who would take delivery had been resolved, however, the newer members started to place vegetable orders as they were concerned about ensuring that customers were getting a sufficient supply. When these issues were raised first on the members' email list and then in a meeting, it was clear that both groups were feeling frustrated. The more established members were concerned about not being able to pay the supplier and how a new delivery could impact the people who might be expected to unpack the goods as they were not arriving in time with the co-op's usual delivery and unpacking rhythms. The newer members had a sense that the veterans were blocking them and that their behaviour showed a resistance to change. For a while this led to an impasse as the younger members decided to step down from the Brockman's order, feeling that everything had become too complicated. Once Brockman's had been added to the payment system, however, another member who had connections in both groups, decided to take on the order, which ran more or less smoothly from then on.

In Ulin's work with wine cooperative in southwest France generational divides also came up. Demarle, for example, who was a member of the Monbazillac cooperative, told Ulin that when Monbazillac started, there was a 'true cooperative spirit' fostered by the profound need to 'survive difficult times together' (1996: 174). Demarle noted that the new generation of cooperative members were completely different though, with different expectations of the cooperative based on their own interests and needs, and a desire for 'greater dynamism' (Ulin, 1996: 174).

For Fareshares, the need that brought the collective together was the inaccessibility of organic, vegan and fairly-traded goods in an era of precarious livelihoods and Anarchist energies. This seemed to foster a strong communitarian and cooperative spirit. While many of the newer members' interests and activities also revolved around these ethical goods, they connected less with the collectivist methods of provisioning embedded in Fareshares' cooperative structures. As with Monbazillac, they seemed to want more dynamism, questioning whether the cooperative, its logics and ways of working still responded to the needs of the here and now.

Not long after the Brockman's issue, I spoke to Ed, about the generational tensions at Fareshares. At that time, Ed, who grew up in the southwest of England was in his mid-fifties and had been a member for around three years.

Ed was drawn to Fareshares for its cooperativism more than its food. He had been living in a housing co-op for around 30 years and despite the inevitable ups and downs he had experienced there due to the co-op's internal politics, he still felt compelled by the cooperative model and felt there was more he wanted to learn and reflect on within cooperativism. He had decided that a grassroots project such as Fareshares might be a good place to do this work.

Ed's own commitment to cooperation could make the fragmentation within Fareshares feel disappointing at times. He told me:

> I think a lot of the skills and the assumptions that go into things like self-organization have sort of atrophied or been eroded over the last 30 years. In 1980, I think about 80% of people were in trade unions and now I think it's about 10%. So . . . those skills and those assumptions about people being able to organize themselves have kind of gone and I'm not sure how you get those back, or how you support or encourage those. It feels like starting from a very low base.

Ed's comments highlight some of the ways in which the actions and events of previous eras have contributed to changing practices, ideals and subjectivities. Since the 1990s, there has been much academic speculation over the nature of politics in Western democracies, and whether we are living in a less political age in terms of participation in mainstream politics and everyday forms of political action (Mouffe 2005; Prosser and Stoker 2017). In his classic book, *Bowling Alone* (2001), Robert Putnam argues that many social ties and forms of civic participation beyond the family, such as union activism, serving on local committees or attending public meetings, have declined in this period, doing much to erode a sense of community, civic participation (a crucial part of a healthy democracy) or 'social capital', while fostering a more individualized society. Similarly to Ed, Sennett argues that within advanced liberal contexts such as the UK, a 'de-skilling' is taking place in relation to cooperation due to various material, institutional and cultural changes happening within society. These, he suggests, have led to greater stratification and atomization, combined with a weakening capacity for cooperation, and also a weakening desire (2013). If the 'acquisition of a skill is embedded in a larger social knowledge about the value of that skill' (Venkatesan, 2010: 158), then the less cooperative context of contemporary Britain and the structures of feeling of the austerity era have inevitably had implications for how people value and perform cooperation (or not).

In terms of contemporary activism, too, various scholars have identified a certain 'unwillingness on the part of individuals to subject themselves to collective structures, norms, or identities' (Sörbom and Wennerhag 2013: 454). This, in turn, is thought to have led to individualized, lifestyle-focused forms of action, which reconfigure the relationship between the individual and society (ibid.). No doubt, the rise of the internet has also changed some of the means and modes of political action as new forms of digitally networked communities have developed (see, for example, Castells 2012) and clicktivism (signing online petitions) has become more popular. It is unsurprising that these changes to the means of organizing would cause tensions for a space formed around the idea of cooperation – an inherently collective act.

It is not uncommon for those within a cooperative to have different values, interests and politics, and as Rakopoulos suggests (2014: 97), 'it is impossible to conceptualise cooperatives as united, cohesive actors in democratic mobilisation over food concerns'. In the Sicilian anti-mafia, agricultural cooperatives he worked with, the ethics of food created class-based divisions, with administrators pushing a food activist agenda that interested them and the co-op's consumers, but not the workers. At Fareshares, there was more agreement around the ethics of food and the values of more sustainable provisioning approaches. Instead, it was cooperativism itself that created generational divisions, both as a means of running the food co-op effectively and, more implicitly, as an activist method. Whittier (1997) suggests that long-running social movements are often made up of different 'political generations'[2] who shape their activism around the ideologies and issues of different eras. While this intergenerationality can be an important factor in helping to keep a movement going, inevitably it also comes with challenges, and in this case, they related to cooperative imaginations and more collectivist politics.[3] It also spoke to tensions between 'residual' and 'emergent' structures of feeling (Vanke 2024). The 'residual' ones being more collectivist and the 'emergent' arguably more individualized.

CHANGING LANDSCAPES

I also had the chance to speak to Lourdes, the original food co-op coordinator at St Hilda's, in the autumn of 2016. We met at a hospice in East London, where she was working – still in the field of community development and volunteer services, but in relation to bereavement and dementia. She told me she missed the fresh fruit and vegetables she used to get from St Hilda's. She reminisced:

> My kids took the piss out of me because I had a little trolley I'd take up to work for my weekly shopping. I do miss that because it was really good stuff and that was what was great. It was really nice food. And that's what I was proud of really, selling that, and the impact it had on the social level.

Lourdes felt both surprised and proud that the food co-op had managed to continue for so long. From Lourdes' perspective, it had always been hard to keep it going in terms of the time she could commit to it (which involved a lot of juggling between her role as volunteer coordinator for the whole centre and as food co-op coordinator), the volunteers she was able to recruit, and the money the food co-op needed to get by.

Even in the New Labour years, it could feel challenging to find money, she told me. With the election of the Conservative-Liberal Democrat government in 2010, however, she felt that 'there was just this prevailing sense of doom. That we all kind of felt that no one would get this project or want to get it'. This resonates with an often felt sense of inevitability that can come with neoliberal restructuring (Anderson 2016: 747). During the New Labour years (1997–2010), there were many attempts to reduce inequalities in health and related diet and nutritional issues as St Hilda's food co-op's work did. Since the financial crisis of 2008, however, both the focus on, and the means of, tackling food-related inequalities seem to have changed. The Labour Party's food policy work towards the end of their time in power stressed the importance of access to 'a decent environmentally and socially sustainable diet' as 'part of the understanding of poverty in the UK in a similar way to the need for decent housing and affordable heating' (Dowler 2014: 163). Dowler (ibid.) suggests that the Coalition government, in contrast, were less interested in food security[4] on a household level. With the shift to the Coalition government, there was also a broader move away from policy focused on the needs of those living on low incomes in areas of multiple deprivation, who were dealing with the consequences of rising food and fuel costs (due to the 2007–8 food and financial crises) along with declining employment, stagnant wages and cuts to benefit provisions. Instead, there was an expectation that people would develop individualized coping strategies and informed consumer choices reminiscent of Thatcher's ethos of an 'enterprise culture' as opposed to the 'nannying' welfare state discussed in chapter 1. Koch and James suggest that this 'shedding' of the state's 'caring responsibilities' is 'both ideological and procedural: from ambitious [post-Second-World-War] top-down directed initiatives and a "one size fits all" approach to an increasingly informal and "flexible" model which blurs the boundaries between state, voluntary and business sectors', therefore creating a reconfiguration of the welfare state in more plural ways (2022: 2). Organizations such as St Hilda's are no doubt a part of this plurality of welfare, despite the precarities that the third sector itself has faced during this period.

While there was still funding available for food co-ops one year on from the Conservative-Liberal Democrat coalition's election in 2010, by the time St Hilda's Local Food project money had finished in 2014, the situation was different, with funding options much reduced. As Jenny put it, 'what we've seen are cuts after cuts after cuts in terms of the community services run at community centres'. This reflects the 'disproportionally large percentage of austerity cuts' that voluntary organizations have faced, which were estimated to be in the region of £1.7 billion between 2010 and 2017 before inflation (Land and King 2014: 932). As Jupp points out, this means that since the beginning of austerity, the 'community and voluntary sector' have been 'working in extremely constrained circumstances, losing grants and income while grappling with increased social need' as a consequence of welfare cuts (Jupp 2022: 27). Jupp suggests that while 'community programmes under new labour were partly framed by a narrative of reducing reliance on 'the state', they nonetheless took place within a context of relatively generous state spending' (2022: 26). Rupert, the director at the community centre during the time of my fieldwork, told me:

> When money was more available it was very difficult for voluntary organizations not to fall into the trap of becoming very dependent, getting that easy money from the local authority. And then when the crash happened in 2008 and public sector funding started to be cut and austerity took hold, it's been very difficult for voluntary organizations after that . . . although somehow, we [the community centre] have managed to just about survive.

Clearly, St Hilda's Food Co-op also managed to survive and continued to work with what it could in order to support people dealing with some of the impacts of austerity. The fact that it formed part of a wider institution (i.e. the community centre), was no doubt significant in its ongoing existence. Since the Lottery money finished, there have been times when the project has had little or no funding. Nonetheless, at these times, the food co-op was supported by the community centre. This undoubtedly put pressure on the centre's own resources, but enabled the food co-op (which had come to be valued) to keep going.

Like the food co-op's budget, Jenny the food co-op coordinator's time was also tight when she first started. She was employed just one day a week at the centre, but regularly found that responsibilities such as ordering the weekly fruit and veg, answering emails and doing admin spread into other days or evenings. Happily, the food co-op secured three years of funding from the London-based independent funder City Bridge Trust in 2016 for a food and advice project. The funding enabled Jenny to increase her employment at St Hilda's to four days a week, letting go of some of the ESOL teaching work she had been doing at colleges and community projects in the local area. The food co-op expanded to two sessions a day on a Thursday – one in the morning and one in the evening in order to give more people access to the project. Each of these sessions was accompanied by an accredited general advice service, which offered help with issues such as benefits, basic housing concerns and debt. At times there was also legal or financial advice on offer in the evenings. All of these extended services were based on the knowledge that there were many people in the area dealing with the consequences of austerity, and they were often further disenfranchised by age, disability or a lack of English language skills. As with many other services, advice has been subject to funding cuts and other resourcing issues, making what St Hilda's offered as a community centre, which works holistically on multiple needs within the community, all the more important in an era when so many people were feeling the strains of economic instability and increasing precarity. The food co-op also started offering healthy living cookery workshops again (some of which I hosted) and training including food hygiene and first aid, all of which were intended to contribute to healthy diets and employability. St Hilda's innovation in relation to the linking of food and advice services within the project highlights Jupp's point that, 'with austerity comes not just less capacity and resources to care, but also new ideologies and politics of care that shift the emphasis and orientations of many services' within the community and voluntary sector (Jupp 2022: 18) – in this case solely from food, to a more holistic project that took into account different pressure points in people's lives.

Where at Fareshares there were questions about what need the food co-op was responding to and how, at St Hilda's, the aims and values of the co-op and community centre combined with a need for funding necessitated constant reflection and evaluation of the project and the ways in which it was responding to local need, available funding calls and their criteria. Responsiveness was, therefore, a key element in the ongoing sustainability of the food co-op and the community centre. It demonstrates the 'immense pressures on communities and community action under austerity, but also the creativity and persistence demonstrated by local activists' (Jupp 2022: 2) such as community centre staff. By the middle of this funding cycle, however, St Hilda's was inevitably already starting to think about where the next pot of money might come from, and how much they would have to adapt their offering to the priorities of that funder. Such precarity inevitably takes up considerable time and energy for those involved with running community projects.

THE PUNITIVE TURN

Alaya, a general advice worker at St Hilda's, who had been working at the centre for twelve years when I interviewed her in the autumn of 2017, felt that things had changed significantly since the election of the Conservative-led government in 2010:

> I think in the past when Labour was in government, it wasn't as severe; there was a lot more financial help available to [advice] clients in the area, and everywhere to be

> honest. It's ever since the Tories have come back into government, especially with the start of the austerity measures, that people have been seeing a huge impact on their finances. There have been benefit cuts, there has been the benefit cap. There has been the bedroom tax[5] . . . and all of these have had a huge impact on clients and the amount of money they've got to live on. The benefit cap, I think, has been the biggest impact, because where people have had a certain amount of money to live on, when it was capped down to a certain amount, they found that it was hard to pay their rent, because most of the deductions were made to housing benefit, so they had to find the extra income to cover their rent or risk losing their home. We've had to look at charities to help meet the shortfall.

One of the Conservative-Liberal Democrat coalition government's first actions when it came to power in 2010 was to announce an emergency budget. Spearheaded by George Osborne in his role as Chancellor of the Exchequer, these austerity measures included a £40 billion package of tax increases, welfare cuts, and public sector pay freezes (Onanuga 2010). This set a trajectory for the Conservative Party, leading the United Nations (UN) to raise serious concerns about the levels of inequality apparent in the UK. In 2016 the UN's Committee on Economic, Social and Cultural Rights went so far as to suggest that the country's austerity measures and welfare reforms could be in breach of its human rights obligations (Leszkiewicz 2016; Mortimer 2016). This was followed up in 2018 with comments from its poverty envoy that '[t]he UK government has inflicted "great misery" on its people with "punitive, mean-spirited, and often callous" austerity policies driven by a political desire to undertake social re-engineering rather than economic necessity' (Booth and Butler 2018).

Many of the cuts to social security for working-age adults and families have also been seen by academics and left-leaning popular discourses as both disproportionate and potentially punitive (Dowler 2014: 161). In particular, the increased application of benefit 'sanctions', which involve unemployment payments being paused or cut if recipients are not seen to be following the rules properly, or showing enough willingness to work, have garnered much attention.

Ed, who I shared a Wednesday afternoon unpacking shift with at Fareshares, told me that post-financial crisis austerity measures felt like a 'war on the poor' to him. Ed grew up in Yeovil in the southwest of England, and having lost his father as a child, the family's finances became extremely tight. This experience gave him a strong sense of working-class identity and consciousness. Ed was concerned about how people suffering from deprivation were portrayed in the media and on TV, the language that was being used to describe poor people, as well as how this was affecting public perceptions. As he told me:

> I suppose I've got used to it now, but certainly for a long time I felt a real shock and dismay about the kind of characterization of working class people . . . the kind of poverty porn that's on the telly and all that sort of stuff . . . it's kind of de-humanizing to the extent that it's almost kind of softening up the wider public to make it legitimate to do absolutely anything to people really . . . And it seems to have an effect. People are genuinely influenced by that and genuinely do see a lot of working-class people as sub-human almost, so yeah, you know, I don't think anybody could have anticipated that 20 years ago.

Having worked in advice services since 2009, Ed had seen the consequences of these post-crisis measures first-hand, and the many ways in which they had impacted people's lives, as well as their physical and mental wellbeing. I spoke to several advice workers during my fieldwork and heard of various instances in which the process of benefit reassessment and withdrawal had driven people to stress-related self-harm or total mental breakdown.

Ed went on to explain that even during Thatcherism, the rhetoric around poverty had felt different to how it did in austerity Britain as it was still framed as 'something that you could escape out of'. Whereas under austerity it was 'something to be punished much more'. He told me that 'there's a definite movement towards the deserving poor and the undeserving poor, which has always been around in the background and that's really being pushed a lot now'. Koch suggests that since 2010, 'the contours of citizenship have changed in the UK as discourses of hyper-moralization have resurfaced' (2018: 34), and this, in turn, has created space for a more punitive regime. Within public and academic debate, many have suggested that the drastic withdrawal of entitlements combined with more punitive regimes around welfare to work ideologies is leading to a return to more overtly moralistic discourses around the 'deserving' and 'undeserving poor' or the 'strivers' and 'skivers' (see, for example, Koch and James 2022: 5; Williams 2013). While these were present even in the early days of the welfare state, when in combination with the growing role of philanthropy and charitable organizations in supporting those in need, they also resonate with more nineteenth-century moralisms and welfare practices (see, for example, Koch and James 2022: 3). As Anderson notes, structures of feeling can resonate around specific figures (in this case 'the poor'), pulling people into certain forms of reasoning (2016: 747). In austerity Britain, policy discourses around collective belt tightening are folded into moral judgement, revaluation and stigmatization, often with class-based and racialized tones.

Structures of feeling can also intensify around specific events (ibid.). Many commentators have argued that austerity, along with the concentration of economic and political power into the hands of an elite few, and the 'refugee crisis', which has seen significantly increased numbers of migrants and refugees arriving in Europe since 2015 (primarily from Muslim majority countries), had much to do with the results of the Brexit referendum and the connected rise in right-wing populism.

Politicians such as Nigel Farage, who founded UKIP (the UK Independence Party) to push for Brexit, gained visibility during this period in Britain, campaigning for British sovereignty and tighter borders. One particularly controversial part of the UKIP campaign was a poster that pictured a long line of mostly non-white migrants and refugees, with the caption 'Breaking Point: the EU has failed us all'. The poster frames migrants and refugees as a threat to Europe and its borders, causing a representative from the Unison union to report it to the police for inciting racial hatred (Stewart and Mason 2016). While defending the poster, Farage made allusions to the risk of Islamist terrorist attacks stating that '[w]hen Isis [the Islamic State of Iraq and Syria, an Islamist group] say they will use the migrant crisis to flood the continent with their jihadi terrorists, they probably mean it'. This clearly folds together leaving the EU with racist structures of feeling that associate threat with Muslim people and more broadly with immigrants. While Islamophobia has been on the rise in the UK since 9-11, it became heightened during and in the aftermath of the Brexit referendum. This is, undoubtedly, a significant issue in multicultural areas such as Southwark and Tower Hamlets, the latter of which houses the biggest Bangladeshi community in Europe.

Ghassan Hage (2003: 20–1) argues that people who have 'lost hope', due to the ways in which global capitalism has changed how the state interacts with society and the level of services or care that it provides, have a tendency to look back towards older forms and ideas of their national society as a 'passport to hope'. In doing so, they draw on a 'national social imaginary' that 'combines an emotional attachment to the nation consisting of ordinary "lower class" people, as well as a mundane critique of social inequality and social injustice' (Vanke 2024: 157). This then produces the kind of 'paranoid' nationalism that events such as Brexit have been said to represent.

Hage suggests that people who are feeling the effects of these changes can come to resent anyone else perceived as being cared for better by the nation than themselves, and all the more if they are of a different nationality. As he puts it (Hage 2003: 20–1), '[t]heir new life condition brings out the worst in them, as it would in any of us'. These experiences can lead them to sympathize with right-wing ideologues, 'who promise a good nation' along with tighter controls on immigration. Nonetheless, such discourses also show how specific structures of feeling have come to resonate around the co-called left-behind, white working class in relation to the Brexit vote, while ignoring the 'squeezed middle' (Bhambra 2017a). This, in some ways, acts to validate white 'racial self-interest' (Bhambra 2017b: S217) and connection to nation, while leaving the actions and beliefs of the white middle class or

Figure 4.1. MAKE BRITAIN HATE AGAIN. Subversive poster in East London in response to Brexit, 2018 © Celia Plender

politicians less scrutinized in relation to potential racism, Islamophobia and xenophobia.

In terms of welfare, the figure of the right-wing 'traditionalist' is not the only one to lament the shrinking state. Although the articulation may be different, much of the left-leaning anti-austerity campaigning that took place in the UK during this period looked back towards the more expansive state of the post-Second World War era, calling for a return to welfarism, the revival of trade unionism and a return to the more traditionally left-wing values that these are seen to represent. In essence, a return to an earlier form of moral economy in which the state was more caring, and the citizens felt more involved in the workings of politics and democracy. As such, this represented a differently orientated version of the national social imaginary in terms of ideological leanings.

Jeremy Corbyn became representative of a party-political shift away from centrist New Labour politics. He was elected as leader of the party in 2015 with a whole movement, known as Momentum, building up to support him in response to widespread opposition to Corbyn within his own party. With Corbyn, the Labour Party returned to some of its bread-and-butter issues, promoting better welfare provisions, working conditions and an anti-austerity stance. Nationalization was also on Corbyn's agenda, with regular calls for a re-nationalized rail network. From his first session of Prime Minister's Questions in Parliament, he also exemplified a populist approach by reading out questions from named members of the public on issues affecting them, such as a lack of affordable housing, benefit cuts and education, in a bid 'to bring a new kind of politics to Westminster' (Corbyn 2016). There were also many anti-austerity marches during this time calling for the expansion of the state and of welfare. I went to some with Jenny from St Hilda's, and others with other friends or my flatmates.

Brexit was an issue that came up often in my fieldwork. In the main, the people that I spoke to from both food co-ops mentioned feelings of concern and disbelief. For some there was a profound sense of loss, and for others a hope that it might not actually happen. Anna from Fareshares told me she could not 'bear it' and that it made her 'want to scream'. She told me she felt very 'frightened for England ... for Britain'. Anna felt that the EU was 'the only thing standing between us and really brutal capitalism' and yet, 'we had 'elected to leave'. She suggested that precarity and the fears it had caused in terms of job security and housing had caused people to 'allow management to walk all over them' and that 'pay and working conditions had collapsed under the cloak of austerity'. She felt that people needed to think more, and that they had not been thinking as they 'sleepwalked' into this situation, and into Brexit. She therefore evoked austerity's enclosure of 'practices of liveability' (Casas-Cortés et al. 2014: 453) and of imaginations (Asara 2020: 20).

Beth also experienced austerity as a dampening of free and imaginative thinking and worried for the sustainability of projects such as Fareshares within such an environment where minds, borders and property were being enclosed by neoliberal capitalism (Krasny 2020: 177–8). She told me that while she went on marches sometimes, she was not sure if they made much of a difference. Anna, by comparison, 'felt roused' by 'the old union banners' when she marched and the 'residual' leftwing imaginaries (Vanke 2024) they represented in terms of workers' rights, resistance and collectivism.

FOOD AND POVERTY

When I asked Alaya what she thought it would take to improve the situation within austerity Britain, which she described as 'harsh', 'very, very tough' and 'depressing', she replied:

> I think politicians need to start living here alongside these people and see how the other half live, because it's all very well for them to sit in their posh houses and make these decisions, and say, so many millions and millions of pounds are being wasted or

> used on people and the welfare system, but the welfare system is there for a reason and these people are genuinely in need. There are many people out there who don't choose to be on benefits, but they have to be on benefits for whatever reason, be it health reasons or personal circumstances . . . can't go out to work, or for lack of education can't get a decent job . . . or can't get a job that pays enough to feed the family, so you have to look at everything. It's almost like they think people choose to live like this. Nobody chooses to live like this. I think the politicians need to become a lot more understanding. Personally, I think it would have been easier and better if Labour had come into government, but obviously, what can you say? It is what it is really. 'Cause it seemed like Corbyn was a bit more in touch with people compared to Theresa May . . . but I'm sure even if he had come into power, his fellow colleagues wouldn't have allowed him to do as much as he probably wanted. But who knows?

Conservative politicians, then, showed a complete 'lack of ability to relate' to normal people's lives from Alaya's perspective (Koch 2017: 110). Her comments mirrored the anger felt about austerity during the 2017 election campaign, that politicians were not only out of touch, but also judgemental and punitive in their approach to people who made use of the benefit system.

By the time of the 2017 election, Theresa May had become the Prime Minister of the Conservative government following the resignation of David Cameron who stepped down the day after the Brexit vote in 2016. Cameron felt it would not be right for him (a remainer) to be 'the captain that steers our country to its next destination' (Cameron 2016).

Just nine months into her tenure as Prime Minister, May made the decision to call a 'snap' general election. Although the election was framed in relation to Brexit, much of the discussion within the media and among the general public, also revolved around austerity and welfare reform. Despite promising an economy that would work 'not for a privileged few, but for every one of us' (May 2016) when she first came to power, some people believed that she was not living up to this claim. In particular, the fact that nurses in full-time employment within the NHS were having to resort to using food banks,[6] led to considerable outrage.

There were various forms of backlash against the Conservative Party and its austerity agenda. A week before the general election, for example, a song titled 'Liar Liar GE2017' by anti-austerity band Captain SKA was heading to the top of the charts. This mocked Theresa May's claims of 'strong and stable leadership' (see Poole, 2017 for more on this slogan). The song also included the trope of nurses using food banks and the rise in child poverty. All proceeds from its sales went to food banks and the People's Assembly's anti-austerity campaign (Weaver 2017). Around London subversive posters and banners bashing Theresa May or promoting Jeremy Corbyn also started to pop up. These included slogans such as 'THERESA MAY. LIAR, LIAR £995 PANTS ON FIRE', which used the popular children's rhyme to poke fun at the Prime Minster while reminding people that she owned a pair of leather trousers worth £995. These had caused uproar in the media in late 2016, as they were seen to send the wrong signal to a country that had been dealing with austerity for several years (Sawer 2016).

Figure 4.2. Liar Liar Pants on Fire. Subversive election campaign poster in East London, 2017 © Celia Plender

Figure 4.3. Teresa May Be Not. Subversive election campaign poster in East London, 2017 © Celia Plender

Within the co-ops too, the election was a site of interest. While political conversations among volunteers tended to be less common at St Hilda's than at Fareshares, many of the people who worked, volunteered or shopped at St Hilda's Food Co-op on the day of the election (Thursday 8 June) mentioned whether they had voted yet or not, reminded others to do so, or acknowledged that they were planning to go to the polling station after their shift or shopping. Although people did not generally say how they intended to vote, there was clearly a sense of significance to a vote that came so soon after a Brexit referendum which had already had a significance impact on the social and political fabric of the UK.[7]

As the discourses around poverty and hunger during the 2017 election highlight, food banks became a particularly emotive symbol of austerity in the UK as increasing numbers of people turned to 'emergency food aid' schemes which cater to those facing significant financial shocks or crises. Benefit sanctions, cuts and changes are some of the most common causes of food bank use in the UK, along with low income and indebtedness (Dowler 2014; Lambie-Mumford 2017; Trussell Trust 2016, 2018). When I spoke to members of the food charity Sustain's food poverty project, Food Power, they agreed that welfare reform was a significant driver of poverty, including food poverty. They also highlighted the added pressures that people faced in cities such as London where housing and the cost of living can be more expensive. Indeed, in a survey of food insecurity in London conducted not long after my fieldwork (the first of its kind in England), one in five adults were found to have low or very low levels of food security, and 60% of these were in work. One in six parents were also said to have children living with food insecurity (Demography and Policy Analysis Team, City Intelligence Unit 2019).

Alaya told me that she had also seen more and more people experiencing poverty and having to access food banks or schemes such as the food co-op over the years. When I asked her whether food often came up in her sessions, however, she told me that:

> It's there, in the forefront of everyone's mind, but it's not something that's mentioned specifically because when they come to us for advice, it's more the threat of losing their home that they are worried about. They do think about how they're going to support their family, how they're going to feed their family, but most people think, 'what if the council take my home, I won't have a roof over our head. How will I manage that?' So, it's more to do with housing and then the debts they fall into that people come to us for help with and obviously getting their benefits put in place.

Expenditure on food is often adjusted in times of hardship by reducing what is bought, substituting for cheaper options or, in some cases, going without for short periods of time or prioritizing the feeding of some (typically children) over others (Caraher and Dowler 2014). Comparatively, housing costs tend to be less elastic (Kirkpatrick and Tarasuk 2011: 285), meaning that they can potentially feel more urgent due to the immediate risk of utilities being cut off or property seized, which goes some way to explain why these were the issues that came up more often at the advice service. Nonetheless, food insecurity is a very real issue, with detrimental impacts on both physical and mental wellbeing.

While I was interviewing a member of Fareshares, for example, they told me that they had needed to use a food bank at one point when they were short of work. This was something that they clearly still felt raw about, causing both their posture and their facial expression to change as they spoke. Although they felt terrible for saying it, they told me they hated the food they got from the food bank as much as they hated the experience of having to be there at all. Food meant a lot to them and they found being denied any choice about what they could eat, along with being limited to highly processed tins and dried goods, tough. They told me:

> There's this real feeling that if that's your entire diet, if that's all you eat or most of what you eat what happens in your mind is 'oh, this is what I deserve, this is all I deserve'. So, again, it's that link between poverty and rubbish food. It's huge, I think if we eat something it becomes part of us physically but also psychologically. It becomes part of our identity . . . that this is what we eat.

Luckily, they only had to visit the food bank once.

Just as the language used to describe recipients of welfare benefits can impact on their sense of identity or self-worth (Patrick 2017: 145), becoming part of the 'machinery' of stigma and inequality (Tyler 2020), my interlocutor's words allude to the potentially damaging impacts of feeding 'rubbish' food to people suffering from financial issues. They too can start to feel like rubbish.

EXPERIENCES OF AUSTERITY

Although discussions framed in terms of 'austerity' rarely came up among those who interacted with St Hilda's Food Co-op, some people involved with the project were feeling the strains of precarious lives. Others were feeling the pressures that welfare reform was putting on their benefit claims and interactions with related statutory services.[8] Various volunteers and customers from the food co-op also made use of the advice service that formed part of the City Bridge funding. The ability to feed their families or themselves was clearly a worry for some, along with housing and basic financial needs. Of the regular volunteers at the food co-op during my time there, a handful were in regular work. Others were actively looking for work, often after their children had reached school age, leaving them with more time to do so. Many had caring responsibilities. A reasonable number were also the recipients of state support in one form or another, ranging from social housing to unemployment benefits or forms of incapacity benefit for those unable to work due to illness or disability. Other volunteers, however, did have more stable livelihoods and lifestyles, or more choice in terms of the work that was on offer to them. This is important to note as there were a diverse and varied range of people and experiences at both food co-ops, representative of the open access models that they worked by, which drew volunteers and customers from different backgrounds and income levels who also had different needs and interests.

For some volunteers, there was a sense of frustration with the state and its welfare representatives. One volunteer told me that she had previously been given a small amount of housing benefit due to her caring responsibilities. She had then been told to give it back as she was not entitled after all, before being offered it again. She decided she would rather manage without it despite the potential entitlement. She was angry at an overly bureaucratic system that was not only disorganized, but had also tried to stigmatize her as someone who had attempted to take more than she should have. To reject this benefit, then, was a way to maintain her dignity and to have some agency ('being an actor as well as acted upon' (Gibson-Graham 2003: 54)) within a political economy that felt very top-down, even if it meant going without money that could have made a difference to hers and her family's life.

At Fareshares, too, various members were experiencing the impacts of welfare reform in one way or another.[9] While some of Fareshares' members worked in well-paid, full-time jobs, others worked for themselves or in part-time jobs, ranging from retail to driving for Deliveroo;[10] some were students, and others received various forms of benefits due to physical and mental health issues. As such, while some had comfortable incomes and lifestyles, others were dealing with various forms of precarity, whether through the nature of the work they did or through circumstance. More than one member mentioned to me that they were going through the reassessment of benefits, leading to considerable stress, and the negotiation of complex rules, regulations and bureaucratic processes. It requires a lot of skill, mental and physical capacity and confidence to complete the paperwork, attend assessment meetings, appeal hearings, and to fight for one's right to these benefits. All of this can end up equating to a full-time job due to the amount of work (as well as stress) involved (Koch and James 2022: 6).

One Fareshares member, Nuala, who had been on benefits for several years due to severe anxiety and depression, explained that it was austerity that had brought her to Fareshares in the first place as the basic items such as grains, pulses and nuts were cheap there. She heard about it from a mental health day centre near to the food co-op (which has now closed down) where various other visitors shopped at Fareshares. She then started volunteering because, in the spirit of mutual aid, she wanted to be able to give something back as well as benefitting from it. She went on to explain that her recent interaction with the benefit system felt 'very frightening'. At the time of our interview in 2017, she was still waiting to be reassessed and transitioned from Disability Living Allowance (DLA) to Personal Independence Payments (PIP),[11] but she said that all of the other people she knew from the day centre who had been transitioned were having their benefits cut. She told me that the sense of fear and anticipation this gave her had really affected what she did. As she explained:

> I think I was a bit more active a couple of years ago. When I had money to do more, to occasionally go to the cinema. I don't have that anymore. So, even though I've really tightened my belt, I also still manage to have less money because they've cut it so much and because I'm trying to save a bit because I'm so frightened of what they are going to do . . . any day now. They've written to me to say that they will call me. And when they call me, I will have four weeks. And then if I don't apply within those four weeks, it could be that they will stop my money instantly. And then if I do apply [for PIP] and get rejected, that'll be eight weeks. So, within eight weeks I could have the bigger amount of my money cut.

She also received Employment Support Allowance, but she said that it was 'a tiny amount'. She explained that her benefits had already been reduced in recent years as her health had improved slightly (which she felt was fair). Nuala suggested, however, that the fact that the state no longer increased benefits in line with inflation meant that the value of what she did still receive had also gone down.

Other researchers have documented similar stories, highlighting how these experiences of being forced to repeatedly prove deservingness can exacerbate psychological distress. As part of this distress, Patrick (2017: 3) argues that these processes of welfare reform not only impact on an individual's 'capacity to live in the present', but also 'to reflect on their past(s) and plan for the future' (see also Harris et al. 2019: 749). As such, this, too, represents the potential closing down of imaginations as the processes of welfare negotiation and the threat of precarity become all encompassing. In the conversations I had with some of the volunteers at Fareshares and St Hilda's, however, while they demonstrated frustration and anger with a punitive system which was treating them as untrustworthy, they tried hard to hold on to their dignity and sense of autonomy. This was done by either fighting for what they saw as a right or extricating themselves from the stress and stigma the system seemed to be piling onto them by refusing the conditional, and retractable gift of welfare.

CONCLUSIONS

During the period of my fieldwork, austerity came to feel increasingly present within the food co-ops and the country, whether as a consequence of personal experiences, public discourses or political events. This lent it an affective quality, described by some as a public mood (Forkert 2017) and others an atmosphere (Denning 2021; Hitchen 2021). According to Sharma and Tygstrup, affectivity is a distributive phenomenon; an 'assemblage of small parts of different provenance, which make up, due to an internal system of relations, an unmistakeable phenomenon, a feeling with a verifiable and identifiable structure' (Sharma and Tygstrup 2015: 5; see also Williams 2015), and this is no less the case for the affectivity of austerity Britain. While its 'structures' (in Raymond William's use of the term (2015)) may not always be entirely tangible, 'somehow we know it is there – we *feel* [and experience] its presence' (Hitchen 2021: 297 emphasis original) across diverse phenomena.

Although some were more directly and detrimentally impacted by the financial implications of austerity than others within the country, arguably, its affective and temporal qualities were more pervasive, leading to multifarious and complex feelings of concern, discomfort, indignation and resentment, along with heightened moral and political discourses, actions and inactions, as this chapter has explored. As Asara points out (2020: 20), radial imaginaries are 'endangered by austerity's multiple regimes of civic, economic, political and ideational enclosure'. Ultimately, however, the complex structures of feeling in austerity Britain both opened up and closed down imaginations, political actions and possibilities in some ways, as the experiences discussed in this chapter highlight.

For Adina, changing times were punctuated by a sense of precarity, temporal malaise and nostalgia for the lost sense of community she connected with the area and project in the late 1980s/early 1990s. This sense of change was also felt within Fareshares and the relationship that different members had to collective practices and approaches to food provisioning and activism more generally. Time was clearly a big concern for many of the current members of Fareshares during my fieldwork, causing tensions in terms of the commitment they could afford to make to the co-op through shifts and jobs, and the classically contentious issue of the time it takes to make decisions using a non-hierarchical, consensus model (Polletta 2012: 12), as discussed in the previous chapter. This kind of work can be both mentally and emotionally taxing. For some, an inability to balance the time commitment and emotional labour needed to be an active, decision-making volunteer-member, with other commitments, values and aspects of their identities (class, mental health, race or ethnicity) could become a barrier to inclusion in the project, or a source of frustration. For some of the newer or younger members less wedded to ideas of anarchism or cooperation, it could also feel inconvenient. Precarious time, therefore, contributed to forms of 'ideational enclosure' (Asara 2020: 20). As 'life under capitalism can make it terribly difficult to find the time and energy to participate in the commons' (Arbell et al. 2020: 59).

Changing times also impacted on notions of the needs Fareshares was or should be responding to, and how a co-op formed in another era with different structures of feeling could address needs and capture cooperative imaginations today. Rakopoulos suggests that the activities of politicized co-operatives become 'purposeful' through the combination of material practice and the articulation of future-orientated goals around social change, 'eventually and hopefully leading to a broader cooperative social movement spilling into a sea of wider consciousness' (2014: 190–1). Through the combination of practice and deliberation, therefore, co-ops can attempt to not only shape the world around them, but also the activities and imaginations of those involved, and beyond. At Fareshares, however, there could be a lack of perceived time or space for deliberation as the apathy about meeting attendance in the previous chapter highlighted, and the desire for efficiency discussed in this chapter reinforces. Combined with changing values and relationships to cooperative skills and practices, this impacted on the workings and aspirations of the project in such an era. Even those who founded Fareshares had their ambivalences. While Martin wondered what the food co-op might be for today, and which needs it was serving, Adina, although more confident about what Fareshares was for (as discussed in chapter 2), struggled to find the time to commit to more than just shopping at the co-op.

While Fareshares seemed to struggle with change in some ways (while being resilient in others as it managed to keep going despite adversity), a necessity to change was built into the fabric of St Hilda's due to the ways in which it had to adapt to a shrinking pool of funding and respond to the changing interests of funders. This inevitably caused pressures in terms of a continuous sense of precarity felt among staff, and in terms of the strains precarity could put on the centre's own resources. It also made St Hilda's more adaptable to change, however, as it was constantly having to respond to changing circumstances, showing the forms of creativity, imagination and resilience that can come out of such circumstance (Jupp 2022). It was this combination of adaptiveness and the centre's aims around deprivation and social exclusion that led to the development of the food and advice project.

In an era of welfare cuts, hyper-moralization around welfare receipt, deservingness and how different kinds of people were valued, this caused members of both projects discomfort and concern. While Alaya and Ed saw the impacts that such an atmosphere was having on their clients, and felt worried and frustrated about the ways in which things were changing within the country, others were having to work out first-hand how to respond to the threat of benefit withdrawal, or the accusation that benefit claims were invalid, and the practical and moral valuations that came with these. On all parts, they felt let down by a state that neither understood them, nor cared. In the minds of people such as Ed it was being deliberately cruel. Such authorities, therefore, lacked 'ordinary personhood and the commitments that flow from it', instead looking out for their own interests while creating feelings of 'us' and 'them' for many people in the country (Koch 2017: 116).

Within Koch's work with residents of a post-industrial English council estate, she found that these kinds of experiences of state failure could make 'relational, affective and social ties' matter to them even more (2017: 116). Through these forms of sociality, Koch (ibid.) and Skeggs (2011) suggest it is not uncommon for other forms of personhood to emerge based on how places and people are cared for in times of social, political and economic change. Building on Skeggs, Koch argues that this creates 'a different political ontology of the self, one which does not take individualism as its self-evident point of departure', therefore, highlighting the ways in which 'politics is always embedded in social life' (Koch 2017: 117).

For many of those involved with Fareshares and St Hilda's East food co-ops, finding spaces of sociality and connection could also feel important as a means of coping within the harsh context of austerity Britain. As Koch and James suggest, within such contexts, the daily interventions and caring practices of those working at the interface of the state, the market, the third sector and everyday citizens can become 'mechanisms for implementing or imagining alternatives to the status quo, however ad hoc or fleeting these might be' (2022: 3). I continue to explore these everyday alternatives in the following chapters. While this chapter has looked at the structures of feeling in austerity Britain, the impacts of political-economic change on the food co-ops, their participants and imaginations, in chapter 5 I return to the issue of community, exploring how this was understood and invoked in two areas undergoing rapid gentrification and regeneration.

NOTES

1. This is what a lot of people in the local area affectionately called the Pullens Estate.
2. Here I view generations a little differently to Mannheim whose work Whittier draws on. Rather than simply taking into account the socio-historical environment of an activist's youth, I argue that the period in which someone becomes politically active and the forms of action they engaged with at that point all play a part in their relationship to, and outlook on, social organization and activist methods.
3. Within her work with worker-run collectives in Berlin in the 1980s, Müller (1991) also noted that 'the younger members did not have equally pronounced political intentions', suggesting that they 'were still trying to find' their political orientation and used their work with the collectives to develop this.

4. The United Nations' Committee on World Food Security defines this as 'the condition in which all people, at all times, have physical, social and economic access to sufficient safe and nutritious food that meets their dietary needs and food preferences for an active and healthy life' (IFPRI n.d.). While this term is commonly used in policy discussions, the term 'food poverty' is often used in media coverage and discussions among the general public. Both are often used interchangeably in academic literature (Lambie-Mumford 2017: 17).
5. The bedroom tax is an informal name given to a rule implemented in 2012 as part of the Welfare Reform Act, which means that housing benefit payments are reduced if a claimant's property is judged to have more bedrooms than they need.
6. In the British context, a food bank is a charitable organization where people can go to get free food parcels of between three and five days' food for an individual or household. They typically receive tins and dried goods, which the food bank received through charitable donation or through arrangements with supermarkets and food waste charities. Food bank users tend to be referred through front-line services such as GP (doctors') surgeries, advice services and Jobcentres.
7. Overall, the 2017 election significantly weakened Theresa May and the Conservative Party's position. The Conservatives lost 22 seats while the Labour Party gained 21. As a consequence, there was a 'hung parliament' in which no party had a strong majority. Ultimately, this led the Conservative Party to form a 'weak' majority which was legislatively supported by the right-wing and socially conservative Northern Irish Democratic Unionist Party (DUP) – a move that greatly concerned many within the centre and on the left.
8. In order to maintain the privacy and dignity of those involved with each food co-op, and to avoid the exoticization of their experiences, I choose not to go into too much detail of individual cases, instead, illustrating the kinds of austerity and welfare related issues that anecdotally arose in each food co-op unless a research participant specifically chose to discuss something of this nature with me during a recorded interview. Names are often changed or left out in relation to these accounts for the same reason.
9. This challenges the perception of local food projects and alternative food networks as spaces purely for middle-class people with comfortable incomes (Goodman et al. 2014: 14).
10. Deliveroo is a take-away delivery service, which has become synonymous with the 'gig' economy in which organizations contract with independent workers on short-term, often flexible contracts or as freelancers.
11. DLA and PIP are welfare benefits intended to help people with long-term health problems or disabilities. PIP was introduced as part of the 2012 Welfare Reform Act to gradually replace DLA. The medical assessments and eligibility for welfare are more regular and more stringent than with DLA. Clearly the name Personal Independence Payment itself has discursive power in relation to individual autonomy and more active forms of citizenship.

REFERENCES

Anderson, Ben. 2016. 'Neoliberal Affects', *Progress in Human Geography* 40(6): 734–53.

Arbell, Yael et al. 2020. 'Contested Subjectivities in a UK Housing Cooperative: Old Hippies and Thatcher's Children Negotiating the Commons', *Geoforum* 110: 58–66.

Asara, Viviana. 2020. 'Untangling the Radical Imaginaries of the Indignados' Movement: Commons, Autonomy and Ecologism', *Environmental Politics*: 1–25.

Bauman, Zygmunt. 1976. *Socialism: The Active Utopia*. Plymouth: Allen & Unwin.

Bhambra, Gurminder K. 2017a, 10 November. 'Why Are the White Working Classes Still Being Held Responsible for Brexit and Trump?', *LSE BREXIT*. Retrieved 21 December 2023 from https://blogs.lse.ac.uk/brexit/2017/11/10/why-are-the-white-working-classes-still-being-held-responsible-for-brexit-and-trump/.

———. 2017b. 'Brexit, Trump, and "Methodological Whiteness": On the Misrecognition of Race and Class', *The British Journal of Sociology* 68(S1): S214–32.

Booth, Robert, and Patrick Butler. 2018, 16 November. 'UK Austerity Has Inflicted "Great Misery" on Citizens, UN Says', *The Guardian*.

Cameron, David. 2016, 24 June. 'Brexit: David Cameron's Resignation Statement in Full', *BBC News*.

Caraher, M., and E. Dowler. 2014. 'Food for Poorer People: Conventional and "Alternative" Transgressions', in M. Goodman and C. Sage (eds), *Food Transgressions: Making Sense of Contemporary Food Politics*. Farnham, Surrey: Ashgate, pp. 227–46.

Casas-Cortés, Maribel et al. 2014. 'The Commons', in Donald Nonini (ed.), *A Handbook of Urban Anthropology*. London: Routledge, pp. 449–69.

Castells, Manuel. 2012. *Networks of Outrage and Hope: Social Movements in the Internet Age*. Cambridge; Malden, MA: Polity Press.

Corbyn, Jeremy. 2016, 3 September. 'Jeremy Corbyn – Today is My 100th PMQs Question as Labour Leader – but I Still Won't Get a Straight Answer from David Cameron (The Independent) – Jeremy Corbyn MP', *Jeremycorbyn.Org.Uk*. Retrieved 13 October 2018 from http://jeremycorbyn.org.uk/articles/jeremy-corbyn-today-is-my-100th-pmqs-question-as-labour-leader-but-i-still-wont-get-a-straight-answer-from-david-cameron-the-independent/.

Demography and Policy Analysis Team, City Intelligence Unit. 2019. *Survey of Londoners Headline Findings*. London: Greater London Authority, p. 21.

Denning, Stephanie. 2021. 'Three Foodbanks in a Decade of Austerity: Foodbank Affective Atmospheres', *Antipode* 53(4): 1018–37.

Dowler, Elizabeth. 2014. 'Food Banks and Food Justice in "Austerity Britain"', in Graham Riches and Tiina Silvasti (eds), *First World Hunger Revisited – Food Charity or the Right to Food?* New York: Palgrave Macmillan, pp. 160–75.

Forkert, Kirsten. 2017. *Austerity As Public Mood (Radical Cultural Studies): Social Anxieties and Social Struggles* (Illustrated edition). Lanham: Rowman & Littlefield.

Gibson-Graham, J. K. 2003. 'An Ethics of the Local', *Rethinking Marxism* 15(1): 49–74.

Goodman, David et al. 2014. *Alternative Food Networks: Knowledge, Practice, and Politics*. Abingdon: Routledge.

Hage, Ghassan. 2003. *Against Paranoid Nationalism: Searching for Hope in a Shrinking Society*. Annandale, NSW: The Merlin Press Ltd.

Hancox, Dan. 2018, 1 April. 'The Unstoppable Rise of Veganism: How a Fringe Movement Went Mainstream', *The Guardian*.

Harris, Ella et al. 2019. 'On-Edge in the Impasse: Inhabiting the Housing Crisis as Structure-of-Feeling', *Geoforum* 101: 156–64.

Hitchen, Esther. 2016. 'Living and Feeling the Austere', *New Formations: A Journal of Culture/Theory/Politics* 87(1): 102–18.

———. 2021. 'The Affective Life of Austerity: Uncanny Atmospheres and Paranoid Temporalities', *Social & Cultural Geography* 22(3): 295–318.

IFPRI. (n.d.). 'Food Security', *International Food Policy Research Institute.* Retrieved 24 February 2019 from http://www.ifpri.org/topic/food-security.

Jupp, Eleanor. 2022. *Care, Crisis and Activism: The Politics of Everyday Life.* Bristol: Policy Press.

Kirkpatrick, Sharon I., and Valerie Tarasuk. 2011. 'Housing Circumstances Are Associated with Household Food Access among Low-Income Urban Families', *Journal of Urban Health: Bulletin of the New York Academy of Medicine* 88(2): 284–96.

Koch, Insa. 2017. 'When Politicians Fail: Zombie Democracy and the Anthropology of Actually Existing Politics', *The Sociological Review* 65(1_suppl): 105–20.

Koch, Insa Lee. 2018. *Personalizing the State: An Anthropology of Law, Politics, and Welfare in Austerity Britain.* Oxford: Oxford University Press.

Koch, Insa, and Deborah James. 2022. 'The State of the Welfare State: Advice, Governance and Care in Settings of Austerity', *Ethnos* 87(1): 1–21.

Krasny, Elke. 2020. 'Precarious Commons: An Urban Garden for Uncertain Times', in Derya Özkan and Güldem Baykal Büyüksaraç (eds), *Commoning the City: Empirical Perspectives on Urban Ecology, Economics and Ethics.* London: Routledge, pp. 177–92.

Lambie-Mumford, Hannah. 2017. *Hungry Britain – The Rise of Food Charity.* Bristol: Policy Press.

Land, Christopher, and Daniel King. 2014. 'Organizing Otherwise: Translating Anarchism in a Voluntary Sector Organization', *Ephemera* 14: 923–50.

Leszkiewicz, Anna. 2016, 29 June. 'The UN Declares the UK's Austerity Policies in Breach of International Human Rights Obligations'. Retrieved 1 July 2024 from https://www.newstatesman.com/politics/uk/2016/06/un-declares-uk-s-austerity-policies-breach-international-human-rights.

May, Theresa. 2016, 13 July. 'Statement from the New Prime Minister Theresa May', *GOV.UK.* Retrieved 7 January 2024 from https://www.gov.uk/government/speeches/statement-from-the-new-prime-minister-theresa-may.

Molé, Noelle J. 2010. 'Precarious Subjects: Anticipating Neoliberalism in Northern Italy's Workplace', *American Anthropologist* 112(1): 38–53.

Mortimer, Caroline. 2016, 29 June. 'The UN Have Said Austerity Policy Breaches Human Rights', *The Independent.*

Mouffe, Chantal. 2005. *On the Political.* London; New York: Routledge.

Müller, Birgit. 1991. *Toward an Alternative Culture of Work: Political Idealism and Economic Practices in West Berlin Collective Enterprises.* Boulder: Westview Press.

Onanuga, Tola. 2010, 22 June. 'Emergency Budget: George Osborne's Speech in Full', *The Guardian.*

Patrick, Ruth. 2017. *For Whose Benefit? The Everyday Realities of Welfare Reform.* Bristol: Policy Press.

Polletta, Francesca. 2012. *Freedom is an Endless Meeting.* Chicago: University Of Chicago Press.

Poole, Steven. 2017, 10 May. '"Strong and Stable Leadership!" Could Theresa May's Rhetorical Carpet-Bombing Backfire?', *The Guardian.*

Powers, Theodore. 2022. 'Austerity', in James Carrier (ed.), *A Handbook of Economic Anthropology.* Cheltenham; Northampton, MA: Edward Elgar Publishing, pp. 461–72.

Prosser, Brenton, and Gerry Stoker. 2017. 'Rise of "Anti-Politics" Produces Surprise Result in the UK Election – and It's Playing a Role in Australia, Too', *The Conversation.* Retrieved 4 March 2021 from http://theconversation.com/rise-of-anti-politics

-produces-surprise-result-in-the-uk-election-and-its-playing-a-role-in-australia-too-78813.

Putnam, Robert. 2001. *Bowling Alone: The Collapse and Revival of American Community*. New York: Simon & Schuster.

Rakopoulos, Theodoros. 2014. 'The Crisis Seen from Below, Within, and Against: From Solidarity Economy to Food Distribution Cooperatives in Greece', *Dialectical Anthropology* 38(2): 189–207.

Sawer, Patrick. 2016, 3 December. 'Conservatives at War over Theresa May's Leather Trousers', *The Telegraph*.

Sennett, Richard. 2013. *Together: The Rituals, Pleasures and Politics of Cooperation*. London: Penguin.

Sharma, Devika, and Frederik Tygstrup (eds). 2015. *Structures of Feeling: Affectivity and the Study of Culture*. Berlin: De Gruyter.

Skeggs, Beverley. 2011. 'Imagining Personhood Differently: Person Value and Autonomist Working-Class Value Practices', *The Sociological Review* 59(3): 496–513.

Sörbom, Adrienne, and Magnus Wennerhag. 2013. 'Individualization, Life Politics, and the Reformulation of Social Critique: An Analysis of the Global Justice Movement', *Critical Sociology* 39(3): 453–78.

Standing, Guy. 2014. *The Precariat: The New Dangerous Class* (Revised edition). London; New York: Bloomsbury Academic.

Stewart, Heather, and Rowena Mason. 2016, 16 June. 'Nigel Farage's Anti-Migrant Poster Reported to Police', *The Guardian*.

Sugarman, Jeff, and Erin Thrift. 2020. 'Neoliberalism and the Psychology of Time', *Journal of Humanistic Psychology* 60(6): 807–28.

Trussell Trust. 2016, 27 October. 'Benefit Sanctions & Foodbank Use', *The Trussell Trust*. Retrieved 7 January 2024 from https://www.trusselltrust.org/2016/10/27/benefit-sanctions-foodbank-use/.

———. 2018. 'The Trussell Trust – End of Year Stats', *The Trussell Trust*. Retrieved 7 January 2024 from https://www.trusselltrust.org/news-and-blog/latest-stats/end-year-stats/.

Tyler, Imogen. 2020. *Stigma: The Machinery of Inequality*. London: Zed Books.

Ulin, Robert C. 1996. *Vintages and Traditions: Ethnohistory of Southwest French Wine Cooperatives*. Washington, DC: Smithsonian Books.

Vanke, Alexandrina. 2024. *The Urban Life of Workers in Post-Soviet Russia: Engaging in Everyday Struggle*. Manchester: Manchester University Press.

Venkatesan, Soumhya. 2010. 'Learning to Weave; Weaving to Learn . . . What?', *Journal of the Royal Anthropological Institute* 16(s1): S158–75.

Weaver, Matthew. 2017, 31 May. '"She's a Liar, Liar": Anti-Theresa May Song Heads to Top of Charts', *The Guardian*.

Williams, Raymond. 2015. 'Structures of Feeling', in Devika Sharma and Frederik Tygstrup (eds), *Structures of Feeling: Affectivity and the Study of Culture*. Berlin: De Gruyter, pp. 20–5.

Williams, Zoe. 2013, 9 January. 'Skivers v Strivers: The Argument That Pollutes People's Minds', *The Guardian*.

Woodly, Deva et al. 2021. 'The Politics of Care', *Contemporary Political Theory* 20(4): 890–925.

CHAPTER

5

CHANGING PLACES, CHANGING COMMUNITIES

THE 'RIGHT' KIND OF CUSTOMERS

When St Hilda's Food Co-op started its evening openings in August 2016 after receiving funding for the Food and Advice Project, the weather was pleasant enough to set up on the pavement outside the centre for the first few weeks. This enabled us to make the most of passing footfall as the new opening hours were getting established. The stall elicited interest from all sorts of different people. As well as asking where the produce came from and whether we grew it ourselves, a lot of the more affluent (often white) customers were also interested to hear about our financial model, wondering whether the food co-op was a means of raising funds for the community centre. Some also asked who the stall was for, unsure of whether a project like this was somewhere where they could or should shop. When we told them that it was a non-profit project that was open to everyone, some chose to pay more than the price of the goods in order to support the co-op and the community centre. This could be as much as £10 for a £3 purchase. Many of the more affluent customers, who lived or worked in the area, were also surprised to see how cheap the goods on sale were, whether organic or not.

One sunny evening, shortly after the evening openings had begun, a white man in his late twenties to early thirties with a beard, striped T-shirt and long hair tied up in a top knot stopped at the stall on his way past. He selected his produce carefully, while didactically commenting on some of the items on the stall. We should be cautious of the non-organic corn-on-the-cob, he told us, as it was likely to be filled with genetically modified organisms. The organic corn probably could have done with staying on the stalk for a few more days, he added. Unsolicited, he went on to demonstrate how to tell if an avocado was good or not by pulling out the stalk and checking whether the flesh underneath was green or black. Having filled his basket with organic vegetables, cut-price non-organic avocados (which were going for 10 pence each as the quality was mixed), and a pack or two of Zaytoun's fairly-traded grains, he made his way towards the till. I could not help but point out the giant courgettes that had grown to the size of marrows, which were in a box next to the till, to see how he would value these. 'They're gleaned', I told him (i.e. gathered from farms that cannot sell them to their usual customers), and he enthusiastically confirmed that he would definitely have one of those. He was going to spiralize it, he told us.[1] After he had ridden away on his bicycle, Mary, an evening volunteer who had recently moved to the area and was keen to get in touch with community projects, wryly commented that he was the 'epitome of a hipster'.[2]

I cannot deny that by pointing the courgettes out to him I was being a little mischievous as an ethnographer, as I wanted to see how this 'hipster' would perceive their value. His positive response to the courgettes confirmed my suspicions about his preferences. Shopping choices, and indeed food itself, can say much about identities (see, for example, Appadurai 1981 on gastropolitics; Bourdieu 2010 on distinction; Clark 2004; Littler 2011 on ethical consumption; Mintz and Du Bois 2002 on food and identity). In this case, the 'hipster' customer marked aspects of his values and status out through consumption of 'ethical' goods. Doing so can also be a means of expressing resistance to the 'dominant lifestyle norms and mainstream consumer sensibilities' in order to reinforce a more alternative identity (Cronin et al. 2014: 3). Within public understandings and academic literature, the kind of consumption choices he was making, which privileged alternative food networks, such as locally produced organic goods sourced directly from the farmer or gleaned courgettes, are typically associated with the middle classes and often whiteness, however inadvertently (see, for example, Goodman et al. 2014; Grasseni 2013; Guthman 2008; Kneafsey et al. 2008; Slocum 2007; Som Castellano 2015).

In those early weeks of the new evening opening, we regularly counted customer numbers, even turning it into a guessing game at 8pm as we waited for the till to print out a 'Z' reading which showed takings and sales numbers for the shift. There was also discussion between Jenny and Rupert about whether we were getting enough of the 'right kind' of customers – that is, less affluent. We were certainly getting customers who were seen as part of the target audience, such as social housing tenants from the nearby Boundary Estate, people using the advice service or just appearing less well-heeled, and some of our morning customers had even started coming twice a day. But we were also getting a higher proportion of organic sales and many of the evening customers did appear to be either more affluent or more 'hipster'.[3]

The changing demographics of the area around St Hilda's framed many of the conversations about the new sessions. There was much discussion of who the community centre wanted to make use of the new sessions, especially as the funding focused on food poverty and general advice, which often related to issues with state benefits (as discussed in the previous chapter). But as St Hilda's also cared about building friendships 'across diverse cultural and social backgrounds' (as discussed in chapter 2), there was some potential negotiation to be done to meet the funding targets and the perceived needs of the less affluent members of the local community, while also making everyone feel welcome at the food co-op. Jenny thought about these issues a lot and we discussed them on more than one occasion. Ultimately, she concluded, all customers were good customers as the more we sold, the lower we could make the mark-up because the delivery costs would remain the same. Despite the associations the organic foods might have with more affluent shoppers, she felt strongly about giving people the choice and, as she put it, 'not assuming how people are going to use what, I recognize, are very limited budgets'. As she explained, 'I don't think it's our role to assume how those budgets might be used'.

Both Shoreditch and St Hilda's East are historically deprived and multicultural areas going through significant processes of gentrification and regeneration, which are changing demographics and access to resources within each area. As both food co-ops worked by the logics of open access to all, as well as a concern for making good food more accessible to people, on low incomes (as discussed in chapter 2), the tensions caused by changing demographics combined with the challenges of rising inequality inevitably threw up complex questions about community, inclusion and the accessibility of the spaces and the foods within them. In this chapter I explore the complex dynamics of gentrification, regeneration and food as well as some of the ways in which community and conviviality are envisaged and practised within this context of change.

While the term 'community' itself is often critiqued within academic literature for its amorphousness and ambiguity (see, for example, Amit and Rapport 2002, 2012; Creed 2006), at both St Hilda's and Fareshares it was regularly invoked as something meaningful and desirable in the face of spatial, demographic and political-economic changes.[4] It also represented a key component of each food co-op's understanding of sociality and of everyday politics. I start the chapter by offering context to the area around St Hilda's, its changing demographics and how this was experienced by members of the community centre. I then move on to the associations between gentrification and certain kinds of foods, and the kinds of structure of feeling and class consciousness these engendered in the area, before exploring the ways in which the food co-op attempted to navigate inclusion within the project. Next, I turn to how feelings of community have changed around the Pullens Estate and the forms of nostalgia and concern this and rapid regeneration projects created for those in the area. Finally, I explore issues of inclusion and visions of safe space at Fareshares.

WAVES OF MIGRATION

During my time at St Hilda's, the area around the community centre was often filled with tourists snapping pictures of the heavily graffitied walls and crumbling urban architecture of Shoreditch and Bethnal Green. Here, Victorian brick railway arches and buildings stood side-by-side with the glass, concrete and polished metal of Shoreditch Overground station and the rows of corrugated steel shipping containers next door, which had been turned into trendy pop-up shops. The colourful sights and smells of Brick Lane were another draw to the area as this has been a hub for the Bangladeshi community for many years. Curry houses, Asian grocers and fabric shops butt up against retro, second-hand clothing stores, independent cafés selling flat white coffees for £3.80 and boutique furniture shops where you would struggle to find anything for under a few hundred pounds, again alluding to the changing demographics in the area.

The East End has always seen flows of migration due, in part, to its location near the City and the docks. Once home to the Huguenot community, who brought silk weaving skills to the area in the seventeenth and eighteenth centuries, during the nineteenth century, many Irish people who left their country due to poverty and famine took up work in East End sweatshops. Then, from the late 1800s onwards, the pogroms of Eastern Europe brought Jewish refugees here (Dench et al. 2006: 15–16; Eade 2001: 125); and since the 1960s, the number of people from the region of pre-partition India known as West Bengal (now Bangladesh) has grown substantially.[5] Today, the borough of Tower Hamlets has the largest population of people from Bangladeshi backgrounds in the UK – around 30% of the inhabitants of the borough in 2018 (Tower Hamlets Council 2018), and Brick Lane is the heart of the Bangladeshi community. Along with curry houses and halal butcher's shops, the street also retained aspects of its earlier history, such as the Jewish bagel shops, which were also seen as a tourist destination at the time of my fieldwork.

According to Dench et al. (2006: 1), from the mid-nineteenth century, up until the formation of the post-Second World War welfare state in Britain, the East End was also a 'breeding ground for social policy ideas and visionary thinking'. This included the foundation of the Boundary Estate in 1886, which was one of the first council-run social housing schemes in the UK. The attractive five-story, red and yellow brick tenement buildings that make up the estate replaced one of the East End's most notorious slums – the Old Nichol (London Borough of Tower Hamlets 2007: 4).[6]

The community centre itself has a long-running connection with the Boundary (as locals often call it), having been located in close proximity to it since only a few years after the Boundary's foundation. As I mention in chapter 2, St Hilda's was founded in 1889 as part of the British Settlement Movement which set up 'colonies of learning and fellowship' in poor urban areas in which working- and middle-class people came together.[7] St Hilda's East was intended to be 'a community of people bound together in the service of the poor' (*St Hilda's East Community Centre* 2010) – a place where 'social problems may be studied and the necessary support given to those prepared to devote themselves to working out reforms amongst women and children' (ibid.). They were to be given help to enable them to 'help themselves' (Beauman 1996: 87).

As St Hilda's East's website acknowledges, the community centre has, 'changed immensely since being established in 1889', and while the founding members 'would still recognise the aims of St Hilda's East today: to combat deprivation and social exclusion through providing education and recreational provision along with social care – activities that enable and empower individuals' (St Hilda's East Community Centre n.d.), they would not recognize the purpose-built, red and black brick building that has housed St Hilda's since 1994. They would also 'be surprised by many of the changes to the surrounding area', the website suggests (ibid.).

Rupert, the centre's director, told me that he felt the estate and the area around Shoreditch and Bethnal Green had 'completely changed' since he first joined St Hilda's in 1987. He started as a community development worker in older people's services and then moved on to campaigning with a pensioners' action group. Rupert continued working with the community centre until 1996. He then came back as director in 2001, a role he continued in until 2020 when he retired. In Rupert's earlier years at the centre, there were still a lot of Bangladeshi families living on the Boundary Estate. He suggested that at that time, it was mainly filled with 'ordinary people' and 'families'. There were also the beginnings of a few 'professionals' moving onto the Boundary.

Since then, a lot of flats had been bought and sold under 'right to buy', or bought and rented out he explained, 'so, there are still Bangladeshi families living on the estate, there are still individuals on lower incomes on the estate, but there are also a lot of professionals and well-off people who might work in the City or something. So, there's a real mixture'.

He also pointed out various buildings in view of St Hilda's that used to be textile and leather factories which are now gone. He told me:

> Now it's completely ... I think gentrified doesn't do justice to the word actually ... it's more than gentrified. It's been completely ... that area's been completely taken over by designer shops ... quite bizarre, very up end, very expensive, aimed-at-tourist clothes shops ... there's a shoe shop, that's actually been there for some years, a designer shoe shop where shoes will set you back at least £250, you know, things like that. So, in terms of the factories and shops that used to exist in the area, a complete sort of cleansing. I'm not sure if you'd call it social cleansing, but some kind of cleansing has taken place which means that in the local area, for the people that are left behind, there are not some of the facilities or the area that was. I'm pretty sure that there are still a hell of a lot of people in the vicinity who are on low incomes.

Tower Hamlets ranks highly on multiple indices of deprivation. It has the highest rate of both child and pensioner poverty in the whole of the UK (Tower Hamlets Council n.d.). In Weavers Ward, where St Hilda's is located, 41.5% of children and 52.4% of older people were in income deprived households at the time of my fieldwork (Tower Hamlets Council 2015). According to Alexander, 'Tower Hamlets has a longstanding association with poverty and social decay' and this is 'strongly linked to its history as a space of immigration and a zone of transition' (2011: 213). Within the Bangladeshi population in Britain, in particular, she notes that there can be significant economic marginalization, with 65% of Bangladeshi families living below the poverty line. Unemployment rates are also considerably higher for people in Britain with Bangladeshi backgrounds compared to white people – four times higher for men and six times higher for women (Alexander 2011: 213).

Over time, the City has encroached on the East End, with offices and city workers moving into the area, while the garment industry, which drew many immigrants there in different periods, has moved further east towards Whitechapel (Eade 2001: 129). As Rupert acknowledged, the area around St Hilda's is seen as a site of rapid gentrification. As well as the city workers who now live there, Shoreditch and surrounding neighbourhoods are also associated with the creative industries and with 'hipsters' as the introduction to this chapter highlighted.

COMMUNITY AND CONVIVIALITY

The proliferation of boutique food and drink businesses (regularly associated with hipsters) is often seen as a significant signal that gentrification has arrived (Hubbard 2016; Joassart-Marcelli et al. 2020). One particularly contentious 'hipster' spot during my fieldwork, which was less than five minutes' walk from St Hilda's East, was the Cereal Killer Café on Brick Lane. This opened in 2014, selling bowls of cereal for three to five pounds. In a TV interview for Channel 4 News, reporter Symeon Brown highlighted some of the objections people felt to such a place by asking if the (white, Irish, bearded) owners thought local residents would be able to afford to eat there. As Brown explained, 'Tower Hamlets is one of the poorest areas in London', a fact that the owner he spoke to was unaware of (Channel 4 2014). Although this process of demographic change and so-called urban renewal has been ongoing since at least the late 1990s (Hubbard 2016), for many current residents, the café became a powerful symbol of the changes happening in the area, and the city more widely. In 2015, the café even became the focus of an anti-gentrification protest by the Anarchist group Class War, which culminated in paint and cornflakes being thrown at the café, while the protesters shouted 'scum' at those inside (Harvey 2015; Hubbard 2016). Such instances, again, highlight how certain structures of feeling, resonant with tension, anger and fragmentation, could coalesce around a figure such as the hipster in austerity Britain.

For Lourdes (British Asian), the original coordinator at St Hilda's food co-op, the fact that there were cafés in the area, such as Cereal Killer and The Boundary 'where local people on low incomes could never afford to go' made a resource such as the food co-op all the more important. As she saw it, with the food co-op everyone involved was:

> part of this evolving sort of thing that happens on a Thursday morning . . . You can just come and chat to your neighbours, different people who live on the estate and just get to know people really that otherwise you wouldn't talk to because now Shoreditch is just very diverse. You've got quite a high income, trendy Shoreditch lot with their beards and then you've got the Bengali community who've been there for a long while . . . and they don't mix. I think London would like to think it's really multicultural, but those communities do not ever mix.

In essence, Lourdes described a form of multiculturalism in which the Bangladeshis and the (often white) Shoreditch hipsters, maintained a 'mosaic model of the multicultural city' in which they led different and separate lives despite their proximity (Rhys-Taylor 2013: 404; see also Wessendorf 2014). Within the 'micro-public' of the food co-op they did mix, however, and as a consequence she felt that this was one of the project's strengths. It was a space of everyday life where 'prosaic negotiations with difference through intimate proximity' took place (see also Amin 2002 on micro-publics; Back and Sinha 2016: 524). In her view this created more meaningful forms of conviviality[8] and community. As she put it, 'a food co-op where you have different people from different classes and backgrounds working together to set the tables, price up the veggies and then in between, chatting about "what are you doing at the weekend?", or "what's this?" That is your community development there'. From Gibson-Graham's (2003: 67) perspective, this is part of capacity building and an ethics of the local, in which 'subjects are made anew through engaging with others' who are different to themselves.

While I was at St Hilda's, the volunteers themselves were often more reflective of the Black, Asian and Minority Ethnic population of the area and of London than they were the white, middle-class hipsters of Shoreditch. Nonetheless, through the activities of the food co-op, people from different backgrounds, age groups, and types of mental or physical ability did come together, chat, and get to know each other, whether volunteering or shopping. As a consequence, this form of conviviality took into account not just ethnic and racial diversity, but a more intersectional range of differences. Inevitably, at times these differences could lead to tensions due to a lack of patience on someone's part, differing methods of communication, lack of knowledge about someone's support needs or, every now and then, inappropriate language or conversations which highlighted difference – an important point to acknowledge as I do not wish to romanticize or overly celebrate these instances of conviviality (Tyler 2017:1891). But in the main, these interactions did seem to work.

Many of the volunteers I spoke to valued the opportunity to mix with and learn from people who were different to themselves (as did I). These interactions were a means of engaging in different forms of affective relations, while also fostering a sense of neighbourliness and connection (Vanke 2024: 189). Working together on the various tasks around the food co-op also created a sense of connection between volunteers, and with customers and members of staff within the centre, which could go beyond the fleetingness of small interactions to produce something more trusting, caring and meaningful for those involved (Tyler 2017: 1904).

MAINTAINING DIVERSITY

Since the Brexit vote, many reports have suggested that racist, xenophobic and Islamophobic hate crimes have risen (Weaver 2018). Within the discourses of both populism and racist, xenophobic or Islamophobic sentiments there can be a sense of nostalgic loss and yearning for a time when Britain is perceived to have been 'better' in terms of living conditions. Within such discourses it is often believed that there was cohesion, and that communities were more racially and ethnically homogenous (Back 2009; Hage 2003: 20–1). Within such a climate, this sense of conviviality, connection and belonging is arguably all the more important.

During my fieldwork, there was a spate of acid attacks in the East End, a proportion of which were directed at Asian Muslims. Although many of these were robberies, some were said to be motivated by Islamophobia. Either way, these attacks caused heightened fears about hate crime among some Bangladeshi Muslims in the area (Lusher 2017). Such incidents not only led to a sense of fear and feelings of otherness, but also had the potential to restrict people's mobility. One Bangladeshi woman stopped coming to volunteer at the food co-op, for example, as she was scared to leave her house after news of the rise in acid attacks. Although Jenny, the coordinator, discussed these issues with others within the community centre to see if there were ways to assist this volunteer or any others who were scared to come to the centre, they struggled to come up with a practical solution.[9]

In relation to diversity, Jenny tried hard to be reflexive about her role as a white woman and the perceived authority figure in a project which often had a majority of Black and Asian volunteers. Racism and intersectionality were topics that she attempted to reflect on in terms of her own work practices and how the food co-op operated. In many ways, this was part of the project's performative work. It was a means of enacting within the food co-op what

Figure 5.1. This Melting Pot is at Boiling Point. Graffiti in Shoreditch East London, 2018 © Celia Plender

Jenny and the centre wished to see more broadly within society. Returning to Alice's words from chapter 2, it was a 'standard of how things can be', which created 'contingency' in the here and now, along with the possibility that things could change (Gibson-Graham 2003: 53). As a consequence, Jenny tried to enforce a zero-tolerance policy towards discrimination of any kind, taking quick and decisive action whenever she witnessed or heard about any form of perceived oppression. In doing so, she attempted to be 'attentive to the forms of division and racism' that can still occur within seemingly diverse environments in which people from different backgrounds were both living and working alongside each other (Back and Sinha 2016: 521).

When an older, white, male customer who often talked in tangents when he came to shop at the food co-op started speaking about 'coloured people', for example, Jenny quickly picked him up on his language suggesting that this was not an appropriate term and that this kind of language would not be tolerated at the food co-op. As Emma (a Black British woman), had just started volunteering that day, Jenny was particularly mindful of ensuring that she felt safe and included at St Hilda's.

Jenny also tried to be attentive to the needs and concerns of those involved with the food co-op as volunteers or customers. She regularly ran surveys and talked to customers to try to ensure that the produce on sale met their needs. Where an item could not be bought from the co-ops' suppliers, such as green bananas and plantain, which some members of the Older People's Project requested, or where the quantity she was required to order from the supplier exceeded the amount the co-op could realistically sell before the produce went bad, she regularly took personal orders and then sought out these items herself in local shops and markets. This dialogue with customers also led to other changes in stock, such as the supply of cans with ring pull lids, which were easier for the customers from the Older People's Project to open.

Due to the mix of people that used St Hilda's, inevitably there could also be frictions within the centre at times. When I interviewed Rupert, for example, he identified the Older People's Project, from which the food co-op had a loyal customer base, as both a success in some ways and in others a site of tension in relation to multicultural conviviality. The majority of the older people who frequented the lunch club were white, English and working class, often born and raised in the East End. There was also a reasonable number of people from the West Indies, many of whom had been resident in the UK since the Windrush era.[10] There was a noticeable absence of Bangladeshi older people, due to the fact that St Hilda's also ran a day centre for Bangladeshi elders on another site (which moved out of the community centre in 2005 when the council invested in a bespoke centre for eldercare targeted at Bangladeshi people, as mentioned in chapter 1). Around half of the staff working with the Older People's Project had Bangladeshi backgrounds, however.

While Rupert acknowledged that this absence of Bangladeshi elders from the Older People's Project was a shame, he still hailed the project a success due to the inter-racial and ethnic (as well as intergenerational) relationships that it fostered. During the time I spent with the older people – either accompanying them to the food co-op and helping them with their shopping, or in the lunch club chatting to them, or doing surveys for the food co-op or Older People's Project – this diversity was not often mentioned. It was, perhaps, treated as commonplace although it was also undoubtedly noticed (Wessendorf 2014). Others embraced diversity, developing strong bonds with the people who looked after them. Doris, a white East Ender in her nineties had a particularly strong connection with Arif, one of the Bangladeshi staff members. She often remarked on their difference in age, ethnicity and gender, deriving both interest and amusement from these dissimilarities. As I spoke to others (whether from Black Caribbean or white British backgrounds), just occasionally less than positive comments would come up about the presence of the Muslim or Asian population in the area.

Within the physical configuration of the room where the Older People's Project was based, race was also a factor, with many of the white, British and Black, West Indian people choosing to sit with people from more similar ethnic backgrounds to their own. All this reflected some of the complexities and contradictions of conviviality and community, nuancing binary portrayals of racial dynamics.

SHARING FOOD, THINGS, SPACE

All of the people I spoke to who had been involved with Fareshares in the late 1980s and early 1990s talked about how the long housing campaign on the Pullens Estate had created a strong sense of community around the area. As Adina recalled:

> There was a fantastic sense of community round here, because all the squatters were being harassed by the council. They were constantly being evicted. And then there was this mass eviction – it was about 1986, I think. Because of this squatters' resistance, the tenants and squatters were really united about saving the Pullens . . . [there was a] really good sense of community.

Elephant and Castle itself was substantially bombed during the Second World War and while the yellow brick tenement buildings that made up the Pullens Estate (which was built around the turn of the twentieth century) survived, many other buildings in the area were destroyed. This led to substantial redevelopment in the 1960s and 1970s, including the first shopping centre in Europe, which was completed in 1965,[11] the tallest residential tower block in London just opposite the shopping centre (Draper House, built 1965),[12] and what was said to be the largest single housing block in Europe (the Aylesbury Estate constructed between 1967 and 1977). The Aylesbury consisted of 2,700 homes, in 60 concrete blocks, all connected by 11 miles of raised pedestrian walkways known as 'streets in the sky' (Beckett 2016; Boughton 2018: 129–30). As all of these superlatives suggest, just as the construction of the Boundary Estate represented an aspirational time for civic architecture and expanding welfare at the turn of the twentieth century, so did the post-war regeneration of Elephant and Castle during the 'Golden Age' of state welfare.

As part of this work, Southwark Council planned to demolish the Pullens (which had been taken into council ownership in the 1970s) in order to construct a large, new council estate in its place. This proposal did not go down well with the estate's tenants, however. Many of them felt a strong sense of community and belonging in the Pullens, and did not want this to be disrupted. Large numbers of tenants were moved on nonetheless, and by 1983, blocks on three streets had been knocked down (mudlark121 2018). In retaliation against the threat of further demolition, the Pullens' tenants mounted a campaign to save and renovate the remaining blocks.

During this period, many of the empty units started to be filled by squatters, which was generally welcomed by the council tenants as the squatters were proactive in maintaining the flats and renovating the plumbing and wiring (Batchelor 2011: 32; mudlark121 2018). In fact, the squatters and tenants became united in their desire to save the Pullens from demolition. After a long campaign coordinated collectively by the two groups (which included the attempted mass eviction of the Pullens' squatters discussed in chapter 1), Southwark finally agreed for both to stay, and started a programme of improvements to the estate. In the long run, many of the squatters were also granted official tenancies (Batchelor 2011: 32–5).[13]

All sorts of events took place to bring people together around the estate to campaign and socialize. People in the area even put on a 'buskers' opera', which was written by Fareshares founder member Adina's boyfriend, to highlight the struggles taking place within the Pullens. There was also a strong sense of connection with Fareshares in the neighbourhood, even from people who did not necessarily shop there. As Martin told me:

> there was this quite unusual sense of community which involved people who were squatters, had been squatters, and people who had been council tenants previously on the Pullens who had refused to leave and then fought to save the estate, and in the early years, twice, the council made quite big efforts to evict [Fareshares]. And among the most vocal of Fareshares' supporters, who really felt aggrieved and 'this is our

> cooperative, this is our thing, you can't touch it!' were people who never used Fareshares, or sort of came in and had a chat sort of thing. And that really struck me that they weren't . . . the food and politics behind it weren't really their thing. But yeah, it really had a sense of ownership about it. 'Hands off our project!'

Long-term Fareshares member Colomba told me that Fareshares was a community 'hub'. She had a sense that the food co-op was an important part of the wider Pullens community – a 'loving, sharing community', as she described it. She recalled, 'volunteers [at Fareshares] were your neighbours and people you knew from the area. People would give each other advice. The Pullens was amazing like that. You couldn't walk anywhere without talking to people'. There was a strong sense of shared affections, and shared resources. She reminisced about how people used to have parties on the roofs of the buildings. As the spaces were undivided, everyone could use them. 'People would often knock on your door – "have you got some sugar, or do you need some oil?"', she told me. 'It was all about sharing. People were sharing food, things, space.' As such, it constituted a form of urban commons that was 'reclaimed, produced, used, and maintained over time through solidarity-based action for the collective' or community (Card 2020: 159).

These people were undoubtedly part of 'a multitude of social networks and narratives of identity and belonging', all of them claimed at different times in different ways by the various members of the area. But the Pullens and the fight for its survival, and by extension Fareshares, provided 'a space in which it was possible . . . for a particular sense of community to emerge' (Crehan 2006: 73). This developed through the 'affective experiences and practices of co-making, co-creation, co-production and helping one another' (Vanke 2024: 63).

As I sat and chatted with Adina and Colomba around the kitchen table of the Pullens flat where Colomba had lived for over two decades, both of them seemed to feel a sense of sadness at the perceived loss of community here. Echoing a classic connection between concepts of community and nostalgia (Creed 2006: 3; Crehan 2006: 73), Adina and Colomba told me how people used to knock on the door, talk to each other face-to-face and make spontaneous arrangements. Few had phones in their homes (especially not the squatters), let alone the newer forms of communication technology that are available to much of the population today. The weakening sense of community that they lamented was framed in relation to these changes to technology as well as lack of time, changing lifestyles (both personally and societally) and changing tenants within the estate and the wider area as a consequence, of 'right to buy' and regeneration. Their words, therefore, demonstrated a residual structure of feeling premised on communitarian values and forms of sociality. This was contrasted with an emergent structure of feeling 'informed by values of neoliberal development', individualism and 'private space' (Vanke 2024: 56).

CRISIS AND 'REGENERATION'

While reminiscing about what it was like to squat in the area in the 1980s, Adina pointed out one of the ironies of London housing today is that 'there were a lot of empty spaces around here. There still are, but you can't get into them – like the fancy new tower bocks owned by Chinese businessmen and Russian oligarchs. All brand new, empty flats, no one lives in them. If you want to live in them, it costs like a million quid'.

Over the last decade or so, the London skyline has changed substantially as slick, new buildings have been erected with the aid of overseas investment – a trend that started soon after the economic crash of 2008 (Sassen 2015). Although an inordinately high number of the super-rich choose to live in London, others merely invest in property there, meaning that there are many 'ghost towers' – luxury blocks of flats bought as investments rather than homes, which are barely occupied. Some have dubbed this kind of construction 'necrotecture' due to the lifeless, empty state of these buildings (Atkinson 2019).

As these buildings have gone up, so too have rental and purchase housing prices in the capital, catalysing the ongoing, UK-wide housing crisis, in which London has been deeply affected (Wilde 2017). This crisis means that many people 'cannot afford their rent and . . . are forced to live in overcrowded or unsuitable conditions' (London City Hall 2017). Home ownership is also out of the question for many Londoners. As Wilde highlights, '[s]ince the early 1980s, a succession of policies has eroded the availability of public housing, removed rights and protections in the private rented sector, aggressively gentrified inner-city boroughs and privileged the interests of developers and speculators over the needs of working-class residents' (2017: 16).

Austerity only worsened the situation, reducing local authority budgets, and implementing caps on housing benefits – the state subsidy that supplements rent for those on low incomes when there is a shortfall (ibid.). One of the starkest consequences of these council cuts was the devastating fire at Grenfell Tower in 2017, a 1970s council-built block in West London. It killed at least 71 people and left many more injured and displaced. Along with inadequate fire safety measures (something that tenants had been raising concerns about for years), it was the consequence of Kensington and Chelsea Council's choice to use highly flammable cladding in a recent refurbishment of the building, as it was cheaper than the fire-resistant kind. Firefighters had never seen a tower block fire escalate so fast or so fiercely.

The tragedy of Grenfell was all the more bitter as Kensington and Chelsea is one of the richest areas in the whole of the UK (Wills 2018). This not only highlighted the extreme disparities between living conditions for people within London, but also 'the deadly inequalities of safety and security that characterize contemporary urban life' (Maddens in Wilde 2017: 16). Grenfell came up often in my fieldsites in the days that followed the fire as we all came to terms with the extent of inequality within the city as well as the fatal consequences of austerity and the housing crisis.

To many of the people I spoke to in Elephant and Castle, the new buildings going up all over the area were towering symbols of affluence in the face of economic inequalities, displacement and changing communities in Southwark and London more broadly. The economic inequalities these blocks represented were on the minds of many of those involved with Fareshares while I was there, and for good reason. In recent years, the Borough of Southwark, where Elephant and Castle is located, has been the 41st most deprived borough in the country (out of 326) and 12th most deprived of the 33 boroughs in London (Southwark Stats n.d.).

Like Tower Hamlets, Elephant (as locals often call it) has also long been a racially and ethnically diverse area. As well as a large number of Black British, African and Caribbean people (around 24.6%) (Krausova 2018: 12), Elephant also has a large Latin American community, which Roman-Velazquez suggests is both the largest and the oldest in the city (2014: 23). Many of the small businesses in and around the area are also owned and run by Black, Asian and Ethnic Minority[14] people. As Elephant was in the middle of another wave of regeneration during my fieldwork, this led to much concern among local residents and activists about local livelihoods and about the maintenance of a racially, ethnically and economically diverse community in the area (Hancox 2018; Roman-Velazquez 2014).

This latest wave of regeneration comprised of a three-billion-pound, 15-year redevelopment programme (Southwark Council 2019), which involved collaborations between Southwark Council and multinational, overseas construction companies such as the Australian firm Lendlease. This was one of the largest schemes of its kind in Europe to date (Sutherland 2008: 4). While I was at Fareshares, many people in the area saw the regeneration as a sign that within the workings of global capitalism and the buoyancy of the British economy, property's role as a commodity was being put above the housing needs of British citizens.

Concerns about regeneration and gentrification led to a range of campaigns and forms of activism within the area: to save the sites earmarked for demolition; to contest the processes of regeneration at work; to fight for higher proportions of social housing to be built within these public–private partnership construction schemes; and to highlight the ways in which they were leading to gentrification in the area. This included protests, and other forms of direct action, both big and small; refusals by tenants to leave their homes on estates set to be demolished; awareness raising walks through the estates; conversations with the press; whole blogs devoted to the gentrification of the area such as Southwark Notes; and much lobbying of the local council by various parties ('35% Campaign' n.d.; 'Latin Elephant' n.d.; 'Walking the Rip-Off' n.d.; Hancox 2018; Hill 2016; see also, for example, Lees and Ferreri 2016; Southwark Notes n.d.). The Infoshop in the same

Figure 5.2. Anti-gentrification poster outside Fareshares, 2017 © Celia Plender

building as Fareshares has been active in various forms of anti-gentrification activism as part of this work, including participating in various walking tours, and hosting visits to Southwark Notes' material in the radical archive they house there. While I was at Fareshares, people would also regularly leave leaflets and posters relating to these issues in the food co-op and other parts of the building.

INCLUSION AND EXCLUSION

Many of the people I worked with at Fareshares had a strong sense of the growing inequalities within the city, and within Elephant and Castle itself. This led to concerns about what kinds of shoppers might be attracted to the food co-op and whether they reflected Fareshares' values or not (both politically and in terms of inclusion). Just as Adam (white, British) raised concerns about Fareshares becoming a novelty for well-heeled incomers to the area (as discussed in chapter 4), I heard other member-volunteers express discomfort at the rising number of visitors to Fareshares who appeared to be more affluent. These were shoppers who were likely to have been drawn to Elephant because of the new housing and new facilities popping up as part of its regeneration. As foods such as avocados and coconut oil, which Fareshares stocked, had become quite trendy in recent years, the concern was that this was an opportunity for these kinds of shoppers to flock in for a bargain. Rather than promoting the forms of community to which the food co-op's motto aspired, there were worries that their interactions at the co-op could also potentially have a more transactional quality.

As for those on lower incomes in the area, there was also a recognition that not everything stocked at Fareshares would be accessible – especially items such as the avocados and coconut oil. Kell (white, British) told me that one of the things they had always appreciated about Fareshares was the 'idea that we provide, or try to provide, vegan organic food that's affordable to people'. They suggested that even with the rising popularity of vegan foods in recent years, many of them still had premium price tags. While they acknowledged that 'people on the dole can't afford to buy much organic vegan food' (as discussed in chapter 2), they suggested that vegan staple foods such as beans, grains and rice were much cheaper at Fareshares and much less packaged. In their own case as a long-term benefit recipient on health grounds they suggested that they could buy items such as walnuts at Fareshares that they would not be able to afford elsewhere. Not that they ate them every day, they added (or could afford to).

Ed (white, British), found the issue of prices at Fareshares particularly troubling as someone who lived frugally due to a combination of personal politics, working-class identity and a low income.[15] Due to his work in advice services, he was also keenly aware of the hardship and financial constraints that some people within the city were facing. He told me that when he had first started at Fareshares, he had compared the prices of various items with similar (i.e. organic or fairly-traded) products at the supermarket out of an interest in accessibility. He had not been pleased with a lot of the results. While many members saw shopping at Fareshares as one of the perks of volunteering there, he generally chose not to. As he explained to me, the co-op already had enough shoppers, so he chose to contribute to the collective in other ways, and get his groceries from cheaper sources such as street markets, and cash and carries.

These questions about inclusion and exclusion mirror classic debates within alternative food network (AFN) literature, in which such schemes are criticized for their elitism (Goodman et al. 2014; Kneafsey et al. 2008) – due to the higher prices which often accompany organic, local, fairly-traded or less industrially produced goods. There have also been calls for more AFNs to attempt to tackle issues of food access or food poverty as well as environmental sustainability, or changes within the global, industrial food system (Caraher and Dowler 2014). Some scholars claim that schemes such as food co-ops and buying clubs have a greater capacity for inclusivity than other forms of AFNs due to factors such as volunteer labour, which keeps mark-ups low (Little, et al., 2010; Renting et al., 2012). Even with a low mark-up, however, some of the organic products at Fareshares could be expensive, even for people who had shopped there before. I remember one occasion when a customer who had recently started shopping at Fareshares due to health-related dietary changes had to put back half of his shopping after tallying up his goods. The organic avocadoes, in particular, went straight back onto the shelf. Instead, he stuck to the cheaper grains and pulses. Nuala (white, Irish), also told me that many of the products that Fareshares sold were out of her price range. There was one whole wall of goods, ranging from organic olive oil to the coconut oil, which felt alien to her due to the price of the items on its shelves. As discussed in the previous chapter, however, it was austerity that had brought her to the food co-op in the first place as other items such as the grains and pulses that Kell mentioned were cheaper. Being able to weigh out exactly how much shoppers wanted was, no doubt, also helpful in managing tight budgets.

THE CREATION OF SAFE SPACE

Zoe, a white Belgian in her twenties, lived round the corner from Fareshares and was studying for a Masters in social sciences when I interviewed her in 2014. She found out about the food co-op after taking a feminist, herbal medicine course with a member of Fareshares who had mentioned the food co-op to the course participants. Zoe started off working on a Wednesday evening, packaging herbs with the same Fareshares member. Later, she also started to attend monthly meetings, sometimes just contributing, but over time also chairing on occasion. Zoe told me that she enjoyed the quiet sociality of three women working together to package herbs. Acknowledging her own privilege, she also explained that she valued the ways in which her involvement with Fareshares created opportunities to interact with people that she might not meet otherwise.

Zoe saw the co-op as diverse in terms of age and class, but less so in terms of race, suggesting that Fareshares was 'pretty white, which is a bit of a problem'. Others also had an awareness that while Fareshares' membership was reasonably ethnically diverse (with members from other parts of Europe, Latin America and Australasia as well as the UK and Ireland), it was majority white with only a limited number of Black, Asian and mixed race members, although customers were more ethnically and racially diverse than the members.

Zoe was not sure why the collective was so white and her uncertainty was echoed by other members, too, although many of them acknowledged Fareshares' whiteness.[16] Founder-member Martin (white, British), suggested that even in the early days, Fareshares was not as diverse as he would have liked it to be, not because their 'efforts at outreach failed', but because they were 'feeble and ill thought out' in his opinion. As a consequence, the project's less diverse environment continued to be reproduced.

As Slocum (2007: 526) points out, whiteness is not uncommon in schemes which attempt to increase access to healthy or organic foods. Although the ideals of healthy food or a healthy environment are not inherently white, 'the objectives, tendencies, strategies, the emphases and absences and the things overlooked in community food make them so'. The spaces themselves can also be socially and culturally coded as white spaces in terms of aesthetics and practices (Guthman 2008: 434). As scholars of whiteness have highlighted, one of its characteristics is its own invisibility, as a 'set of cultural practices that are usually unmarked and un-named' (Frankenberg 1993: 1).[17] Adopting overt anti-racist practices requires considerable, work, reflection and scrutiny of an organization's internal culture and structures however (Slocum 2006: 340), and within this, arguably there needs to be some recognition of the racial structuring of whiteness and its consequences. While many members of Fareshares clearly had an openness to and an interest in racial diversity that suggested a 'cosmopolitan disposition' (Noble 2013: 167), they did not necessarily have a clearly thought out set of reflexive practices or tools to foster and reinforce a more racially inclusive environment.

Capacity was no doubt also a factor in a project which was always inherently precarious, leading people to feel like there was limited time and space to do much more than work on keeping the project going, however much they might want to.

Nonetheless, the food co-op could feel inclusive in other ways. As Zoe explained, 'the bookshop is very Anarchist, we're at the kind of soft, hippy side of that, but because of that people believe in community, believe in inclusiveness . . . maybe they don't always know how to do it necessarily, but they have this initial openness and wanting to commit to treating people with respect'. As Zoe saw it, many within the co-op were 'not living standard lives'. They were often politically aware and conscious of the ways in which these ways of living had radical elements, and she enjoyed being part of such an environment. While she did not feel that Fareshares was 'changing the world' she felt that they were creating different social dynamics. Others also mentioned the fact that they valued Fareshares' non-conformity and the ways in which it reminded them that other ways of life were still possible despite the ways in which alternative spaces and imaginations felt like they were being 'squashed', as one member-volunteer put it (as discussed in the previous chapter).

'I suppose we are a community in a way', Kell, told me, 'full of oddballs, non-conformists and vegans'. As a consequence of this, the notion of safe space was important to Kell's ideal of the kind of workplace, non-business and community that Fareshares was attempting to create. Kell continued, 'I think we enable a safe space for all those people that modern consumer society doesn't allow themselves to be . . . It's a safe space for people who don't conform to not conform'. Kell valued this from both a personal and political perspective as a queer person and an Anarchist. Nuala, who worked on the same shift as Kell, also appreciated the queer-friendly nature of the space, although she speculated that this could potentially be dependent on who was actually running each shift, therefore reflecting shift workers' individual values rather than necessarily being consistent throughout the co-op and its shifts. She was unsure, however, as she had not been there very long and was still getting to know others within the collective.

As Boni (2018: 395) defines it, safe space is a 'comfortable, respectful space that allows freedom of expression of opinions and practices. It relates to a physical place, which people treat as *theirs* and to metaphorical space constructed through social relations'. Like cooperative practices, it is also processual, requiring considerable 'relational work which is put into making and preserving' it (ibid.). This safe space not only attempted to counterpose the kind of consumer culture that Kell referred to, but arguably also the forms of disenfranchisement born of neoliberal capitalism and the traditionalism of rising right-wing populism that were so pervasive during this time.

As Barrett (2010) points out, however, what may feel safe for some, may not always feel safe for others.

CONCLUSIONS

The day after I had my induction at St Hilda's, I was invited back for a visit to a local chocolate shop, which was open to all volunteers at the centre as a way of saying 'thank you' for their work at St Hilda's. The shop was two roads over from the community centre and almost every shop on that street sold 'artisanal' or 'boutique' goods of some kind with prices to match. At the chocolate shop, even the smallest chocolate bar (28 gram) cost four pounds while a 100-gram bar was seven. Many of the volunteers had mixed feelings about the tasters we were offered here, and as we left, I noticed that one piece had been dropped discreetly into a corner of the shop. As many of the volunteers acknowledged, they preferred milk chocolate, and even the milk tasters they tried here were not entirely to their liking.

I often found myself thinking back to this as we tucked into boxes of Cadbury Roses, Celebrations or other more industrially produced milk chocolates to celebrate various occasions, ranging from birthdays and leaving do's to Christmas or Eid celebrations at the end of Ramadan. Each box, which was typically provided by Jenny, would have cost little more than a pound per 100 grams, and they always went down well. As the incident with the Cereal Killer café highlights, trendy food outlets are often seen as the 'harbinger of things to come' in terms of the processes of dispossession and displacement that gentrification can lead to (Alkon et al. 2020: 5). They can also be exclusionary to long-term residents who may not have 'the time, financial resources, and/or cultural capital to enjoy them', as our chocolate shop visit highlighted, despite the chocolate shop's best intentions (Joassart-Marcelli et al. 2020: 36). Food as well as the sites where it is sold and consumed can, therefore, be deeply implicated in processes of boundary-making and exclusion, however inadvertently.

While food projects featuring local, organic and fairly-traded food are often also part of the package of new arrivals in gentrifying areas, in the case of St Hilda's and Fareshares, the co-ops predate these recent processes, catering to a broader demographic. Due to the wider projects in which each food co-op is located and what these represent socially and ideologically (i.e. a community centre and a radical, left-wing collective), they also lack some of the classic social and sensory semiotics of such 'alternative food spaces'. Nonetheless, the gentrification and regeneration of Shoreditch and Elephant and Castle had brought a different demographic into each project during my fieldwork, leading to reflection within the co-ops about who was using them, who they were and should be for, and how each project experienced and understood community.

During periods of rapid political-economic change, specific identity groups can also be thrown into the spotlight. This has the potential to create divisions and antagonisms within local areas, as the example of the Cereal Killer café in Shoreditch highlighted, or within whole nations, as has been seen with the rise of national populism and the so-called culture wars. Imogen Tyler (2015: 506) notes that the figure of the 'middle-class urban hipster' came into usage after the financial crisis of 2008. This was at the same time as the revival of the notion of the benefit scrounger discussed in the previous chapter. Tyler suggests that 'these class figures are pitted against each other, ruthlessly employed to divide people along a vampiric axis of blame for diminishing social resources'. Arguably, political energies can, therefore, become misdirected at other everyday people rather than the architects of austerity and neoliberal housing politics. In the context of Brexit and austerity Britain, race, ethnicity and religion have also been significant factors in these antagonistic divisions.

Back and Sinha (2016: 517) suggest that London, which was once 'an imperial centre', is now 'a key junction or crossroads within the circuit of global neoliberal Capitalism, an exemplar of what Doreen Massey calls the "throwntogetherness" of urban life'. This relates to the ways in which diverse entities (different kinds of people, different foods and temporalities) can gather together to 'foster a particular "here and now"' within a specific space (Anderson 2008: 230). It is, therefore, inevitable that these attempts at community building and conviviality can cause their challenges. 'Places and people are defined not by singularity and coherence but by multiplicity and ambiguity' (Eade 2001: 6).

While such identity-based divisions and antagonisms can work to divide and fragment, in contexts such as St Hilda's and Fareshares, the structures of feeling produced by austerity Britain made notions such as community all the more compelling. For St Hilda's, it was a means of bringing people from different backgrounds together in the face of demographic change and financial challenges. At Fareshares, it offered a space to be different from the political mainstream, where alternative political-economic practices and identities could be embraced and fostered. As such, it was a key component of their everyday politics as a 'counter-space' of care and conviviality (Goldstein 2017; Vanke 2024). Their 'micro-practices' of community making, therefore, represented a form of everyday struggle through 'quiet' kinds of power (Vanke 2024: 174). As much of the literature on conviviality points out, however, it is a skill that must be learned and maintained (see, for example, Passes and Overing 2000; Noble 2013). For conviviality to work well, therefore, it requires considerable work and reflexivity. While this chapter has explored themes of community, diversity and inclusion as they were imagined and enacted within both food co-ops, in the following chapter I turn to the issue of mutual aid and the complex interplay between different logics of aid and exchange as they played out at both food co-ops within the context of growing humanitarian sensibilities around food poverty.

NOTES

1. Spiralizing is a technique whereby vegetables are cut into thin ribbons which are often eaten raw in the place of carbohydrates such as pasta or noodles. Spiralizing has been fashionable in the last few years, especially among health-conscious cooks.
2. Mary was a white, Irish, structural engineer who had recently started volunteering after work as a means of getting to know the area better as she had just moved there.
3. Although high in cultural capital, this is a group which is often associated with creative, entrepreneurial or freelance jobs meaning hipsters' work lives and finances can be more precarious (Hubbard 2016).
4. My exploration of community, here, draws on 'what community *is understood to be* within' my 'research participants paradigms' (Rakopoulos 2017: 151 emphasis original).
5. There has, however, been a presence of people from the Sylhet region of what is now called Bangladesh since the eighteenth century (Dench et al. 2006).
6. It is interesting to note that few, if any, of the 5,719 people evicted from the Old Nichol were able to move into the new estate as the rents were around double that of the slum (Haines 2008; Durlacher 2012). This offers a long view of the ways in which regeneration can impact on communities.
7. While other well-known East End settlement communities, such as Toynbee Hall in Whitechapel and Oxford House in Bethnal Green, were set up by educated men from smart Oxford University colleges, St Hilda's East was founded by a group of women. They were all former pupils of Cheltenham Ladies' College, a smart school for girls aged 11–18 in Gloucestershire, southwest England. The community centre was named St Hilda's East, in reference to St Hilda's Hall and College at the University of Oxford and Cheltenham Ladies' College respectively (Beauman 1996: 86–7; see also Phillips 2010; St Hilda's East Community Centre 2010).
8. A term attributed to Gilroy in relation to multiculture, used to describe 'the processes of cohabitation and interaction that have made multiculture an ordinary feature of social life in Britain's urban areas and in postcolonial cities elsewhere' (Gilroy 2004: xi).
9. Some months after I finished my fieldwork, another incident called 'Punish a Muslim Day', which called on people to launch violent attacks on Muslim people on 3 April 2018 (see Baynes 2018 for details), also stopped many staff members and volunteers from attending the community centre for that day. I heard details of this soon afterwards on a social visit to the centre. It was clear that this had been an upsetting experience.
10. The boat HMT Empire Windrush docked in England in 1948, bringing hundreds of people from the Caribbean to the UK. This landing became emblematic of a wider migration from the West Indies to the UK. People who came over at this time are

often described as 'The Windrush Generation' (see Campbell 2024 for more on the Windrush Generation).

11. In 2020 this was knocked down as part of the redevelopment of the area to be replaced with a mixture of housing, shops, restaurants and other entertainment options as well as a new building for the nearby London College of Communication.
12. Where I lived in the early 2000s.
13. It is worth noting that the Boundary Estate also has connections to significant squatting action in Tower Hamlets. In the 1970s, living conditions for this burgeoning Bangladeshi community were often poor. Multiple families were packed into low-quality, private rental properties and semi-derelict buildings. As a consequence, some Bangladeshi people started to squat. Over time, many chose to join the active squatters' movement in the area to occupy empty buildings including empty council properties, which were numerous. By 1976, the Bengali Housing Action Group (BHAG) had formed to connect the various Bangladeshi squatting groups. It also facilitated the occupation of prospective new squats, and a waiting list of those who needed homes. According to Dench et al. (2006: 46), through this housing activism and campaign work, many within the Bangladeshi community were also developing a better understanding of their rights as British citizens. This work along with the sheer volume of Bangladeshi squatters in the area around Brick Lane eventually put sufficient pressure on the local council and the Greater London Authority to rehouse many of the Bangladeshi squatters into properly maintained homes as official council tenants (Dench et al. 2006: 46–49). These properties included the Boundary Estate (Durlacher 2012).
14. I use the term Black, Asian and Minority Ethnic with the acknowledgement that these are overly large and general categories, which represent people who can have very different experiences, income levels and identities.
15. In fact, he was even the author of a self-published book about living on a budget, which had been stocked at the Infoshop at one point.
16. I regularly asked member-volunteers who the members were and who the customers were, and many noted very quickly that they felt the members were quite white. Kell, however, felt that the situation was a little better than it had been in the past. One of their shiftmates was a person of colour, which may well have factored into this. As with other identity markers, therefore, no doubt different shifts also felt different in relation to race and ethnicity.
17. While I subscribe to Goodman et al.'s (2014) call for more reflexivity in alternative food movements in relation to issues of inclusion and exclusion, I do not include these sensitive issues in an attempt to criticise Fareshares. Instead, I see them as an important component of an exploration of power, structure (which can include 'racial structuring' (Frankenberg 1993: 1)), social practices, and the complexities within these. I also acknowledge that having been a (white, British) member of the collective, I am no less implicated in the reproduction of white space at Fareshares.

REFERENCES

'35% Campaign'. (n.d.). Retrieved 7 January 2024 from http://35percent.org/.

Alexander, Claire. 2011. 'Making Bengali Brick Lane: Claiming and Contesting Space in East London', *The British Journal of Sociology* 62(2): 201–20.

Alkon, Alison Hope et al. 2020. 'Introduction: Development, Displacement, and Dining', in Alison Hope Alkon et al. (eds), *A Recipe for Gentrification: Food, Power, and Resistance in the City*. New York: NYU Press.

Amin, Ash. 2002. 'Ethnicity and the Multicultural City: Living with Diversity', *Environment and Planning A* 34(6): 959–80.

Amit, Vered, and Nigel Rapport. 2002. *The Trouble with Community: Anthropological Reflections on Movement, Identity and Collectivity*. London: Pluto Press.

———. 2012. *Community, Cosmopolitanism and the Problem of Human Commonality*. London: Pluto Press.

Anderson, Ben. 2008. 'For Space (2005): Doreen Massey', in Phil Hubbard et al. (eds), *Key Texts in Human Geography: A Reader Guide* (New edition). Los Angeles: SAGE Publications Ltd, pp. 225–34.

Appadurai, Arjun. 1981. 'Gastro-Politics in Hindu South Asia', *American Ethnologist* 8(3): 494–511.

Atkinson, Rowland. 2019. 'Necrotecture: Lifeless Dwellings and London's Super-Rich', *International Journal of Urban and Regional Research* 43(1): 2–13.

Back, Les. 2009. 'Researching Community and its Moral Projects', *Twenty-First Century Society* 4(2): 201–14.

Back, Les, and Shamser Sinha. 2016. 'Multicultural Conviviality in the Midst of Racism's Ruins', *Journal of Intercultural Studies* 37(5): 517–32.

Barrett, Betty J. 2010. 'Is "Safety" Dangerous? A Critical Examination of the Classroom as Safe Space', *The Canadian Journal for the Scholarship of Teaching and Learning* 1(1).

Batchelor, R. 2011. *The Pullen's Story 1879–2011*. London: Self-published.

Baynes, Chris. 2018, 10 March. 'Terror Police Investigating Letters Calling for "Punish a Muslim Day" Attacks', *The Independent*. Retrieved 7 January 2024 from http://www.independent.co.uk/news/uk/crime/punish-muslim-day-letters-points-islamophobic-hate-crime-counter-terrorism-police-bradford-a8249571.html.

Beauman, Katherine Bentley. 1996. *Women and the Settlement Movement*. London: The Radcliffe Press.

Beckett, Andy. 2016, 13 July. 'The Fall and Rise of the Council Estate', *The Guardian*.

Boni, Zofia. 2018. 'It's Safe: Food as a Way of Expression for Children in Warsaw', *Children's Geographies* 16(4): 393–404.

Boughton, John. 2018. *Municipal Dreams: The Rise and Fall of Council Housing*. London; Brooklyn: Verso.

Bourdieu, Pierre. 2010. *Distinction: A Social Critique of the Judgement of Taste*. London: Routledge.

Campbell, Adina. 2024, June 19. 'Who Were the Windrush Generation and What Is Windrush Day?', *BBC News*. Retrieved 24 November 2024 from https://www.bbc.com/news/uk-43782241.

Caraher, M., and E. Dowler. 2014. 'Food for Poorer People: Conventional and "Alternative" Transgressions', in M. Goodman and C. Sage (eds), *Food Transgressions: Making Sense of Contemporary Food Politics*. Farnham, Surrey: Ashgate, pp. 227–46.

Card, Kenton. 2020. 'Contradictions of Housing Commons: Between Middle-Class and Anarchist Models in Berlin', in Derya Özkan and Güldem Baykal Büyüksaraç (eds), *Commoning the City: Empirical Perspectives on Urban Ecology, Economics and Ethics*. Abingdon: Routledge, pp. 159–76.

Channel 4. 2014, 12 October. '"Stop This Interview" – Cereal Café Dodges Poverty Question', *Channel 4 News*. Retrieved 1 July 2024 from https://www.channel4.com/news/cereal-cafe-opens-in-london-but-can-it-survive.

Clark, Dylan. 2004. 'The Raw and the Rotten: Punk Cuisine', *Ethnology* 43(1): 19–31.

Creed, Gerald W. 2006. 'Reconsidering Community', in Gerald W. Creed (ed.), *The Seductions of Community: Emancipations, Oppressions, Quandaries* (Illustrated edition). Santa Fe: School for Advanced Research Press.

Crehan, Kate. 2006. 'Hunting the Unicorn: Art and Community in East London', in Gerald W. Creed (ed.), *The Seductions of Community: Emancipations, Oppressions, Quandaries* (Illustrated edition). Santa Fe: School for Advanced Research Press.

Cronin, James M. et al. 2014. 'Covert Distinction: How Hipsters Practice Food-Based Resistance Strategies in the Production of Identity', *Consumption Markets & Culture* 17(1): 2–28.

Dench, Geoff et al. 2006. *The New East End: Kinship, Race and Conflict*. London: Profile Books.

Durlacher, Chris. 2012. 'The Secret History of Our Streets Series 1. Arnold Circus.' *BBC Two*, Retrieved 11 July 2023 from https://www.bbc.co.uk/programmes/b01kvkw6.

Eade, John. 2001. *Placing London: From Imperial Capital to Global City*. New York: Berghahn Books.

Frankenberg, Ruth. 1993. *White Women, Race Matters: The Social Construction of Whiteness*. University of Minnesota Press.

Gibson-Graham, J. K. 2003. 'An Ethics of the Local', *Rethinking Marxism* 15(1): 49–74.

Gilroy, Paul. 2004. *After Empire: Melancholia or Convivial Culture? Multiculture or Postcolonial Melancholia by Paul Gilroy*. London: Routledge.

Goldstein, Piotr. 2017. 'Post-Yugoslav Everyday Activism(s): A Different Form of Activist Citizenship?', *Europe-Asia Studies* 69(9): 1455–72.

Goodman, David et al. 2014. *Alternative Food Networks: Knowledge, Practice, and Politics*. Abingdon: Routledge.

Grasseni, Cristina. 2013. *Beyond Alternative Food Networks: Italy's Solidarity Purchase*. London: Bloomsbury Academic.

Guthman, Julie. 2008. 'Bringing Good Food to Others: Investigating the Subjects of Alternative Food Practice', *Cultural Geographies* 15(4): 431–47.

Hage, Ghassan. 2003. *Against Paranoid Nationalism: Searching for Hope in a Shrinking Society*. Annandale, NSW: The Merlin Press Ltd.

Haines, Gary. 2008. 'Boundary of Old Nichol's Vice, Filth & Death', *East London Advertiser*. Retrieved 13 March 2019 from https://www.eastlondonadvertiser.co.uk/news/heritage/boundary-of-old-nichol-s-vice-filth-death-1-666236.

Hancox, Dan. 2018, 3 July. 'Save the Elephant: The Fight to Protect South London's "Anti-Westfield"', *The Guardian*.

Harvey, Will. 2015, 28 September. 'I Was Part of the Cereal Killer Cafe Protest – Here's Why', *The Guardian*.

Hill, Dave. 2016, 7 June. 'Latin Southwark Seeks Its Place in Elephant and Castle's Future', *The Guardian*.

Hubbard, Phil. 2016. 'Hipsters on Our High Streets: Consuming the Gentrification Frontier', *Sociological Research Online* 21(3): 1–6.

Joassart-Marcelli, Pascale et al. 2020. 'The Taste of Gentrification: Difference and Exclusion on San Diego's Urban Food Frontier', in Alison Hope Alkon et al. (eds), *A*

Recipe for Gentrification: Food, Power, and Resistance in the City. New York: NYU Press, pp. 31–53.

Kneafsey, Moya et al. 2008. *Reconnecting Consumers, Producers and Food: Exploring Alternatives*. Oxford; New York: Berg Publishers.

Krausova, Anna. 2018. *Elephant and Castle: Mapping Super-Diversity in the 2011 UK Census* (Working Paper No. 142). Oxford: Centre on Migration, Policy and Society, University of Oxford.

'Latin Elephant'. (n.d.). Retrieved 4 April 2019 from https://latinelephant.org/.

Lees, Loretta, and Mara Ferreri. 2016. 'Resisting Gentrification on Its Final Frontiers: Learning from the Heygate Estate in London (1974–2013)', *Cities*, Special Issue: Resistance to Social Housing Transformation 57: 14–24.

Littler, J. 2011. 'What's Wrong with Ethical Consumption?', in T. Lewis and E. Potter (eds), *Ethical Consumption: A Critical Introduction*. London: Routledge, pp. 27–39.

London Borough of Tower Hamlets. 2007. 'Boundary Estate Conservation Area'.

London City Hall. 2017, 30 August. 'Tackling London's Housing Crisis', *London City Hall*. Retrieved 7 January 2024 from https://www.london.gov.uk//what-we-do/housing-and-land/tackling-londons-housing-crisis.

Lusher, Adam. 2017, 3 July. 'What is the Truth behind Claims East London Muslims Are Being Targeted by Acid Attackers?', *The Independent*. Retrieved 7 January 2024 from http://www.independent.co.uk/news/uk/crime/east-london-acid-attacks-muslim-resham-khan-jameel-muhktar-south-asian-residents-race-hate-crimes-a7821701.html.

Mintz, Sidney W., and Christine M. Du Bois. 2002. 'The Anthropology of Food and Eating', *Annual Review of Anthropology* 31(1): 99–119.

mudlark121. 2018, 6 December. 'Today in London Housing History, 1986: Pullens Estate Squatters Resist Eviction, Walworth', *Past Tense*. Retrieved 7 January 2024 from https://pasttenseblog.wordpress.com/2018/06/10/today-in-london-housing-history-1986-pullens-estate-squatters-resist-eviction-walworth/.

Noble, Greg. 2013. 'Cosmopolitan Habits: The Capacities and Habitats of Intercultural Conviviality', *Body & Society* 19: 162–85.

Passes, Joanna, and Alan Overing (eds). 2000. *The Anthropology of Love and Anger: The Aesthetics of Conviviality in Native Amazonia*. London: Routledge.

Phillips, Anna. 2010. *St. Hilda's East: The Story of a Community*. London: St. Hilda's East Community Centre.

Rakopoulos, Theodoros. 2017. *From Clans to Co-ops: Confiscated Mafia Land in Sicily*, The Human Economy (Vol. 4). Oxford: Berghahn Books.

Rhys-Taylor, Alex. 2013. 'The Essences of Multiculture: A Sensory Exploration of an Inner-City Street Market', *Identities* 20(4): 393–406.

Roman-Velazquez, Patria. 2014. 'Latin Americans in London: Claims over the Identity of Place as Destination', in Ricardo Campos et al. (eds), *Popular and Visual Culture: Design, Circulation and Consumption*. Newcastle upon Tyne: Cambridge Scholars Publishing, pp. 23–40.

Sassen, Saskia. 2015, 24 November. 'Who Owns Our Cities – and Why This Urban Takeover Should Concern Us All', *The Guardian*.

'The Secret History of Our Streets Series 1'. 2012, 7 November. *Arnold Circus*.

Slocum, Rachel. 2006. 'Anti-Racist Practice and the Work of Community Food Organizations', *Antipode* 38(2): 327–49.

———. 2007. 'Whiteness, Space and Alternative Food Practice', *Geoforum* 38(3): 520–33.

Som Castellano, Rebecca L. 2015. 'Alternative Food Networks and Food Provisioning as a Gendered Act', *Agriculture and Human Values* 32(3): 461–74.

Southwark Council. 2019, 15 March. 'Elephant and Castle', *Southwark Council*. Retrieved 7 January 2024 from https://www.southwark.gov.uk/regeneration/elephant-and-castle.

Southwark Notes. (n.d.). 'Southwark Notes – Whose Regeneration?' Retrieved 7 January 2024 from https://southwarknotes.wordpress.com/.

Southwark Stats. (n.d.). 'Southwark: Statistical Databank'. Retrieved 7 January 2024 from https://www.southwarkstats.com/public.php?d=D0002&p=P0002&s=S0018.

St Hilda's East Community Centre. (n.d.). 'History'. Retrieved 1 July 2024 from //sthildas.org.uk/about/history/.

St Hilda's East Community Centre. 2010. *Community Memories Archive*. Retrieved 7 January 2024 from https://sthildas.org.uk/about/archive.

Sutherland, Patrick. 2008. *Home: The Elephant and Castle* (Vol. 1). London: London College of Communication. Retrieved 7 January 2024 from http://ualresearchonline.arts.ac.uk/6173/.

Tower Hamlets Council. 2015. *Deprivation in Tower Hamlets: Analysis of the 2015 Indices of Deprivation Data*. London: Tower Hamlets Council Corporate Strategy and Equality Service.

———. 2018. *Borough Profile 2018: Population*. London: Tower Hamlets Council, p. 13.

———. (n.d.). 'Income, Poverty and Welfare', *Tower Hamlets*. Retrieved 7 January 2024 from https://www.towerhamlets.gov.uk/lgnl/community_and_living/borough_statistics/Income_poverty_and_welfare.aspx.

Tyler, Imogen. 2015. 'Classificatory Struggles: Class, Culture and Inequality in Neoliberal Times', *The Sociological Review* 63(2): 493–511.

Tyler, Katharine. 2017. 'The Suburban Paradox of Conviviality and Racism in Postcolonial Britain'. *Journal of Ethnic and Migration Studies* 43(11): 1890–906.

Vanke, Alexandrina. 2024. *The Urban Life of Workers in Post-Soviet Russia: Engaging in Everyday Struggle*. Manchester: Manchester University Press.

'Walking the Rip-Off'. (n.d.). *Charting the Elephant*. Retrieved 4 April 2019 from http://chartingtheelephant.com/projects/walking-rip-off/.

Weaver, Matthew. 2018, 16 October. 'Hate Crime Surge Linked to Brexit and 2017 Terrorist Attacks', *The Guardian*.

Wessendorf, Susanne. 2014. *Commonplace Diversity: Social Relations in a Super-Diverse Context*. Basingstoke: AIAA.

Wilde, Matt. 2017. 'Embryonic Alternatives Amid London's Housing Crisis', *Anthropology Today* 33(5): 16–9.

Wills, Ella. 2018, 24 May. 'Revealed: The Two London Boroughs with the Highest Disposable Incomes in the UK | London Evening Standard'. Retrieved 7 January 2024 from https://www.standard.co.uk/news/uk/revealed-the-two-london-boroughs-kensington-and-chelsea-and-hammersmith-and-fulham-with-the-highest-a3847921.html.

CHAPTER

6

THE POLITICS OF AID, EXCHANGE AND PRICE

MORAL DILEMMAS

One Saturday afternoon, an East African man came into Fareshares at a quiet moment when no one was in the shop. He explained to Alison and me (both white European),[1] who were working the shift, that he was 'a little bit homeless at the moment' and asked if we could give him any crisps or other food. Alison explained that it was a volunteer-run project and a co-operative, so we could not offer him anything on behalf of the collective. Neither of us had any cash on us, so, unfortunately, we could not buy him anything with our own money either (the co-op was cash only). After he had said 'ok' and left the shop, Alison looked troubled. She was clearly torn between her personal humanitarian[2] desire to help him, and the responsibility of being a collective member to do right by the food co-op. Not only did she feel that we could not make the decision to give away food on behalf of the collective, she was also worried about the impact it could have on Fareshares' finances if it became known as a place that gave out donations, therefore setting a precedent for a charitable form of aid (Graeber 2011: 110–11) which diverged from Fareshares' organizational model.

'He looked very tired', she said, 'I think he must have been homeless for a while'. Shortly afterwards, she went into the back of the building and returned with a 'skip key' for unlocking supermarket bins. She went out onto the street to find him and give him the key. Apparently, he did not want it when she offered though. She told me that it would have felt like an amazing gift to her if she had been offered one when she had just started sourcing food from bins. We both agreed that he may not have felt comfortable with the idea of eating food from bins, however.

Alison explained that when she first arrived in London, she had gone 'skipping' a lot. She was struggling to make ends meet, and it helped her to get by. A friend had shown her how. They often visited supermarket bins, in which, she told me, 'you'd get really good stuff', including whole packs of croissants still in date. 'All just thrown away'. She worked with a crew which made the whole thing feel easier and safer. They also went to markets sometimes. At Borough Market, she recalled, they would each focus on different foods, visiting the traders and the bins to see what was being thrown out. Some traders would be waiting for them as it saved them from having to pack everything up or throw it away. Others were less happy to hand over their produce for free. But the crew would always come back with rich pickings. After some time, Alison's working situation improved and so did her income, which meant she did not need the free food as much as she had. As a consequence, when her crew started to disband, she did not do too much to try to find a new one, or choose to go skipping on her own.

The rest of the shift at Fareshares that Saturday was reasonably quiet. We only served about six customers and took around £180, which included a large pre-order of organic flour and yeast for a new customer who was getting into making his own bread. While the fruit and veg that needed to sell out by that point had done, we still had two loaves of bread left over at closing time. We would usually give these away to others in the building, or take them home, as the food co-op would not be open again until Thursday. On this occasion, we both acknowledged that we should have suggested that the homeless man came back at closing time. Alison looked around the street for him again, but could not find him, so we agreed that we would each take a loaf home unless we saw him again after we had left the shop. Just a few doors down the man said 'hello' to us from one of the Pullens' building's doorways, so we offered him our bread. He seemed happy enough to accept. Alison finally looked satisfied that we had been able to do something to help him without compromising the co-op, its finances or its ideology. As we sat in a local café eating a falafel sandwich each before other food co-op members arrived for the monthly meeting, she acknowledged that it had not been a busy shift, but she felt that we had achieved something that day by being able to offer the homeless man some bread.

Issues of surplus food and charitable giving are always loaded with moral dilemmas and power discrepancies. If a gift should never be refused (Caplan 2017: 17; see also Mauss 2002), then this goes some way to explain

Alison's surprise at the skip key's refusal. Clearly, eating what others throw away also has many different social and cultural connotations though. Skip diving was both a lifestyle choice and practicality for Alison, which sat comfortably within her ideology as an activist, a vegan and a leftist (see Clark 2004 for more about the social value of skipping and left-wing ideology). For a homeless person, eating other people's rubbish could have very different associations, ranging from concerns for safety and legality to feelings of otherness and abjection.

Along with issues of personal and organizational ideologies, or of reciprocity, the story also raises questions about notions of aid within the cooperative model and within Fareshares itself. In this chapter, I explore Fareshares and St Hilda's East's relationship to mutual aid, how each conceptualized and negotiated this in relation to practices of aid and exchange, and the politics of price that these involved. In doing so, I highlight how their organizational models and logics could become disrupted in an era of growing inequalities, in which charitable practices were increasingly being invoked in response to the consequences of austerity, a 'policy dogma' which Rakopoulos (2018: 2) argues 'aims to change social formations and re-evaluate the worth of people's lives'. Through this exploration I show the tensions this could create, and the ways in which these changed the power balance, or performativity of mutual aid orientated practices. At times, these imbalances simply created discomfort for those involved, at others, when differences within and between organizational logics and personal values could feel irreconcilable, they grew stronger, leading to what founder member Martin described as 'awkwardnesses' in the context of unequal needs.

IDEALS OF MUTUALITY

Since the Rochdale Pioneers first came together in 1844 to found a consumer cooperative, the concepts of self-help and mutual aid have been at the heart of the cooperative imaginary and the movements' response to issues of poverty and access to affordable and safe food (as discussed in the Introduction). By pooling their time, resources and efforts, the Pioneers were able to buy food in bulk for the mutual benefit of all the co-op's members, therefore helping themselves and each other. Within this ideology, everyone was perceived as being in need of help, but also able to give it. The interaction between collectivist ideals of self-help and mutual aid configured the relationship and power dynamics between aid givers and receivers very differently to the more common philanthropic and humanitarian practices of the time (Koven 2004; Scheuer 2011). The latter typically reinforced the hierarchy between givers and receivers (Kropotkin 2014: 179).

Mutual aid also contested the class-based stratification at the heart of Victorian charitable giving, whereby middle-class philanthropists decided on the moral worth ('deserving' or 'degenerate') of working-class people as they decided who to give aid to (Skeggs and Loveday 2012: 473). Instead, mutual aid was premised on ideals of solidarity rather than charity (Spade 2020). In Kropotkin's words, this simultaneous role of giving and receiving is a means of bringing 'the individual to consider the rights of every other individual as equal to his own' (Kropotkin 2014: 8). In its ideal form, as Firth suggests (2020: 67), mutual aid 'recomposes social bonds and community rather than reproducing commodified power relations'. As such, she argues that it is a 'highly politicised phenomenon' with prefigurative properties due to the ways in which it links 'non-hierarchical relationships' with a 'structural critique of capitalism'. In the case of food co-ops, this is often interlinked with notions of alternative and solidarity economies (as discussed in the Introduction and chapter 2), which attempt to draw on 'non-market idioms and ideas' relating to moral and social values (Pratt and Luetchford 2013: 10; see also Rakopoulos 2014) rather than the forms of depersonalized self-interest and value calculation that formal market rationality entails (however much these ideal typical forms end up overlapping).

Like the Rochdale Pioneers, Fareshares' form of cooperativism contained elements of self-help and mutual aid, albeit differently configured to the Pioneers in some ways. When Fareshares first set up in the late 1980s, organic, fairly-traded and vegan goods were not easily accessible and often prohibitively expensive. Many of the people who got involved with Fareshares were also on low incomes. By providing more affordable, 'ethical' goods, Fareshares therefore fed the food needs and the ideologies of the local activist and squatter community of which it was a part, while reinforcing a sense of collectivity (Gudeman 2008). As well as serving this group of like-minded people, there was a desire from the very beginning for the project to be a resource for the wider neighbourhood. This was one of the reasons not to have a prescriptive membership model.

Despite the lack of a formal membership policy, the people who shopped at Fareshares were also expected to pull their weight, however, not least by paying for the goods they wanted. As discussed in chapter 2, they were required to bag their own goods and clean up if they spilled the bulk grains and pulses they weighed out. They also added up the price of their own goods, before telling the volunteer-member on shift how much it came to. There was no need to show the items to the person behind the counter and for many years there were very few checks to see if people were paying the correct amount. More recently, however, after a period of particularly bad financial difficulty, 'chits' were introduced for customers to write a list of the items they were buying and their quantities so that there was some form of record for each purchase. These sat on the food co-op's counter during my fieldwork period along with pens and calculators so that shoppers were able to add up their list of items more efficiently. While some volunteers had started to double check these numbers in order to avoid under and over payments caused by human error, others still worked on trust, accepting the figures presented to them by each shopper.

This system served various ideological functions, creating a different sense of connection and solidarity between those selling and buying the food co-op's stock; stock that should be seen as a mutual resource, a commons, just as the space itself was. The shoppers' participation in these transactions reconfigured the relationship between sellers and buyers, along with the conventional Capitalist roles that each performed. This resonates with the values of other alternative food provisioning projects, such as the solidarity purchase groups of Northern Italy that Cristina Grasseni studied in the years following the financial crisis. These, she argues, represent attempts to create 'economies of trust' within some 'sectors' of capitalism in which values such as respect and solidarity 'shift economic practice away from the sole consideration of profit maximization' (2013: 29). All these practices were part of Fareshares' performativity as an alter-Capitalist space. They were intended to create a less consumerist exchange, while also building forms of trust and sociality, which are so fundamental to the practices and values of mutuality (Gudeman 2008; Graeber 2011: 94–102 here described as 'communism'; Pratt and Luetchford 2013: 186–9).

Paper signs and handwritten whiteboard messages around the food co-op also encouraged shoppers to volunteer, highlighting which shifts were currently in need of help. Others asked for stationary, participation in other food co-op activities such as cleaning days or odd jobs like fixing shelves or door hinges. If shoppers could not offer time to volunteer on a regular basis, then contributing to these other resources still fostered forms of 'communal exchange' (Gudeman 2008: 39) along with opportunities for customers to acknowledge their own sense of responsibility to the project, desire for it to keep running and willingness to contribute resources. It also showed an appreciation for the member-volunteers who did show up week after week to keep the doors open. One final means of contributing was through donations. On the counter, there was a pot for people to leave their spare change, which helped with the co-op's running costs, along with a reminder that this was a volunteer-run, non-profit project. While I was at Fareshares, there could be as much as twenty pounds in the donations jar at the end of the day, or as little as a few pennies.

THE POLITICS OF AID

Being open to all raised questions about who benefitted from Fareshares' model of mutuality and who got left out; or to return to Kropotkin's words, whose 'rights' were considered and whose were not. As O'Neill points out, mutuality depends on a 'rough equality of vulnerabilities' (2018: 112), and through its acknowledgement and the mutual support that it engenders, this form of vulnerability has the scope to be resistive (Butler et al. 2016: 1) and performative as a different form of social organization and model of responsibility, aid and community. When the needs of some become significantly greater than others, however, this shatters the illusion of equal needs as it did when the homeless man came into Fareshares. A compulsion to be charitable also disrupts the model by introducing a vision of charitable aid, which 'does nothing to enhance solidarity' (Douglas in Mauss 2002 [1925]: x) or foster mutual ties. As a consequence, these unequal charitable relationships can slip back into forms of paternalism ('liberal' rather than collective care (Ticktin in Woodly et al. 2021)), in which one's own vulnerability is forgotten and replaced instead with perceptions of vulnerability as weakness or passivity which requires more hierarchical forms of support rather than solidarity (Butler et al. 2016).

Many scholars have bemoaned the loss of a perceived 'Golden Age' of twentieth-century welfare in which there was rising employment and wages, with greater social benefits and collective justice. The free-market oriented form of economy that has developed in its place is said to lack a conscience and be tied up with more competitive and calculative practices (see, for example, Bauman 2000; Harvey 2007; see also Muehlebach 2012: 6). Muehlebach, however, suggests that morality has not been lost. Just as it was a fundamental aspect of the liberal market of the Pioneers' era, it also works in 'productive tension' with a neoliberal market order. One of the ways in which this becomes evident is through an emphasis on the role of volunteers in acts of aid and care (2012: 24–6).

Through the processes of responsibilization, it is argued that these volunteers are crafted into ethical, or moral citizens due to this 'orientation towards the common good' (Hyatt 2002; Muehlebach 2012; Ogawa 2010; Paley 2001; Rozakou 2016). Where the state's parameters have changed in relation to how it assesses the legitimacy of need and suffering in terms of the provision of aid (as demonstrated through welfare reform), 'ethical' citizens fill in these spaces, motivated by compassion and moral conviction (Muehlebach 2012; Ticktin 2011).

In the context of austerity, many people have felt compelled to act out of a humanitarian desire to support people who have been most acutely affected by austerity and welfare withdrawal, such as the elderly, the sick, the disabled, or those who find themselves homeless or in need of emergency food. Where other humanitarian issues can feel daunting in size and complexity, those which operate in a 'humanly graspable scale' (Malkki 2015: 9), such as food aid, can feel all the more compelling. Hunger is an issue that people feel they can actually *do* something about by simply giving food or time (Poppendieck 1998). While many of those who give may come from

Figure 6.1. Cream of Food Bank Soup. Subversive artwork commenting on austerity Britain in Shoreditch East London, 2017 © Celia Plender

the middle class (a group that Rozakou (2016) and Muehlebach (2012) identify as a common focus of this form of responsibilization), others may start to donate or volunteer in order to give something back, having previously been recipients of such schemes.

In the UK, the number of emergency food aid schemes has grown exponentially since 2010. From April 2016 to March 2017, for example, the largest food bank organization in the UK, the Trussell Trust Foodbank Network, provided 1,182,000 parcels containing three days of emergency food to adults and children (Trussell Trust 2017). This was up from 61,468 in 2010–11 (Trussell Trust 2012). While the number of food banks and other emergency food schemes has gone up considerably in this period, so too has the number of people turning to them. Food surplus charities, such as FareShare,[3] have also grown considerably, facilitating food provision for thousands of different community groups (FareShare n.d.). The third or voluntary sector, rather than the state, is responsible for much of the work that goes on in relation to emergency food aid.

As for the UK government, during the austerity years it regularly denied any connection between changes in the social security system and increased use of food banks (Dowler 2014: 169). Instead, it suggested that supply created demand, and as Dowler (2014: 160) notes, the practice of charitable food provision not only came to be 'recognized by the state at national and local levels', but also 'endorsed, enshrined and encouraged'.[4]

Much as the community food access schemes of the New Labour era were criticized as sticking plaster solutions, as mentioned in chapter 1 (Dowler and Caraher 2003), food banks are considered even more so (Lambie-Mumford 2017). Ticktin (2011: 19–20) argues that charitable or humanitarian acts, which are performed to relieve the suffering of those in need (in this case the hungry), can end up filling in for more politically driven forms of action that fight for rights or attempt to foment positive structural changes. In doing so, these forms of compassion can become a means of 'doing politics' despite the lack of a political mandate or set agenda. As a consequence, she argues, such acts can end up reinforcing inequalities, however inadvertently.

AWKWARDNESSES

Tensions around inequality and charitable giving had been part of Fareshares from the very beginning as Martin, one of the founder members of Fareshares, recalled:

> I guess it was always one of the regrets and *awkwardnesses* of running a strictly non-profit organization . . . you couldn't give things away. You couldn't say that things were

> free because it was going along with the idea that it's not yours in the first place and you're just paying cost price for what they want. You've got no way of saying 'oh have this for nothing because I know you are in a difficult position'. You could do that personally. You could buy something for someone, which I did, but there wasn't a mechanism for collectively authorizing people to take what they needed when they couldn't afford it, which I didn't like . . . You could give everything away, but you could only do that once because it's effectively the same money coming back week after week, that you were buying the next lot with, and that's the beauty of it, but it only works if it does come back. Yeah, it would be an inherently good thing to do and a grand gesture, but you can only do it once if you give the whole stock away (emphasis added).

Martin's comments reinforce the ideological belief that the co-op and its goods were a form of commons belonging to everyone involved, but also no-one. This non-alignment with the dominant Capitalist narratives about the value of food formed part of Fareshares' performative work by creating spaces for alternative practices and ideals (Vivero-Pol et al. 2019: 2; see also Wright 2010).

Arguably, giving goods away on behalf of the collective could also mean that the food co-op's members were claiming ownership of the goods in question in order to donate them, unless they took the time to seek out consent from all those involved before completing the action. Martin's comments also raised questions about how far Fareshares' vision of community stretched, whose needs it could or should be meeting, and how a model premised on Anarchist ideals, which often include a belief in spontaneous order, can become rigid.

While I was at Fareshares, many of the volunteers were concerned with austerity, inequality and their consequences, as discussed in the previous two chapters. For some, austerity showed the strength of mutual aid, for others its cracks. For example, when I asked Kell about the project's politics, they put the food *co-op* into contrast with the food *bank*. Kell told me, 'you're not giving things to people in a very one-way traffic basis and it's not based on pity or largesse or paternalism or anything else. It's not a hierarchy in that sense', therefore once again invoking the performativity of non-hierarchical practices and an understanding of shared vulnerabilities. Yet, as a long-term benefit recipient, Kell had no illusions about the fact that not everyone would be able to afford the prices at the food co-op, highlighting tensions between Fareshares' ethos in relation to typically more expensive ethical goods and the needs of people on lower incomes in the area as discussed in the previous chapter.

Critiques such as Kell's, which engage with the differences between solidarity and charity are not uncommon in activist circles. In austerity-stricken Greece, for example, Theodossopoulos and his research participants faced a dilemma about the implementation of food bank-style aid schemes in response to the crisis. Some suggested, on Marxists grounds, that these reinforced the status quo rather than challenging it. Others argued that 'you cannot stay passive and do nothing' in times of crisis, believing that such political arguments are 'an excuse for inaction' (2016: 176).

For some at Fareshares, volunteering there was also seen as a means of doing something by improving access to more affordable, healthy and 'ethical' food in an area that was still diverse in terms of income levels, race and ethnicity. Nonetheless, they were also aware that beyond the bulk sacks of wholegrains, many of the goods stocked in the food co-op would be inaccessible to people on very low incomes. In informal conversations, some raised questions about how the co-op was, could and should be serving the local community (a 'community' that sometimes seemed to be imagined as less well off than the members who aired these concerns). Yet these issues never seemed to be raised at the monthly meetings. Indeterminacies such as this persisted throughout my time at Fareshares with no one coming to any firm conclusions about how they could be resolved. Instead, the time and headspace of many volunteer-members was taken up with the already challenging job of keeping a non-hierarchical, non-profit project running while managing busy lives and personal precarities.

In the moments when members were forced to face the awkwardnesses that disparities of need created, however, solutions had to be found. In such instances, members often turned to individualized, 'piecemeal fixes' (Forbess 2022; see also Bear 2014) rather than longer-term solutions. While Alison turned to surplus food during our encounter with the homeless man, a strategy that sat comfortably within her own values and did nothing to undermine the co-op's finances or logics in relation to exchange, others found different workarounds. In the early days of my fieldwork, for example, I discussed the active role shoppers played in bagging and tallying their own goods and the trust that this necessitated with Ava. She told me that there was one regular shopper who she and her shiftmates were sure was stealing from the shop. They chose to turn a blind eye, however, as they were aware that the shopper was struggling financially. While this approach avoided the discomfort of confrontation, and the vivification of ideological conflict between a humanitarian compulsion to help and an organizational ethos that sat apart from charitable aid, it was clearly not ideal for the food co-op's finances.

Martin also found his own solutions to these organizational dilemmas during his time at Fareshares. He explained:

> It's the back side of the coin of not being able to turn people away or restrict what they buy because you have a strong suspicion that they're really well-heeled in the same way that you can't really let people who you have a strong suspicion are having a relatively hard time of it economically take things for nothing or half price . . . the way to

> do that is to make it clear that you are buying it for them. You are personally sustaining the loss, it's not the project.

In moments of encounter, which rendered these inequities and the accompanying awkwardnesses more acute, switching hats between collective member and individual citizen out of a sense of solidarity enabled volunteers to negotiate between the structures of the co-op and their own values. Inevitably, these individualized and piecemeal fixes side-stepped rather than addressed issues of inequality, however, despite a desire for an equitable society and food system. In doing so, they also potentially blurred the boundaries between mutual aid and humanitarianism, and the differing logics of collectivity and individualism, solidarity and charity, and the hierarchies contained in each.

THE NEED FOR A FIXED PRICE

Martin's comments also highlight some of the same practical, financial concerns that Alison raised about the survival and financial sustainability of the co-op's activities, and how this interacted with Martin's personal, moral desire to do good by helping others in greater need than himself. If the principles by which the Rochdale Pioneers operated, now known as the Rochdale Principles, were based on the accrual of financial surplus that could be shared among the co-op's members through a dividend based on purchases (Birchall 1994: 57), and in their contemporary form include support and potential investment in the local community (International Co-operative Alliance n.d.), then the decision to operate as a non-profit project undoubtedly changed the meaning and value of the goods that the food co-op sold, the dynamics of community and the logics of aid at Fareshares. From the very beginning, Fareshares had operated on a basis of non-profit. At first, this meant no mark-up on the goods at all, which was possible as this was a squatted space with very few overheads, as discussed in chapter 1. Over time the mark-up crept up to 10% and then 15% as the food co-op's rent, utility bills and, at times, its deficit, grew.

Despite the project's desire to operate outside of the Capitalist logics of wage labour, private ownership and profit maximization, as Martin's comments highlighted, it was still reliant on capital if it wanted to keep going, and its capital was tied up in its stock. The co-op's goods, therefore, had to have a fixed exchange value in order for the project to be sustainable. While this commensurability enabled value to keep circulating within the food co-op's network (Pratt and Luetchford 2013: 16), it also ran the risk of driving out other, more social and moral values (ibid. 2013: 189). In so doing, it put into tension the relationship between mutual sharing and market commerce, highlighting the dialectical relationship that Gudeman identifies between exchange premised on social ties and forms of community (mutuality) and more impersonal forms of trade (markets), which simultaneously oppose and overlap each other (2008).

Vivero-Pol et al. (2019: 2–3) argue that '[t]he social construction of food as a commodity . . . denies its non-economic attributes', including its status as a human right and an element of culture 'in favour of an exclusive focus on its tradable features'. Doing this works to neglect some of the social features embedded in these goods, as well as the relationships they reinforce, or create. Viewing these foods, instead, as belonging to no one, and to everyone, worked to 'neutralise' their Capitalist qualities (Müller 1991: 25). In the case of Fareshares, protecting the food co-op's capital, and avoiding the hierarchical act of charitable giving, also meant side-stepping rather than addressing issues of inequality despite a desire for an equitable society and food system.

I asked Martin whether there were often situations in which he wished he could give things away. After discussing 'the back side of the coin of not being able to turn people away' and the drawbacks of not being able to offer flexibility in the pricing at Fareshares, he went on to tell me how he saw the ability to give *sales*, rather than *goods*, away as both a freedom and a benefit of a model in which profits are not required and more consumerist models of consumption are not the aim:

> One of the advantages of not having to [make a profit], because no one is trying to make a wage of it, and in the days where there really were no overheads and you could be more absolutist about the whole cost price, there was no profit in selling more. In fact, you were liable to lose more . . . From the early days, we sold Whole Earth baked beans, and quite often Safeway's [supermarket], as it was then, would be doing a loss leader on it. And people would keep an eye out and when they were doing a loss leader, we'd have a sign up saying 'you can get these cheaper in Safeway's'. You would be foolish if you were trying to make money out of it.

There was, therefore, not necessarily a need, or desire to increase sales. The lack of profit motive reinforced the food co-op's credentials as an alternative economic project, emphasizing social ties and values (i.e. mutuality) rather than the logics of formal market rationality (self-interest, profit maximization and so on) (Pratt and Luetchford 2013: 9). You can still hear similar sentiments today about how it is not necessarily a benefit to the project to have more shoppers. These days, such comments are often made on the grounds that there is only so much space to store stock and so many people to volunteer, making this a demand on available resources rather than a means of improving the food co-op or becoming more successful in conventional market terms.

Aside from the awkwardnesses of charitable giving, Martin also highlighted how Fareshares' model of mutuality could become disrupted by differing perceptions of the value of the goods on sale and their exchange:

> Sometimes, particularly when . . . and this would impinge on the thing about different cultural expectations as well . . . sometimes people would want to haggle over the vegetables or . . . and that was tricky because obviously there is something by that because you have to make decisions about 'oh we've got to get rid of these, they're not going to be so good by tomorrow', but yes, it's awkward when someone says I'll give you 20p for this head of broccoli when you know you've had to pay twice as much for it.

Volunteering at Fareshares often involved negotiating a range of personal ethics along with the dual roles of autonomous volunteer and member of a collective that attempted to work by consensus. Collective members had to demonstrate an ability to use initiative to take the day-to-day decisions a shift required, while also being mindful of the necessity to represent the collective and its interests. Within Fareshares' ideal of mutuality, shoppers also had a role to play, as I have discussed here, and if they did not conform to these ideals of mutuality, this not only destabilized the food co-op's performative power, but could also create discomfort or hostility between volunteers and shoppers. Like Martin, I experienced the discomfort of a customer attempting to haggle, though only once. This occurred on a Saturday shift when I was working alone. At the time, I felt very aware of my dual position as autonomous, decision-making individual and collective member.

While this kind of bargaining was rare in my experience, the most common cause of friction was shoppers who were unaware that this was not an ordinary shop. Responses could range from confusion to frustration, impatience and indignation, even if a volunteer attempted to explain the way things worked, or to help with the weighing scales and calculations. While some people would turn around and leave, deeming the transaction too far from their expectations of a quick purchase, others would get into the swing, enjoying the novelty of this alternative shopping experience. Inevitably, these frictions could lead to discussions of where the projects' practical and ideological boundaries lay. Among some of the more committed co-operators in the project, for example, there was a belief that in an ideal world, all those who shopped at Fareshares should also volunteer in the spirit of mutuality and equality, ensuring that labour itself became one of the cooperative's commons (Akbulut 2020). Interactions between Fareshares' volunteers and shoppers could, indeed, feel uneven, highlighting the necessity of reciprocating gifts (in this case the gift of time and energy) in relatively equal measure if this system of mutuality is to work on fair and even terms (Graeber 2011: 119).

THE VALUE OF GIFTS AND SURPLUS FOOD

St Hilda's also had many features that distinguished it from the classic consumer cooperative model promoted by the Rochdale Pioneers. As discussed in chapter 3, Jenny, the coordinator, and others at the community centre readily acknowledged that St Hilda's weekly food stall was not exactly a 'proper' cooperative as it lacked the membership structures and decision-making practices associated with the model. Instead, it was a project within the broader structure of the community centre (a registered charity). It had its own paid coordinator, who was an employee of the centre (Jenny) who made the bulk of the decisions, but relied heavily on volunteers to keep the project running.

Coming from a workers' co-op background, Jenny still felt a connection to the principles of cooperation and mutual aid, however. She encouraged us to make autonomous decisions about some aspects of the day-to-day running of the food co-op, in order to foster a greater sense of shared time, labour and care among participants. Because of this, most volunteers were aware of their position as both recipients and givers of support, once again creating a porosity between those who give help and those who receive it (Malkki 2015) and therefore a sense of mutuality.

Like Fareshares, St Hilda's was also a non-profit project, although its financial model was premised more on affordability and access than principles of alter-capitalism. Here, too, there was a mark-up that covered the delivery costs from Community Food Enterprise (CFE), their non-organic fruit and vegetable supplier, as well as the cost of any breakages or wastage. Although the project did not make a profit, gifting and discounting seemed to be less of an issue here than at Fareshares. When new volunteers started, they often received items on sale in the food co-op – such as food co-op tote bags and recipe books (as I did). On special occasions or instances of ill health, food co-op volunteers or regular customers might also receive a gift from the stall.

Regular customers sometimes also asked for discounts at St Hilda's. Unlike with Fareshares, however, this did not seem to cause too much discomfort for either party. One Bangladeshi woman, in particular, regularly came at the end of the morning shift for discounted garlic and ginger, while a Bangladeshi man who often came by in the evening with several young children would sometimes buy up all the apples, oranges and other fruit left on the stall at the end of the evening if he could get a good price for them. Jenny explained to me that this meant more fresh fruit and vegetables were getting out into the area, and fresh produce could be bought in by the food co-op the following week, when these goods would otherwise have been discounted anyway.

Issues of charitable feeding also came up at St Hilda's, and they raised various questions about the value of food, food surplus and different forms of aid. While St Hilda's offered aid by providing support to volunteers, and affordable fresh fruit and vegetables to the local neighbourhood, it was also regularly singled out as an aid recipient by a range of actors including its own suppliers, supermarkets and food charities, which donated food surplus to a range of food banks, social cafés, charities and other community food schemes. Although St Hilda's had no intention of becoming a food bank, the food co-op was a project with a focus on access to affordable food, so, such donations could still make sense within its logics. The community centre was also working hard to balance its books, so free produce for the Older People Project's lunch club or other projects in the building, were well received.

At the food co-op itself, it could still cause tensions or 'awkwardnesses' however – to use Martin from Fareshares' term. Again, these awkwardnesses often hinged on visions of community, equal access and inequalities of need. When I first started with St Hilda's, one of their vegetable suppliers, CFE, would regularly bring us food donations, such as tinned soups with short shelf lives or day-old supermarket breads as they had connections with various supermarkets and food surplus charities. These were usually sold at around ten pence per tin or loaf, and always went down well with the customers. Customers from the Older People's Project were particularly enthusiastic as many of them enjoyed soup, soft white bread and a good bargain – and it definitely was a bargain rather than charity from their perspective. Over time, other produce also started to arrive, such as sacks of onions and potatoes. With these, Jenny often gave the chef in the Older People's Project first dibs. The rest was then sold at the food co-op for very low prices, such as twenty-five pence per kilo, making each onion worth one pence or less. This elicited surprise from some of the customers when their goods were weighed up and the prices rung through at the till. From others there was, again, the sense of getting a good bargain.

One week, two large boxes of oversized courgettes arrived with CFE's delivery. As Karim, the driver, was unloading the food co-op's order for the week, he explained to me that CFE had picked them up from a nearby farm as part of a gleaning initiative, whereby leftover crops were collected from commercial farmers if they could not be sold to supermarkets. Some of these were then redistributed to food co-ops, food banks and other community food projects that CFE worked with. After I had relayed this information to Jenny, she started to think about how we should price them, feeling very aware that we had received the giant courgettes for free. In the end she decided that we should let customers decide how much they wanted to pay for them.

On that day, the stall was outside and at the busiest times, Jenny was on the till while another volunteer and I were weighing and bagging goods. At other times we all rotated between the till, the scales and packing the blue plastic shopping bags. While the stall was outside, we always had a little more footfall, and this tended to include some of the more affluent residents of the area discussed in the previous chapter. I noticed that Jenny did not always mention the option to make a donation when pointing the courgettes out to some of our regular customers. Instead, she asked if they wanted a few before placing them in their shopping bag. With those who seemed more affluent, we all tended to mention the donation. This proved awkward for many of the customers as they were unsure how much to give. They were keen to check the numbers with us, even though we did not have a fixed price in mind either. In the end, many opted for around a pound, which, in relation to the general cost of items on the stall, especially the non-organic produce, was a lot of money. In fact, it was around the price of the organic marrows of the same size that we had been selling on the stall.

If the need for a fixed price at Fareshares and the rigidity that this could create was the cause of many awkwardnesses there, here the cause was the deviation from the equivalence of goods and money, which also challenged the equivalence of the people involved with the exchange (Graeber 2011: 108). The introduction of these free foods called into question the nature of the exchange for those told about the option to make a donation – who was in need, who was helping whom, and what constituted a fair price for these goods. While we, as food co-op coordinators and volunteers, were unsure what to charge for something that had been donated to us, those told they could pay what they wanted did not know whether to respond to the offer of oversized courgettes as customers receiving a bargain, service users making the most of what was on offer, or as patrons offering donations to a revenue generating project for the community centre. This uncertainty over the forms of accounting of people and things involved in the exchange (Graeber 2011: 89) led to awkwardnesses for all involved.

The introduction of these goods also created a valuation and differentiation of different customers. While the food co-op had a desire to be inclusive and accessible to all, it also had a clear idea of who its services were tailored towards and a strong awareness of the ways in which the demographics of the area were changing (as discussed in chapters 4 and 5). This was reflected in Jenny's understanding of the customers most in need of the community centre's services, which in this case came in the form of free, over-sized courgettes. As a consequence, she shifted between modalities of exchange (Graeber 2011: 113), each with its own logics and moral principles. Jenny's actions in relation to who to give the courgettes to for free sat within the food co-op's organizational ethos and commitment to its funders around food poverty and access to affordable, fresh fruit and vegetables. Yet they also involved the often 'dominant logics' of service provision in relation to identifying deservingness (Koch and James 2022: 3). This highlights the diverse and at times competing logics by which a project can run, but also the ways in which situations of diverse levels of need can create tensions between these logics. The following week, Jenny decided to drop the donation entirely and just give the vegetables away, which became the standard practice for all donated vegetables from this point onwards.

RECIPROCITY AND REDISTRIBUTION DILEMMAS

During my time at St Hilda's, issues of food surplus and charitable feeding continued to come up, and here, too, they raised various questions about value, reciprocity and responses to disparate levels of need. Sainsbury's was the first supermarket chain to contact the food co-op about taking some of their surplus food.[5] As a food *co-op* as opposed to a food *bank*, St Hilda's attempted to enact forms of collective self-help and community support through access to more affordable fresh fruit and vegetables. It was also a community space where people from different backgrounds could come together and feel included and supported, and a project which offered opportunities to gain work skills. This represented something quite different to food aid. The scheme still fell within the constellation of food insecurity alleviation schemes, however, in terms of the other organizations that were in its network (including surplus food providers), the aims of the scheme itself and the kinds of funding it sought out. As such, Jenny could still see some positives in relation to food surplus donations, how they benefitted the centre and the food co-op's participants. While working through these issues, though, she spoke to the Thursday evening advice worker to get her thoughts on the arrangement, and Lisa seemed to think it could be a good thing provided it was not a resource that people came to rely on. Once again, this could lead the food co-op into different territory in terms of its ethos, and as I will describe here, the food donations were not necessarily all that consistent.

Jenny's first pick up from a large branch of Sainsbury's in Whitechapel provided a bumper selection of tins, bags of grains and other packaged items. Apparently, they had been dealing with another community food scheme up until this point, but as they had not proved particularly reliable recently, there was a backlog of surplus goods. Jenny brought the goods back to the community centre on her bicycle, with a bike trailer that had been gathering dust in the centre's basement for some time. This was stacked high with tins, grains and other (mainly) dried goods. While some items such as baked beans and large sacks of rice went directly to the chef of the Older People's Project's lunch club, others were portioned off for the centre's advice project, which ran at the same time as the food co-op. The rest went onto a table in the food co-op, with a sign that read 'FREE for local community. Please Help yourself' [*sic*]. Many people who shopped at the food co-op did take a tin or two irrespective of their means, and again, they seemed to see this as a perk rather than 'aid' or 'charity' of any kind. Some of the members of the Older People's Project were particularly pleased to get some freebies and even a few who did not shop regularly at the food co-op popped in to see if there was anything they liked the look of on the table. The free table, therefore, acted as a common resource within the community centre, extending its mutual ties through communal sharing (Gudeman 2008), while avoiding any awkwardnesses born of unequal need or access.

As Lambie-Mumford points out, 'participating in the commercial process of shopping defines food experiences in the UK today, and this market-based experience (where people exercise choice and consumer power) is the socially recognized way in which people acquire food for themselves and their families' (2017: 58). St Hilda's food co-op worked within the logics of this socially recognized and acceptable form of food acquisition. Again, this differentiated the food co-op from other food aid schemes such as food banks, in which service users can feel stigmatized or 'othered' by having to accept their own poverty and need for help (ibid. 2017: 57); or prove their 'deservedness' for aid (Cloke et al. 2010: 105), which is as much a common factor in emergency feeding (Lambie-Mumford 2017). In many food banks, service users have little or no choice about what they receive in their food parcels, and this also accentuates the otherness of this means of food acquisition. Implementing a free table at the food co-op helped to avoid these dynamics. As such, the food co-op pushed back against the increasingly dominant model of food aid, which has taken hold in the UK since 2010 by framing the foods it stocked as either goods for sale or perks that anyone visiting the food co-op was entitled to take.

Jenny was very aware of the situations that different volunteers were in, however. As a consequence, volunteers often confided in her about their lives and the issues they were dealing with in relation to anything from benefits to housing, health or family problems. She told me that on occasion, if she knew someone was particularly struggling financially, she had invited them to go into the store cupboard to take what they wanted from the selection of supermarket goods. This meant they did not have to face the stigma of others seeing that they were in need, which could have arisen if Jenny had offered them goods more publicly, or the risk of appearing to take more than their fair share of a common resource if it was on the free table. In doing so, she simultaneously employed two different logics of apportionment

Figure 6.2. Free table at St Hilda's, 2017 © Celia Plender

(Gudeman 2008: 39) – one alluding to universalist values of equal access and the other to the identification of greater need. Finding flexibility within St Hilda's operational model enabled Jenny to employ different redistributive principles 'to achieve objectives that are simultaneously ethical and pragmatic' (Forbess 2022: 43). This fulfilled the project's remit and her own professional and personal desire to support those in need. While Fareshares' members had to switch hats in order to make such gestures, the structures of the project and Jenny's role as coordinator with care and support responsibilities enabled her to give these goods away on behalf of the project, rather than herself. Nonetheless, these acts still represented quick fixes rather than longer-term solutions to the issue of inequality, or the food co-op's ability to address unequal need.

On the next occasion that Jenny went back to the branch in Whitechapel, at an agreed time, the staff seemed surprised to see her and there was nothing for her to take away, aside from some bananas that were so old that she said they were not even good enough to give away. After a few more failed attempts at communication, the relationship fizzled out.[6]

Shortly afterwards, the charity FareShare, which uses surplus food to tackle food poverty and food waste issues, contacted Jenny and facilitated a partnership between the food co-op and another supermarket chain, Tesco. FareShare had designed an app called 'Food Cloud', which connected supermarkets with community projects as part of their Community Food Connections programme (Caplan 2017: 20). This was targeted at projects that worked on issues of food insecurity. This partnership had its issues too, however, as much of what the branch offered to begin with was day-old croissants and doughnuts from their bakery counter. The first time these arrived, they caused some excitement at the community centre as many of the projects (such as the Older People's Project and the crèche) had a nice selection of mid-morning snacks. The food co-op also had a pile on the table in the tea and coffee area. After a couple of weeks, the novelty wore off, however, giving way to questions about health and the value of such items to the food co-op and the centre. 'We don't have any say whatsoever in what we're given', Jenny explained. 'We can choose not to take it. That's our choice really, but the other stuff has to be negotiated, which has taken a little while to do.' To begin with, Jenny felt uncomfortable being picky about what the supermarket was giving her, again highlighting some of the social discomfort that can arise when a gift is rejected. As Jenny explained, 'you know, it's a donation, so we appreciate the donation. But we are also conscious of the health of the community'. While she generally believed in balance rather than abstinence when it came to a healthy diet (with plenty of healthy fruit and vegetables in there, of course), she was worried that all these bakery goods would tip the scales in the wrong direction. 'We were going to end up passing on a lot of sugar', she explained. After talking to the local branch about this a few times, they started offering more fruit and vegetables, which went straight into the Older People's Project kitchen. Requests for tins were less successful, as the supermarket branch was also working with other partners, and Jenny suspected some of these, such as local food banks, might have been 'a better fit' for the scheme.

CONCLUSIONS

Political-economic change has long been a catalyst for food cooperative activities, and at the heart of these practices is the desire to build some form of supportive community, while making food more affordable and accessible to selves and others. The models that food co-ops adhere to and their relationship to self-help, mutuality, aid and price can vary substantially, however, depending on their institutional ethos, practices and the values of those involved.

At both Fareshares and St Hilda's, the dynamic between a desire for equal access to all, the meaning and value attached to the goods in each non-profit project and the flexibility of the organizational model in relation to price and need all contributed to the creation and avoidance of tensions generated by different values and expectations around an exchange, and deeper awkwardnesses born of inequalities of need, which drew organizational and personal values and practices into tension.

At Fareshares and St Hilda's East, food is perceived as something other than a simple commodity. Instead, it is the social medium around which the complex organizational ethos of each food co-op is enacted. Yet the price and exchange value assigned to food and the ways in which others interact with a food co-ops' goods can still impact on its social values and its effectiveness at representing the food co-op's ethos. At Fareshares, the social and ideological values of the collective determined the exchange value of the food itself. To deviate from a fixed price risked destabilizing the aspects of the food co-op's performative work as an anti-Capitalist project premised on mutual aid, while also having the potential to impact on its financial sustainability. But, by sticking closely to this model, some people's needs were recognized more, while others were excluded. This was an awareness that sat particularly uncomfortably in moments of encounter when such disparities had to be addressed, therefore leading to 'piecemeal fixes' (Forbess 2022). At St Hilda's the arrival of surplus food also challenged the project's organizational practices while raising questions about the appropriate financial value and apportionment of the goods themselves. Again, this caused tensions between notions of equity based in exchange and an organizational ethos and project funding which targeted people on lower incomes. The value attached to the items and who they were made available to, therefore, had to be considered carefully.

As Goodman et al. (2014: 30) argue, the practices of local food initiatives are still 'messy, and bound up in imperfect politics' even if they attempt to work reflexively, acknowledging the 'imperfection of their actions' while pursuing their goals, and this is clearly borne out in these moments of exchange as different values and visions of aid interact with each other. In contexts of austerity, where needs and access to basic necessities can become all the more unequal, there is much space for the kinds of tensions and awkwardnesses elaborated here. As grassroots projects and third sector organizations come to fill in the gaps left by the withdrawal of welfare, the personal attitudes and values of those in key positions can 'make a mark on the ways the organizations are structured and function' (Vargas-Cetina 2005: 230). Many within such organizations have deeply held beliefs about equality and inclusion (Koch and James 2022: 12), yet they find themselves navigating situations and structures which make it hard to find ideal solutions to issues of mutuality and increasing inequality. Within the distribution of (often limited) resources, ranging from food, to housing, advice, care or other forms of aid and support, grassroots and third sector organizations are forced to negotiate between the immediacy of need and complex and, at times, contradictory organizational models and personal values (see for e.g. Forbess 2022; Garza 2022; Koch and James 2022; Theodossopoulos 2016). Inevitably, it can be difficult to find a 'moral balance' between these competing values, logics and needs (Garza 2022: 118), therefore leading to blurred boundaries between different forms of aid (Rozakou 2017), and the values and hierarchies inherent within them. Such situations can, therefore, produce more 'ambivalent' forms of politics, which are 'inevitably entangled with the shifting structures and atmospheres of welfare provision' (Jupp 2022: 36). While this chapter has explored the tensions, or awkwardnesses between issues of access, aid and exchange and the complex politics within this, in the Conclusion, I return to the question of what constitutes the (everyday) politics of food co-ops.

NOTES

1. I choose to give details of identity markers here to signify the potential cultural as well as ethnic and racial difference between Alison and me, and the homeless man. As the subjects of humanitarian aid are often imagined as people of colour in distant countries by aid givers in the Global North (Malkki 2015: 7), arguably this adds a resonance and potential power dynamic to the situation. I am unsure exactly which country the man was from. Having worked with people from Somalia and Ethiopia before, though, I made this assumption based on his accent.
2. In the sense of a moral desire to alleviate human suffering (Malkki 2015).
3. Anecdotally, Martin Oddsocks told me that one of the founders of the food surplus charity FareShare used to volunteer at Fareshares, and that this is where they got the name from. According to Martin, FareShare even used a similar font and design to Fareshares when it first started. When I asked him what he thought about all this, he did not seem too bothered, suggesting that the name might be more appropriate to a food sharing scheme such as theirs anyway.

4. At the start of 2019, however, the work and pensions secretary, Amber Rudd, acknowledged that there was a connection between the roll out of Universal Credit (a catch-all benefit which is replacing others such as housing benefit, income support and child tax credits) and the rise in food bank use in the UK (BBC 2019).
5. A common supermarket corporate social responsibility strategy in the UK.
6. Jenny concluded that it seemed as if Sainsbury's might be in the process of putting a new system for dealing with their surplus in place, which meant that the relationship with St Hilda's had got a little lost along the way.

REFERENCES

Akbulut, Bengi. 2020. 'Cooperative Economies as Commons', in Derya Özkan and Güldem Baykal Büyüksaraç (eds), *Commoning the City: Empirical Perspectives on Urban Ecology, Economics and Ethics*. London: Routledge, pp. 193–206.

Bauman, Z. 2000. 'Special Essay. Am I My Brother's Keeper?', *European Journal of Social Work* 5–11.

BBC. 2019, 11 February. 'Rudd Links Food Bank Rise to Benefit Mess', *BBC*.

Bear, Laura. 2014. '3 For Labour: Ajeet's Accident and the Ethics of Technological Fixes in Time', *Journal of the Royal Anthropological Institute* 20(S1): 71–88.

Birchall, Johnston. 1994. *Co-op: The People's Business*. Manchester: Manchester University Press.

Brindle, David. 2015, 1 June. 'A History of the Volunteer: How Active Citizenship Became the Big Society', *The Guardian*.

Butler, Judith et al. (eds). 2016. *Vulnerability in Resistance*. Durham, NC: Duke University Press.

Caplan, Pat. 2017. 'Win-Win? Food Poverty, Food Aid and Food Surplus in the UK Today', *Anthropology Today* 33(3): 17–22.

Carenotes Collective (ed.). 2020. *For Health Autonomy: Horizons of Care Beyond Austerity – Reflections from Greece*. Brooklyn: Common Notions.

Clark, Dylan. 2004. 'The Raw and the Rotten: Punk Cuisine', *Ethnology* 43(1): 19–31.

Cloke, Paul J. et al. 2010. *Swept up Lives? Re-Envisioning the Homeless City*, RGS-IBG Book Series. Chichester: Wiley-Blackwell.

Dowler, Elizabeth. 2014. 'Food Banks and Food Justice in "Austerity Britain"', in Graham Riches and Tiina Silvasti (eds), *First World Hunger Revisited – Food Charity or the Right to Food?* Palgrave Macmillan, pp. 160–75.

Dowler, E., and M. Caraher. 2003. 'Local Food Projects: The New Philanthropy?', *The Political Quarterly* 74: 57–65.

FareShare. (n.d.). 'What We Do – Fighting Hunger and Food Waste', *FareShare*. Retrieved 7 January 2024 from https://fareshare.org.uk/what-we-do/.

Forbess, Alice. 2022. 'Redistribution Dilemmas and Ethical Commitments: Advisers in Austerity Britain's Local Welfare State', *Ethnos* 87(1): 42–58.

Garza, Ana P. Gutiérrez. 2022. '"Te Lo Tienes Que Currar": Enacting an Ethics of Care in Times of Austerity', *Ethnos* 87(1): 116–132.

Goodman, David et al. 2014. *Alternative Food Networks: Knowledge, Practice, and Politics*. Abingdon: Routledge.

Graeber, David. 2011. *Debt: The First 5,000 Years*. New York: Melville House Printing.

Grasseni, Cristina. 2013. *Beyond Alternative Food Networks: Italy's Solidarity Purchase*. London: Bloomsbury Academic.

Gudeman, Stephen. 2008. *Economy's Tension: The Dialectics of Community and Market* (NED-New edition). New York: Berghahn Books.

Harvey, David. 2007. *A Brief History of Neoliberalism* (New edition). Oxford: Oxford University Press, USA.

Hyatt, Susan Brin. 2002. 'From Citizen to Volunteer: Neoliberal Governance and the Erasure of Poverty', in Judith G. Goode and Jeff Maskovsky (eds), *The New Poverty Studies: The Ethnography of Power, Politics and Impoverished People in the United States*. New York: NYU Press, pp. 201–35.

International Co-operative Alliance. (n.d.). 'Cooperative Identity, Values & Principles | ICA', *International Co-operative Alliance*. Retrieved 4 March 2021 from https://www.ica.coop/en/cooperatives/cooperative-identity.

Jupp, Eleanor. 2022. *Care, Crisis and Activism: The Politics of Everyday Life*. Bristol: Policy Press.

Kenny, Tara, and Colin Sage. 2018. 'Food Surplus as Charitable Provision: Obstacles to Re-Introducing Food as a Commons', *Routledge Handbook of Food as a Commons*. Abingdon, Oxon; New York: Routledge.

Koch, Insa, and Deborah James. 2022. 'The State of the Welfare State: Advice, Governance and Care in Settings of Austerity', *Ethnos* 87(1): 1–21.

Koven, Seth. 2004. *Slumming: Sexual and Social Politics in Victorian London*. Princeton: Princeton University Press.

Kropotkin, Peter. 2014. *Mutual Aid: A Factor in Evolution* (W. Jonson, ed.). Charlestown, SC: CreateSpace Independent Publishing Platform.

Lambie-Mumford, Hannah. 2017. *Hungry Britain – The Rise of Food Charity*. Bristol: Policy Press.

Malkki, Liisa. 2015. *The Need to Help: The Domestic Arts of International Humanitarianism*. Durham, NC: Duke University Press.

Mauss, Marcel. 2002 [1925]. *The Gift: Forms and Functions of Exchange in Archaic Societies*. London; New York: Routledge.

Muehlebach, Andrea. 2012. *The Moral Neoliberal: Welfare and Citizenship in Italy*. Chicago: University of Chicago Press.

Müller, Birgit. 1991. *Toward an Alternative Culture of Work: Political Idealism and Economic Practices in West Berlin Collective Enterprises*. Boulder: Westview Press.

Ogawa, Akihiro. 2010. *The Failure of Civil Society? The Third Sector and the State in Contemporary Japan*. Albany, NY; Bristol: State University of New York Press.

O'Neill, John. 2018. 'Food, Needs and Commons', in Jose Luis Vivero-Pol et al. (eds), *Routledge Handbook of Food as a Commons*. Abingdon, Oxon; New York, NY: Routledge, pp. 103–20.

Paley, Julia. 2001. 'The Paradox of Participation: Civil Society and Democracy in Chile', *PoLAR: Political and Legal Anthropology Review* 24(1): 1–12.

Poppendieck, Janet. 1998. 'Want Amid Plenty', *Monthly Review* 125–36.

Pratt, Jeff, and Pete Luetchford. 2013. *Food for Change: The Politics and Values of Social Movements*. London: Pluto Press.

Firth, Rhiannon. 2020. 'Mutual Aid, Anarchist Preparedness and COVID-19', in John Preston and Rhiannon Firth (eds), *Coronavirus, Class and Mutual Aid in the United Kingdom*. Basingstoke: Palgrave Macmillan, pp. 57–112.

Rakopoulos, Theodoros. 2014. 'The Crisis Seen from Below, Within, and Against: From Solidarity Economy to Food Distribution Cooperatives in Greece', *Dialectical Anthropology* 38(2): 189–207.

———. 2018. 'Introduction: Austerity, Measured', in Theodoros Rakopoulos (ed.), *Global Life of Austerity: Comparing Beyond Europe: 17*. New York: Berghahn Books, pp. 1–16.

Rozakou, Katerina. 2016. 'Crafting the Volunteer: Voluntary Associations and the Reformation of Sociality', *Journal of Modern Greek Studies* 34(1): 79–102.

———. 2017. 'Solidarity #Humanitarianism: The Blurred Boundaries of Humanitarianism in Greece', *Etnofoor* 29(2): 99–104.

Scheuer, Jeffrey. 2011, 19 January. 'Origins of the Settlement House Movement', *Social Welfare History Project*. Retrieved 1 January 2024 from https://socialwelfare.library.vcu.edu/settlement-houses/origins-of-the-settlement-house-movement/.

Skeggs, Beverley, and Vik Loveday. 2012. 'Struggles for Value: Value Practices, Injustice, Judgment, Affect and the Idea of Class', *The British Journal of Sociology* 63(3): 472–90.

Spade, Dean. 2020. *Mutual Aid: Building Solidarity During This Crisis*. London: Verso.

Theodossopoulos, Dimitrios. 2016. 'Philanthropy or Solidarity? Ethical Dilemmas About Humanitarianism in Crisis-Afflicted Greece', *Social Anthropology* 24(2): 167–84.

Ticktin, Miriam. 2011. *Casualties of Care: Immigration and the Politics of Humanitarianism in France*. Berkeley: University of California Press.

Trussell Trust. 2012, 26 April. 'UK Foodbanks Double Numbers Fed in One Year', *The Trussell Trust*.

———. 2017, 25 April. 'UK Foodbank Use Continues to Rise', *The Trussell Trust*. Retrieved 1 January 2024 from https://www.trusselltrust.org/2017/04/25/uk-foodbank-use-continues-rise/.

Vargas-Cetina, Gabriela. 2005. 'Anthropology and Cooperatives: From the Community Paradigm to the Ephemeral Association in Chiapas, Mexico', *Critique of Anthropology* 25(3): 229–51.

Vivero-Pol, Jose Luis et al. (eds). 2019. *Routledge Handbook of Food as a Commons*, Routledge Handbooks. Abingdon, Oxon; New York: Routledge.

Woodly, Deva et al. 2021. 'The Politics of Care', *Contemporary Political Theory* 20(4): 890–925.

Wright, Erik Olin. 2010. *Envisioning Real Utopias*. London; New York: Verso.

CONCLUSION

THE EVERYDAY POLITICS OF FOOD CO-OPS

SENSING THE POLITICAL

Since the Rochdale Pioneers opened their cooperative society in 1844, the cooperative model has captured many imaginations – including those of anthropologists. As Nash and Hopkins (1976: 4) tell us:

> Cooperative forms of organization are interesting for anthropology precisely because they are interesting for those who live them; they are relevant to a theoretical anthropology precisely because they are conceived in order to be lived. It is this element of willful [*sic*] control of one's own social forms that makes movements toward cooperative forms of organization an essential part both of the human experience and of anthropology's field of study.

By examining the imaginary of two food-focused cooperatives in contemporary Britain, I have highlighted the ways in which this idea still captures people's imaginations today in response to a range of different needs, concerns and vulnerabilities. By exploring the social worlds of St Hilda's East and Fareshares, I have attempted to show the complexities and contradictions at play within the model and its enactment. As I have argued, cooperatives are shaped as much by their histories and contexts as they are by their participants and the present moment. These contexts do much to inform their relationship to concepts of autonomy, ownership and authority, as well as their negotiations of politics, aid and care.

Throughout my fieldwork, I often found myself thinking back to my encounter with Brian, who left Fareshares out of disappointment with its politics. This made me ask myself what 'the political' looks like, how it sounds and feels. I therefore regularly asked people whether Fareshares was political and if so, how. Despite the ambivalences documented in this book, Fareshares did still *feel* political to most of the members I spoke to. Not all of them were able to fully articulate what constituted its political content beyond its radical history and Anarchist roots. Nonetheless, many members shared 'convictions and ideas that are in opposition to the principles of the dominant Capitalist society' (Müller 1991: 25) in some ways. This, and in most cases, the food politics that the co-op practised, were where they saw political potentiality. Like many food co-ops that have come before, then, Fareshares attempted to be a counterculture to capitalism in some ways, reimagining in practice the aspiration of less alienated forms of work, sociality, care and consumption. In doing so, the food co-op's members tried to 'rethink the elusively simple act of provisioning on different economic, moral, and social premises'. '[S]hared practices and discourse about the economy' within such spaces 'at once constrain and enable collective deliberation and political imagination' (Grasseni 2013: 174). At St Hilda's too, while its members were less articulate about the political content of the project, their understanding of the project still opened up capacities to image something other than mainstream food and economic systems, therefore developing capacities to imagine other possibilities (Gibson-Graham 2003).

So, what is a food cooperative from this perspective? Rather than a total social institution, in which those involved are cut off from the wider society, its logics, values or impacts, or straightforward businesses, it acts as a 'counter-space' (Goldstein 2017) in which it is possible to step back and reflect on aspects of how things are and how they could be. From Gibson-Graham's perspective (2003: 54) such projects function as part of an 'imaginative infrastructure', which can be used to cultivate alternative subjects and practices. For Federici, the commons itself is a 'way of organizing society', of conceiving relationships between people, production and resources along more collective and cooperative lines, and it is something that needs to be reproduced in our everyday lives to build capacity for struggle and for transformation (Federici in Carenotes Collective 2020: ix–xvi). Food co-ops, therefore, have the capacity to open up spaces of hope, possibility and imagination, as well as encountering obstacles and dilemmas (Wright 2010).

While the practices in both food co-ops attempt to think beyond capitalism in some ways, inevitably many of them are still embedded within the structures and common sense of capitalism. As Anna Tsing puts it, '[c]ontemporary commerce works within the constraints and possibilities of capitalism (Tsing 2015: 5). Equally, capitalism itself now has 'a decidedly moralized face; a moral neoliberal that exists as a correlate to its market counterpart' (Muehlebach 2012: 50). Fair Trade mechanisms and forms of ethical consumption are clearly intertwined with this more moral form of capitalism. By caring through food for people, the environment or the economy, arguably, shoppers enacted the forms of ethical citizenship that Muehlebach (2012) identifies with the moral neoliberal. Rather than succumb to 'a kind of critical melancholy' (Land and King 2014: 924 after Gibson-Graham 2006), however, if we read these activities within Fareshares' and St Hilda's own terms, or indeed, those of the cooperative more generally, they still leave space for performativity.

Gibson-Graham suggest that to study and work with alternative economic practices is a 'performative ontological project', which helps to make 'diverse economies' more '"real", more credible, more viable as objects of policy and activism, more present as everyday realities that touch all our lives and dynamically shape our futures' (Gibson-Graham 2008: 618). This reading also contests understandings of capitalism as constant unwavering progress, showing ways in which it can be more patchy (Tsing 2015: 5), meaning alternatives are more possible (Gibson-Graham 2006).

Building on Sedgwick, Gibson-Graham suggest that such activities are often dismissed by 'strong' theory as 'capitalism in another guise or as always already coopted'. This shows, they argue, that we need to adopt a different orientation towards theory, which moves away from critique to think about how 'to energize and support "other economies"', therefore opening up space for their becoming rather than closing it down (Gibson-Graham 2008: 618).

I argue that the same can be said for everyday politics more broadly. How can those of us interested in everyday forms of political action energize and support these activities through our research by thinking and theorizing in different ways? In doing so, can we expand their capacities and make their transformative potential more credible despite some of the complexities and inconsistencies of the kinds of politics described in this monograph (Gibson-Graham 2008: 618–20)? Perhaps this can help us to take more seriously the resonance of some of the quieter, more subtle forms of political action taking place within these spaces, which can be deeply meaningful and transformative for those involved in terms of their everyday lives and imaginations.

EVERYDAY PEOPLE AND ORDINARY LIVES

In 2020, I went back to St Hilda's to volunteer with a shopping service set up by the food co-op to support vulnerable people who were not able to leave their homes due to Covid-19. The 'shop and drop' had a similar organizational logic to the food co-op. Jenny coordinated it, but there was also a core team of volunteers who helped with the orders, shopping, bag packing and deliveries. In an interview I conducted with Jenny during this period, she told me:

> Politics is about change and transformation of power, isn't it? I don't know how much the things we do as people within a community ... how much that changes things from the top. But I think it's important for all of us at the bottom ... it's about the everyday and just supporting people to live ordinary lives, which should be everybody's right.

Jenny felt that not everyone was given that right in contemporary Britain due to the structures of power within the country and the impact of years of neoliberal policy reform, which had been further compounded by austerity cuts and now the pandemic. She went on to tell me, 'it's definitely felt like the state and the people with power ... do not value a lot of us basically ... some people are left behind, they're forgotten. Getting someone's shopping is very small', she continued, 'it's like a thimble in a giant swimming pool towards addressing that, but it kind of feels like the whole interaction that goes with it, hopefully changes some of that for people'.

As Koch (2017: 108) experienced with her research participants on a post-industrial English council estate, Jenny defines politicians through their 'lack of loyalty and care' for those on the margins. The politicians' stance, therefore, stands outside of Jenny's and the food co-op's values in relation to local sociality, solidarity and caring practices. As such, her comments provide an 'interpretive framework' related to 'person value', context and care by which politicians and the state should be judged (ibid.: 115).

Through the social interactions within the food co-op and shop and drop and attempts at valuing people differently the project tried to work performatively to imagine what a more inclusive and caring society might look like. Jenny felt that these kinds of affective interactions *were* political. But she also saw them as very local, questioning the role of acts such as helping people with their grocery shopping in a wider 'transformation of power'. Throughout our conversation, she often stopped to ask me whether the things she was describing were *actually* political, demonstrating a mixture of conviction and uncertainty, which resonates with the common perception of activism and 'the political' as bigger or less everyday.

Abrahams (1992: 329–30) defines political action 'as a form of human behaviour that involves the negotiation, alteration, or entrenchment of social values and resources'. Martin et al. (2007: 79) build on this to suggest that activism emerges from the everyday and entails the development of new social relations. While they suggest that everyday activism can also have nascent qualities in relation to political action and movement formation, they point out that 'the concept of resistance' does not necessarily always 'adequately capture the full scope of the outcomes of activism', highlighting the ways in which it can transform everyday lives and communities while also changing power dynamics (Martin et al. 2007: 81).

Within the context of austerity, Matt Wilde emphasizes the significance of affective activism as a means of revaluing people who have been stigmatized by austerity. He frames this as 'militant care', arguing that 'to take responsibility for the well-being of a stranger becomes an act of militancy' within this environment of judgement. He suggests that it refuses to 'pathologise' people who are struggling, instead foregrounding 'mutual aid as an alternative model of value' (2022: 33). Arguably, such attempts at inclusivity are all the more meaningful in an era where racist and xenophobic sentiments are also on the rise. 'As a politics, affect can create feelings of possibility in the context of hegemonic ideology and hopelessness', Gerda Roelvink suggests. Affect, therefore, 'expands the political field' by widening awareness of possibilities and the practices that might capture these possibilities to create meaningful change (2010: 112). In this vein, I have tried to broaden understandings in this book of the kinds of contexts in which 'struggles against austerity might take place' and the ways in which these go beyond what might traditionally be considered activism (Jupp 2022: 29).

Federici argues that 'communalism has to be built into every struggle' if we are to come closer to recuperating our 'collective capacity to make decisions about our lives' and the building of a society that is more focused on self-government, sharing and collective responsibility (i.e. commoning) (in Carenotes Collective 2020: xii). This she sees as particularly urgent in an era in which an extractivist relationship to land, nature and other resources continues to cause destruction, displacement and enclosure (Federici in Carenotes Collective 2020: xi–xiii). From Federici's perspective the kinds of communal activities around resource management and fostering more collective and caring social relationships seen in food co-ops such as St Hilda's and Fareshares are, therefore, vital components in reproducing a different kind of everyday life and society. In Sitrin's terms, these are part of ongoing 'everyday revolutions in social relationships' (Sitrin 2012: 3) which have the potential to foster new political imaginations. The more people have the chance to experience such practices, the more such activities link up enabling people to work in coalition across difference, the more opportunities there will be for wider transformations (Federici in Carenotes Collective 2020: xiv; Hobart and Kneese 2020: 9).

Due to its structures and position within the community centre – a registered charity – St Hilda's East Food Co-op has always had an ambivalent position between a community service and something more alternative. In the face of neoliberal welfare reform, such voluntary projects are often framed in relation to their incorporation into the workings of neoliberal welfare (Cloke et al. 2017; Koch and James 2022) – 'sticking plaster' responses to need or inequality (Jupp 2022: 1–2), and a depoliticization of solidarity as care comes to stand in for more transformative politics (Muehlebach 2012; Ticktin 2011). People can become the subjects of 'regimes of care' (Ticktin 2011) through inequality and hunger. Their status as aid recipients can also wound, as charity 'does nothing to enhance solidarity' (Douglas in Mauss 2002 [1925]: x). Instead, it has the potential to reinforce the position of the donor and recipient within a hierarchy of inequality.

While some forms of politics may become eroded by the intertwinement of compassion, care and moral sensibilities, as I have highlighted here, others may also emerge, however complex or ambivalent their form. In Ticktin's (2011: 223) work, she attempts to open 'the way to think about how we might care differently'. Rather than respond to the 'exceptional' and therefore 'legitimate' suffering subject, who is often racialized or gendered, she suggests 'not making exceptions when it comes to questions of inequality' or 'suffering', but instead working towards equity.

Within each food co-op we see a complex interplay between the political imaginary of the food co-op and its participants and the lived reality of austerity Britain. It is in the spaces between the two that tensions often arise. At St Hilda's, while the food co-op's funding is premised on the acknowledgement of inequality, Jenny tried hard to reframe the forms of care and aid on offer by acknowledging the needs and legitimacy of all to access food. Within the context of an area of London in which there are growing inequalities along lines of race, ethnicity, class and ability, this undoubtedly caused its challenges at times.

At Fareshares, the collective's activities also proposed a different model of aid, or collective care in response to charitable giving. As Kell told me when I asked about the nature of politics at Fareshares:

> It's a space where people who want to do something political with a small 'p' that don't necessarily want to lie down in a road or hide in a tree or . . . I mean, a lot of what used to be what we did politically has now been taken over by charities so there's a lot of that and there's also been a lot of disempowerment because of the laws involving street protests . . . So, I think it's very hard to be a political animal and do something productive and so unless you're going to work in a specific project which might be more charity orientated when you give things to people like a food bank for instance, what Fareshares does is gives people opportunities to be political in a very different way. You are self-organizing, so you are learning a whole set of skills. You're not giving things to people in a very one-way traffic basis and it's not based on pity or largesse or paternalism or anything else. It's not a hierarchy in that sense.

The model of equity and mutuality that Kell referred to is clearly based on the assumption of relatively equal needs and vulnerabilities (O'Neill 2018: 112). When confronted with severe disparity, however, this could create conflicts between humanitarian compassion and mutual aid. As discussed in the previous chapter, moments of encounter with stark inequality in both co-ops often led to piecemeal fixes rather than longer-term approaches and solutions.

Rather than dismiss or condemn the actions of each food co-op's participants as ineffective or apolitical in the mode of 'strong theory' (Gibson-Graham 2008: 618), my aim here is to highlight the challenges and ambiguities of doing work premised on mutual aid, care and cooperation within the context of austerity Britain, as well as highlighting its possibilities (in alignment with Wright's emancipatory social sciences (2010)). A process of attempting to value people differently and contest the acceptance of the idea of the suffering subject and the inequalities that come with it can clearly still be meaningful in how food co-op participants try to foster different social relationships and subjectivities. Cloke et al argue that 'in the meantime', practices such as those of food banks, or in this case food co-ops, can also create spaces of being in common in which political and ethical re-evaluations can take place opening up potential 'ruptures in the art of the possible within Capitalist realism' (Cloke et al. 2017: 708). They therefore caution against thinking in binaries about resistance and neoliberal incorporation (Cloke et al. 2017: 721).

In an interview with St Hilda's volunteer Katie in 2020, when I asked her about the project's politics she told me, 'I always think that where the state should supply things it's better that the state supplies it', showing a concern for the ways in which community projects can become part of the configuration of neoliberal welfare. She had been volunteering at the shop and drop while the college where she worked as an ESOL teacher was closed during the pandemic lockdowns.

'I wouldn't like charity to be a substitute for the state, as it kind of is in the United States', she continued. Coming from the US, where food banks have been endemic for a long time (see, for example, Poppendieck 1998), when Katie first saw them growing in prominence in the UK, she 'just knew' they would be here to stay even if others thought they were temporary. As she saw it, they had become 'structural' now, filling in some of the spaces left by welfare withdrawal. Federici and Caffentzis also have their concerns about such forms of co-option of commons-based activities arguing that one of the tasks for those interested in social transformation is to ensure that 'the commons that we create are truly transformative of our social relations and cannot be co-opted' (Caffentzis and Federici 2014: i98). The ways in which the food co-op and its volunteers can become folded into the mixed economy of welfare, therefore, again highlights the cooperative's malleability, which can be both a strength and a potential weakness.

Despite Katie's concerns about charity becoming part of a reconfigured welfare system she told me, 'at the same time, I am all for kind of more cooperative models or experimental things or people trying to do things differently, not replicating charitably the job of the state but trying to find other ways'. Inevitably, forms of everyday politics are 'messy' and imperfect (Jupp 2022: 4). In the context of austerity, they not only elucidate visions of how things could and are being done differently (Jupp 2022: 4), but also how 'shifting practices of the welfare state and collective organisation of care in society' have become 'entangled' in complex ways. To undervalue or under-recognize the 'other ways' that Katie mentions, however, runs the risk of overlooking the political resonances and 'capacities' (Gibson-Graham 2003) that these more ambiguous forms of community organizing can foster – the radical forms of care and aid they attempt to enact, how people are valued and how people come together. All of these have the potential to open up spaces of hope, reorientation and transformation, however messy or entangled (Cloke et al. 2017; Jupp 2022: 3; Wright 2010). 'New visions of the welfare state and the economy are needed, but these might arise from paying attention to "entangled" practices and politics of care in the here and now as well as looking to the future' (Jupp 2022: 21). As Jupp (ibid.: 28) points out, while community action can change 'small scale realities', it does not necessarily always impact on wider political discourses and spheres. The key, therefore, is how we bring these struggles together (Federici in Moraes and Brant 2016: 212).

REFERENCES

Abrahams, Naomi. 1992. 'Towards Reconceptualizing Political Action*', *Sociological Inquiry* 62(3): 327–47.

Caffentzis, George, and Silvia Federici. 2014. 'Commons Against and Beyond Capitalism', *Community Development Journal* 49: i92–105.

Carenotes Collective (ed.). 2020. *For Health Autonomy: Horizons of Care Beyond Austerity – Reflections from Greece*. Brooklyn: Common Notions.

Cloke, Paul et al. 2017. 'The Geographies of Food Banks in the Meantime', *Progress in Human Geography* 41(6): 703–26.

Gibson-Graham, J. K. 2003. 'An Ethics of the Local', *Rethinking Marxism* 15(1): 49–74.

———. 2006. *A Postcapitalist Politics*. Minneapolis; London: University of Minnesota Press.

Gibson-Graham, J. K. 2008. 'Diverse Economies: Performative Practices for "Other Worlds"', *Progress in Human Geography* 32(5): 613–32.

Goldstein, Piotr. 2017. 'Post-Yugoslav Everyday Activism(s): A Different Form of Activist Citizenship?', *Europe-Asia Studies* 69(9): 1455–72.

Grasseni, Cristina. 2013. *Beyond Alternative Food Networks*. London: Bloomsbury.

Hobart, Hi'ilei Julia Kawehipuaakahaopulani, and Tamara Kneese. 2020. 'Radical Care: Survival Strategies for Uncertain Times', *Social Text* 38(1 (142)): 1–16.

Jupp, Eleanor. 2022. *Care, Crisis and Activism: The Politics of Everyday Life*. Bristol: Policy Press.

Koch, Insa. 2017. 'When Politicians Fail: Zombie Democracy and the Anthropology of Actually Existing Politics', *The Sociological Review* 65(1_suppl): 105–20.

Koch, Insa, and Deborah James. 2022. 'The State of the Welfare State: Advice, Governance and Care in Settings of Austerity', *Ethnos* 87(1): 1–21.

Land, Christopher, and Daniel King. 2014. 'Organizing Otherwise: Translating Anarchism in a Voluntary Sector Organization', *Ephemera* 14: 923–50.

Martin, Deborah G. et al. 2007. 'What Counts as Activism? The Role of Individuals in Creating Change', *Women's Studies Quarterly* 35(3/4): 18.

Masquelier, Charles. 2017. 'Beyond Co-optation: Revisiting the Transformative Function of "Workers' Self-Directed Enterprises"', *Socialism and Democracy* 31(2): 53–72.

Mauss, Marcel. 2002 [1925]. *The Gift: Forms and Functions of Exchange in Archaic Societies*. London; New York: Routledge.

Moraes, Alana, and Maria A.C. Brant. 2016. 'SILVIA FEDERICI: "Our Struggle Will Not Succeed Unless We Rebuild Society": An Interview with Silvia Federici', *Sur – International Journal on Human Rights* 13(23): 203–13.

Muehlebach, Andrea. 2012. *The Moral Neoliberal: Welfare and Citizenship in Italy*. Chicago: University of Chicago Press.

Müller, Birgit. 1991. *Toward an Alternative Culture of Work: Political Idealism and Economic Practices in West Berlin Collective Enterprises*. Boulder: Westview Press.

Nash, June, and Nicholas S. Hopkins. 1976. 'Anthropological Approaches to the Study of Cooperatives, Collectives, and Self-Management', in June Nash et al. (eds), *Popular Participation in Social Change: Cooperatives, Collectives, and Nationalized Industry*. The Hague; Paris: Mouton Publishers, pp. 3–32.

O'Neill, John. 2018. 'Food, Needs and Commons', in Jose Luis Vivero-Pol et al. (eds), *Routledge Handbook of Food as a Commons*. Abingdon, Oxon; New York: Routledge, pp. 103–20.

Poppendieck, Janet. 1998. 'Want Amid Plenty', *Monthly Review* 125–36.

Roelvink, Gerda. 2010. 'Collective Action and the Politics of Affect', *Emotion, Space and Society* 3(2): 111–18.

Sitrin, Marina A. 2012. *Everyday Revolutions: Horizontalism and Autonomy in Argentina*. London; New York: Zed Books Ltd.

Ticktin, Miriam. 2011. *Casualties of Care: Immigration and the Politics of Humanitarianism in France*. Berkeley: University of California Press.

Tsing, Anna Lowenhaupt. 2015. *The Mushroom at the End of the World: On the Possibility of Life in Capitalist Ruins*. Princeton: Princeton University Press.

Wilde, Matt. 2022. 'Eviction, Gatekeeping and Militant Care: Moral Economies of Housing in Austerity London', *Ethnos* 87(1): 22–41.

Wright, Erik Olin. 2010. *Envisioning Real Utopias*. London; New York: Verso.

INDEX

www.ingramcontent.com/pod-product-compliance
Lightning Source LLC
Chambersburg PA
CBHW051834080625
27730CB00004B/12
9781805399810